# the art of argument

## an introduction to the informal fallacies

## TEACHER'S EDITION

by **aaron larsen**
and **joelle hodge**
with **christopher perrin**

*The Art of Argument Teacher's Edition*
© Classical Academic Press, 2010
Version 8.0

**ISBN: 978-1-60051-061-8**

All advertisements, logos, company names, and slogans were created for this text and are purely fictional. Any resemblance to real companies, corporations, advertisements, logos, or slogans, past or present, is unintentional and purely coincidental.

Socrates, Tiffany, and Nate illustrations by **Ryan Toews**
"Dialogue on Appeals to Emotion" by **Andrew Davis**
"Love Is a Fallacy" by **Max Shulman**
Cover and advertisements by **Rob Baddorf**

**Classical Academic Press**
515 S. 32nd Street
Camp Hill, PA 17011

*www.ClassicalAcademicPress.com*

PGP.02.19

# Let's Argue!

Have you ever heard an argument from a friend that didn't seem right? Perhaps you knew that something was wrong with an argument but could not figure out just what the problem was. Well, after studying this book, you will know just what is wrong with bad arguments, and you will even learn the names for the ways that arguments can be bad. You will learn the most important "logical fallacies"—twenty-eight of them to be exact. A logical fallacy[1] is an occurrence of bad or incorrect reasoning, and we hope you will learn to sniff out bad reasoning like a hound dog.

All twenty-eight of the fallacies are listed with their definitions on the inside covers of this book. We encourage you to review them often until you have them memorized and they are part of your permanent mental framework. You will note that the twenty-eight fallacies are divided into three basic categories: **fallacies of irrelevance**, **fallacies of presumption**, and **fallacies of clarity**. Simply put, this means that when people **reason** badly they may err in one of three basic directions: they can make points that just don't relate to the issue (irrelevancy); they can make assumptions that are not justified or necessary (presumption); or they can use language that confuses and muddies the argument (clarity). As you learn to evaluate arguments, you will soon be asking yourself questions such as, "Is his point **relevant**? What does his argument **presume**? Is she being **clear**?"

While you can review all twenty-eight of the fallacies at any time (even now!) we will nonetheless proceed chapter by chapter and cover each of these fallacies in turn, providing several examples of each and giving you opportunities to sniff out fallacies in the form of written arguments (bad arguments) and in sixty-five magazine advertisements that each contain one of the twenty-eight fallacies. Yes, advertising is full of fallacies! We have created each of these advertisements ourselves, so you must know now that the products and services they advertise are imaginary. We think you will enjoy them and they will provide you with some good practice in detecting fallacies that occur in our everyday lives. Occasionally we will even ask you to create some of your own fallacies.

You will also note that this text contains a series of ongoing dialogues with the famous Greek philosopher Socrates (400 BC), who is somehow able to travel through time and talk with a couple of college students named Tiffany and Nathan. As Socrates talks with Tiffany and Nathan he will teach them about the logical fallacies (what else?) and you will have the benefit of listening in.

You will see that the book is divided into three units, six chapters, and twenty-eight fallacies. Unit 1 is about **relevance** and contains fourteen fallacies. Unit 2 is about **presumption** and contains eleven fallacies. Unit 3 is about **clarity** and contains three fallacies. At the beginning of each unit there is a page of definitions and fallacies that you will master during the unit. We recommend that you memorize these definitions early on and then deepen your understanding of them as you go. Regular practice and review will enable you to detect fallacies quickly and to reason well.

---

1. The word "fallacy" comes from the Latin word *fallacia*, which means "deceit," "trick," or "fraud." The Latin verb *fallo, fallere, fefelli, falsum* means "to deceive." From *fallacia* and *fallo* we also get our English words "fallacious" and "false." The Latin roots of "fallacy" remind us that a fallacy can be both a deception and a trick.

When you come across a word that is difficult, you will likely find it defined in the glossary at the end of the book. Many of the words that appear in **bold** in the text will also be defined in the glossary. There will also be some logical and technical terms in the glossary that you will not find in the text, but that will help you learn additional vocabulary related to the study of the informal fallacies. Studying the glossary will also serve as another way to review the fallacies and the essential content of the book.

For a fun way to review some of the fallacies, you will enjoy "Bill and Ted's Excellent Election: A Theatrical Play Demonstrating the Common Fallacies." You can simply read the play, but it also can be produced as a brief play that will be enjoyed by schools and homeschool co-ops. The play is included in Appendix A at the end of the book.

You will also enjoy Max Shulman's story, "Love Is a Fallacy," which shows how the logic you learn can be used against you—even in romantic matters. Shulman's story is included in Appendix B.

Please note that this text will represent fallacies from many different sources. Fallacies are present on the political left and right (and in the middle) and in the arguments of people of all kinds of political, religious, and cultural viewpoints. No one "school of thought" is fallacy-free!

In the pages of *The Art of Argument*, I hope you enjoy your study of reasoning gone wrong as you learn how to make reasoning go right. Your friends and acquaintances should beware, for after you have mastered the logical fallacies, you won't be so easily tricked.

Christopher A. Perrin, Ph.D.
Publisher

# Fight Fair! How to Make an Argument Without Starting an Argument

As you may have guessed, this is a "how-to" book, but one of a rather special sort. Its goal is to introduce the reader to the art of arguing like a philosopher. Don't get turned off by any ideas you have about how philosophers argue before a few terms are explained. First, here are some questions to answer:

What do you think of when you hear the word "logic"?

Answers will vary.

What comes to mind when you hear the word "argument"?

Answers will vary.

*Perhaps the principal*

*objection to a quarrel*

*is that it interrupts*

*an argument.*

*—G.K. Chesterton*

What is meant by "argue"? The above subtitle (Fight Fair! . . .) is a deliberate play on two meanings of this word. In the most common, or "negative" sense, "having an argument" implies an emotional disagreement. This is not what is meant when we refer to how philosophers should argue. (Some of them have been known to slip-up, of course. As philosophers, however, they should know better.)

The Latin word *argūtus* means "clear, bright, distinct or penetrating." The Latin noun *argūmentum* means "evidence or proof." The Latin verb *arguō* means "to prove or reveal." To the Latin mind, an argument was not necessarily an emotional disagreement, rather it was an attempt to reveal what was true on the basis of evidence and **reason**. In short, to argue is to provide rational reasons for or against an idea or action.

Philosophers are expected to argue in the "positive" sense. They try to convince, or persuade, others of their points of view by giving reasons to support them. From the early Greek philosophers who sought truth based on reason, to Peter's New Testament exhortation to "be ready to give the reason for the hope that is in you" (1 Peter 3:15, author paraphrase) to the modern law courts where prosecutors seek to prove their cases "beyond a reasonable doubt," there remains a tradition of respectful argumentation. Philosophers, as you shall see, are those who love wisdom and who enjoy respectfully arguing.

In fact, learning how to present your views carefully through the use of logical arguments in the positive sense is a very important skill to learn if you want to avoid arguments in the negative sense.

Obviously, there is far more to it than this. Learning how to deal with differences of opinion in a way that minimizes unnecessary conflict involves many skills, especially skills in reading, or understanding, other people. After all, the same verse in 1 Peter cautions the reader to frame his arguments with "gentleness and respect."

If you wish to avoid emotional disagreements that are completely unnecessary, gentleness and respect are a good starting point. You must, however, also learn to follow the rules for arguing like a gentleman or a lady and a philosopher.

If you are sure your arguments are addressing the real issue in a relevant way (following the principle of **relevance**), others will be less likely to think you are trying to distract them from the main issue. They will not view your arguments as a personal affront to themselves (or others). However, if you violate the principle of relevance in your **debate** by introducing facts, issues, and concerns that distract from the main issue, others may note your efforts to dodge the issue and become frustrated with you.

If your arguments do not contain unnecessary assumptions (following the principle of **presumption**), it is likely that others will not think you are trying to trick them. On the other hand, if you make unjustified, unstated assumptions (such as assuming that only new ideas are better than old ideas, or old better than new) you may irritate others.

If your arguments contain clear language (following the principle of **clarity**), others will be less likely to misunderstand you. If you speak unclearly by using words in two difference senses or by speaking with unjustified or pretended precision (especially with numbers or statistics), you will likely confuse others and hinder a respectful argument.

So, in your arguments with others, seek to stay relevant, presume nothing illegitimate, and speak clearly. That's fighting fair and makes for enjoyable arguments with friend and foe.

## A. ANSWER THE FOLLOWING:

1. How can people argue "positively"? How can people argue "negatively"?

People argue "positively" when they engage in discussion and debate without personal attack, bickering, or quarreling in order to discover, clarify, and more fully understand what is true, correct, or wise. People argue "negatively" when they engage in discussion and debate while also bickering, quarreling, and personally attacking each other, with little regard for actually discovering, clarifying, and more fully understanding what is true, correct, or wise.

2. How do people sometimes violate the principle of relevance when arguing?

Oftentimes people make arguments that are simply not relevant to the issue at hand. Whenever someone argues for something, or introduces facts, issues, testimonies, and evidence that do not truly bear on the issue at hand, he or she is violating the principle of relevance.

3. How do people sometimes violate the principle of presumption when arguing?

Whenever people assume (or presume) something that is illegitimate in the course of making an argument they violate the principle of presumption. Usually people make these assumptions in a stealthy, hidden manner that is hard to detect.

4. How do people sometimes violate the principle of clarity when arguing?

Whenever people make arguments using language in a way that is confusing, tricky, or deceiving they are violating the principle of clarity.

# Critical Thinking as a Way of Life

By mastering the "art of argument," you will learn not only to argue like a philosopher, but also to think clearly like a philosopher, as well. The use of the word "philosopher" in this book does not mean someone who majors in philosophy in college or has a PhD in the subject. It is meant to be defined in its original, oldest sense, coming from a combination of two Greek words, *philos*, meaning, "loving" and *sophia*, meaning "wisdom." In its original sense, then, the word "philosopher" means "lover of wisdom."

A philosopher (the greatest example of which may be Socrates) is someone who takes a passionate interest in discussing the most important things in life. This includes such "deep" issues as what is "really real" (**metaphysics**) and how we know what we know (**epistemology**). On the other hand, it also includes an interest in thoughtfully evaluating others' recommendations concerning everyday issues, such as what to believe, who to vote for, and whether or not to buy product "X."

Evaluating the arguments of others is one of the most important and foundational skills that any person can have. This is, perhaps, more true today than it has ever been. The world bombards us with all sorts of recommendations about what to buy, what to believe, and what to do.

Politicians and advertisers often find it easy to manipulate people's emotions, or to convince them by misleading or confusing them. After all, in this least philosophical of all periods of Western history, this has become an acceptable behavior. Just because something *is* a certain way, however, doesn't mean it *ought* to be that way. (See the is-ought fallacy on page 142.) Just because others are doing the wrong thing doesn't mean you should. (See the *tu quoque* fallacy on page 42.)

In addition to evaluating the arguments of others, you will sometimes find that you need to make your own recommendations to others about what to do, what to believe, and yes, perhaps even what to buy. The question is how are you going to go about it? Rather than resorting to trickery, you will probably be much more satisfied if you make your recommendations with integrity. In the field of logic, that means avoiding manipulation and deception. It means arguing like a gentleman or lady, one who "fights fair," rather than arguing like a demagogue, one who resorts to sneaky and manipulative tricks to get the results he wants. In truth, arguing like a gentleman or lady is the first step toward learning to argue like a philosopher.

Not only is it the right thing to do, it also works. It doesn't always work as quickly as demagoguery, but in the end it will be much more effective; those you convince will be convinced for the right (logical) reasons.

## It Does Not Follow: A Word About *Non Sequitur*

From one perspective, all the fallacies you will study can be grouped under the general category of faulty conclusions that "do not follow" from their premises. The Latin phrase *non sequitur* means "it does not follow." Therefore, any argument that presents a conclusion that does not follow from its premises can be called a *non sequitur*.

For example, if we argue that since Senator Johnson is under investigation for tax evasion we cannot accept his proposal for building a new bridge, we have committed a *non sequitur*. From the fact that Senator Johnson is under investigation for tax evasion it does not follow that his proposal for bridge building is unacceptable. This kind of fallacy is called an *argumentum ad hominem* ("argument to the man") fallacy, which is a fallacy that seeks to abuse the person making the argument instead of addressing the real issue.

Let's look at another example. If a used book seller were to say, "Never buy a new book over an old book—it is the old books that contain hard-won wisdom," we could charge him with a *non sequitur*. It simply does not follow that just because a book is old it will contain wisdom. Nor does it follow that just because a book is new it will not contain wisdom. This fallacy, as you will learn later, is called "chronological snobbery"; it is committed when someone tries to discredit or approve of something merely by appealing to its age.

## Does It Follow?

When you are presented with an argument, it is helpful to ask yourself if the conclusion truly follows from the premises. If you sense you have a *non sequitur* before you, it is good to probe further. Why doesn't the conclusion follow? Is the **premise** relevant (relevance) to the issue or conclusion presented? Does the argument or premise assume or presume (presumption) something that is hidden but unacceptable? Is the premise clear (clarity)?

By violating the principles of relevance, presumption, or clarity, all the fallacies you study will in one way or another feature conclusions that do not follow from their premises or the evidence to which they appeal. They are all versions of a *non sequitur*. As you embark on your study of the informal fallacies, this will become increasingly clear.

## *Argumentum ad* What?

You will notice that many of the fallacies have Latin names. The first one you will learn is called the *argumentum ad hominem* (argument to the man), often called the *ad hominem* fallacy for short. In fact, most of the fallacies with Latin names will be abbreviated this way, with the word *argumentum* being assumed. For example, the *argumentum ad populum* (argument to the people) may simply be called the *ad populum* fallacy.

What Is Logic?
Critical Thinking as a Way of Life

11

**A. DEFINE:**
Define the words below by referring to the lesson you have studied and by looking them up in a good dictionary. Record the etymology (history or linguistic origin) of as many words as you can. For example, the word "etymology" comes from two Greek words: *etumos* ("the real" or "the true") and *logos* ("reason," "word," or "study").

1. Philosopher:

Taken from the Greek words *philos* (loving) and *sophia* (wisdom), the word philosopher literally means

"lover of wisdom." In a more technical and contemporary sense it means "student of philosophy."

2. *Philos*:

Greek for "loving."

3. *Sophia*:

Greek for "wisdom."

4. Metaphysics:

This word is derived from the Greek phrase *ta meta ta physika*, meaning the works that came "after the 'Physics.'" The "Physics" refers to a group of thirteen treatises written by Aristotle on physics and natural sciences. Aristotle's works "after Physics" (after these thirteen treatises) were called "Metaphysics." Metaphysics came to mean that branch of philosophy that examines the nature of reality and deals with the question "What is really real?"

5. Epistemology:

This word comes the Greek word *epistasthai*, which literally means "to stand upon," but is understood figuratively as "to understand or know." (When you can "stand upon" an idea, then you really know it!) Epistemology is therefore the branch of philosophy that studies the origin, nature, methods, and limits of human knowledge and deals with the question "How can we know what we know?"

5. Socrates:

Socrates was the mentor of Plato, who wrote down much of what Socrates taught in the form of dialogues. Socrates is considered by many to be one of the chief founders of Western philosophy.

## B. FURTHER RESEARCH:

Write a short essay answering both of the following questions. Use available classroom resources, Internet sites, or library resources.

1. Why do you think the authors of this book consider that Socrates may be the greatest example of a philosopher?

   **This essay should include points similar to the following:**

   a. Socrates is great in the sense of being famous and well-known, even outside of those who study philosophy. He was one of the first philosophers (he was born around 470 BC).

   b. Socrates is great in the sense that he has had a great influence on the development and history of Western philosophy. His student, Plato (also a famous philosopher), recorded many of Socrates' teachings in the form of dialogues. These dialogues have a great, enduring influence in the history of philosophy and literature.

   c. Socrates is great in the sense that he personified the quintessential "lover of wisdom." He constantly asked questions of himself and others in order to discover wisdom.

2. Why do you think it will be valuable to study informal logic? Why do you think British writer G.K. Chesterton said, "Perhaps the principal objection to a quarrel is that it interrupts an argument"?

   **This essay should include points similar to the following:**

   a. Studying informal logic will help students to protect themselves against faulty, deceptive arguments.

   b. Studying informal logic will help students to craft arguments that are relevant and clear.

   c. Chesterton's comment that a quarrel interrupts an argument shows that he thought respectful argumentation to be valuable and useful—not to mention enjoyable.

# Formal vs. Informal Logic

The first two lessons in this book were something of a pep talk. Now let's take some time to define logic and its two main subdivisions: **formal logic** and **informal logic. Logic can be defined as "the art and science of reasoning."** While this is a course in informal logic, it is helpful to know the main characteristics of both formal and informal logic. After studying this course in informal logic, we encourage you to study our companion text, *The Discovery of Deduction*, which is on formal logic.

Formal logic is about pure reasoning in the abstract. It usually focuses on deductive reasoning; that is, it focuses on types of arguments in which the premises[1] imply a necessary conclusion. For example:

**Premise 1:**     All birds have wings.
**Premise 2:**     A cardinal is a bird.
**Conclusion:**   Therefore, a cardinal has wings.

In this type of argument (often called a syllogism), the conclusion must be true (a cardinal has wings) as long as the premises are true. When the proper form is followed, we can have a valid argument that is actually nonsensical and untrue. For example:

**Premise 1:**     All birds have horns.
**Premise 2:**     A poodle is a bird.
**Conclusion:**   Therefore, a poodle has horns.

This argument (or syllogism) is **valid**, meaning that its form or structure is correct. If it were true that all birds have horns and that a poodle is a bird, then it must follow that a poodle has horns. However, in this argument, the premises happen to be false even though the form is correct. So, the argument is **valid in form**, but not **sound** because of the false premises.[2] If the premises were true, then the argument would be both valid and sound, like the first argument!

You can see that in formal logic, form is very important: that is why it is called *formal* logic.[3] In fact, in the study of formal logic, a student learns very quickly to replace ordinary words, such as "all birds have wings," with symbols, such as "all B are W" (for "all birds are wing possessors"). If the *form* of an argument is what's important in formal logic, then the *content* of the argument (what we are arguing about) is more or

---

1. Premise are reasons or propositions given in an argument that supports or leads to a conclusion.
2. The word "sound" in logic means that an argument is free from defect or fallacy. It is possible for an argument to be valid (having correct form or structure) but still not be sound if the premises are false.
3. Note that *forma* is Latin for "form" or "shape."

less interchangeable. When symbols such as "B" and "W" represent **categories** such as "birds" and "wings," this kind of formal logic is called **categorical logic**. When the symbols are joined together to form statements or propositions, as in "all B are W," we are entering the realm of **propositional logic**. When we use propositional logic, the symbols are joined together with other symbols that replace words such as "and," "or," "not," or "implies." These connecting symbols are called **logical operators**. We use "Λ" for "and" and "V" for "or" and "~" for "not." For example, we can represent "Either a cardinal is a bird or it is not a bird" as "B V ~B."

Now you have had a brief introduction to formal logic, with its subcategories of categorical and propositional logic. This course, however, focuses on informal logic. Informal logic is not so concerned with form or structure. Rather, it is concerned with arguments made using everyday, ordinary language. It also tends to emphasize *inductive* rather than *deductive* reasoning. The Latin word *deducere*, from which the English word "deduce" is derived, means "to lead down or away." Therefore, **deductive reasoning** is reasoning that starts with premises that "lead down" to a necessary conclusion. Deductive reasoning can be described as "whole-to-part" reasoning. The Latin word *inducere*, from which the English word "induce" is derived, means "to lead" or "bring in." **Inductive reasoning**, therefore, can be described as "part-to-whole" reasoning. We begin with particular facts and try to prove a general conclusion. Inductive reasoning involves "bringing in" certain facts to an argument in an attempt to prove a more general point. For example, I may "bring in" the facts that every bird I have seen flies in order to prove that all birds fly. In other words, inductive reasoning often works toward generalizations that are reasonably accurate. However, because the form of inductive arguments does not lead to absolute certainty, these arguments are only more or less probable. For example, does my experience of seeing birds fly prove that all birds fly? No. In fact, we know that the ostrich is a bird that can run very fast but cannot fly.

While deductive arguments, therefore, are said to be either valid or invalid, inductive arguments are said to be either strong or weak. Deductive logic addresses things that are either "black" or "white," while inductive arguments deal in "shades of gray."

| *Formal Logic* | *Informal Logic* |
|---|---|
| • Deductive reasoning | • Inductive reasoning |
| • Either valid or invalid | • Either strong or weak |
| • Certainty (given the premises) | • Probability |

**A Word About Informal and Formal Fallacies**
As you well know, this book is about the informal fallacies, also called logical fallacies. The informal fallacies are weak, poor, and fallacious arguments that occur in common language. These fallacies are not fallacious because of matters of form or structure, but because they violate principles such as relevance, presumption, and clarity. You will be studying these principles and how they are violated throughout this book. There are such things as formal fallacies, too, and they occur when an argument violates established forms that syllogisms should take. You can study these formal fallacies in *The Discovery of Deduction* or similar texts.

The most fundamental difference between informal logic and formal logic is that informal logic deals almost entirely with ordinary-language arguments. In fact, one historian of logic described informal logic as "dialectical logic."[4] He meant that it is the language of debate and of the interchange of ideas between people, as opposed to the logic of one man reasoning all by himself.[5]

One danger of overemphasizing formal logic at the expense of informal logic is that the study of logic can lose its "dialectic interplay," its sense of a back-and-forth exchange between real people. Logic can be both an art and a science. That is, it can be treated in a way that focuses on the practical and artistic (logic as an art) or it can be treated in a way that is exact and academic (logic as a science). Both approaches are important; however, the first approach (logic as an art) has been neglected. That is why this book is called *The Art of Argument*; it is intended to remedy this past neglect. Its intent is to focus on things that can help and encourage you in "dialectical activities," such as debates, mock trials, and discussions. This book focuses on everyday language arguments.

In fact, future courses of this logic series will have built-in sections designed to give you "how-to" instruction in debates and mock trials. First, though, you need to hone your critical-thinking skills by learning to critique the arguments of others. In doing this, informal logic is "where the rubber meets the road." This book begins by studying a number of bad arguments commonly known as "fallacies." By learning to detect bad arguments, you will learn how to avoid them yourself and how to make good arguments as well.

In the next section, you are going to eavesdrop on a conversation about some of the practical implications of good and bad reasoning. Use your imagination and picture a TV room at a typical college, where Socrates is about to engage in a rather interesting conversation.

---

4. C.L. Hamblin, *Fallacies* (London: Methuen, 1970 ), 9.

5. According to this outlook, many ways of approaching inductive logic could actually be classified as "formal logic." (A good example of this could be an in-depth study of scientific reasoning, using John Stuart Mill's canons for establishing causality, as is done in Irving M. Copi's logic curriculum, *Introduction to Logic*.) That is because inductive arguments can also be analyzed in ways that focus only on the form or structure of the argument and in ways that don't involve the back-and-forth, interpersonal dimension of debate between people.

**What Is Logic?**
Formal vs. Informal Logic

## A. DEFINE:

1. Logic:

The art and science of reasoning.

2. Formal Logic:

Reasoning in the abstract, with a focus on deductive reasoning, in which the validity of an argument is based solely on the form of the argument and the premises imply a necessary conclusion.

3. Informal Logic:

Logic that deals with ordinary-language arguments that tend to emphasize inductive rather than deductive reasoning. The form of an argument is less the issue than the weight of the evidence.

4. Deductive Reasoning:

Whole-to-part reasoning that determines the validity of a formal argument. The conclusion of such an argument must, necessarily, be true if the premises used to support it are true.

5. Inductive Reasoning:

Part-to-whole reasoning used to determine the validity of an informal argument by starting with evidence that can be observed and compiled and works toward generalizations.

## B. FURTHER RESEARCH:

Write a short essay answering the following questions. Use available classroom resources, Internet sites, or library resources.

1. What are the main differences between deductive and inductive reasoning?
   Deductive reasoning is emphasized by formal logic and is whole-to-part reasoning, or reasoning that begins with accepted premises that imply a conclusion. Inductive reasoning is emphasized by informal logic and is part-to-whole reasoning that begins with particular facts and seeks to prove a general conclusion.

2. What do you think the benefits of studying formal logic might be?
   The study of formal logic enables a person to pay attention to the forms that arguments take, familiarizing him with the ways in which premises may properly lead to conclusions (valid arguments) and the ways in which they do not lead to certain conclusions (invalid arguments).

3. What do you think the benefits of studying informal logic might be?
   The study of informal logic promotes an awareness of the ways in which arguments are used in ordinary, everyday language and imparts an ability to detect many common fallacies employed in arguments using everyday language.

**What Is Logic?**
Formal vs. Informal Logic

# Dialogue on Logic . . . and Propaganda

*Setting: Lobby in a college dormitory*

**Socrates:** Excuse me, would you mind my asking what you are doing?

**Tiffany:** I'm watching TV. Isn't that obvious?

**Socrates:** Not so obvious as you might think. Your eyes, and mind, appeared to be elsewhere for a moment.

**Tiffany:** Oh. Well, it was just a boring commercial. I was thinking about something else while it was on.

**Socrates:** Boring? On the contrary; I think that commercials make some of the most interesting television these days.

**Tiffany:** Really? Why would you say that?

**Socrates:** Well, to begin with, they're often much more funny and clever than the silly sitcoms aired so often these days. But that's not my main reason. For the most part, I like them because they are so filled with propaganda.

**Tiffany:** Propaganda! Isn't that a bad thing? What is propaganda anyway, and why would you want to listen to it?

**Socrates:** Whoa, whoa! One question at a time. I think that first I should answer your second question, in which you asked what **propaganda** is. In its most basic meaning, the sense in which I am using it, it means any sort of technique that people use to get other people (usually people that they don't really know personally) to do or to believe something that they otherwise might not. Commercials often use propaganda to get people to buy things.

**Tiffany:** So why would you want to listen to people trying to get you to buy things? Do you like shopping?

**Socrates:** Not really. You can see from my outfit that I'm not exactly at the height of fashion.

**Tiffany:** Yeah, I was just about to ask you about that. Where do you do your shopping, at the Sears White Sale? Don't you get cold in that get-up?

**Socrates:** Actually, I was often made fun of in my day for absentmindedly forgetting my cloak. And, no, I did not shop at a white sale. I purchased this from the tailor back in my country.

**Tiffany:** What is your country? And what is your name, by the way?

**Socrates:** I am Socrates, and I am from ancient Athens.

**Tiffany:** Sure, and I am Cleopatra, Queen of Denial.

**Socrates:** Pleased to meet you. Mind if I call you Cleo for short?

**Tiffany:** No, no; my name's not Cleo. It's Tiffany.

**Socrates:** Then why did you say your name was Cleopatra?

**Tiffany:** Because you said your name was Socrates.

**Socrates:** My name *is* Socrates.

**Tiffany:** Look, I don't want to argue with you.

**Socrates:** But I would love to argue with you.

**Tiffany:** Why would anyone like to argue?

**Socrates:** Well, let me first explain. By "argue," I don't mean engage in petty squabbling. I think that may be what most people mean most of the time when they say the word "arguing." Let me turn the question to you. What would you do if someone asked you why you believe what you believe?

**Tiffany:** Well, I suppose that I would give them reasons.

**Socrates:** In that case, you would be making an argument, at least in the sense in which I mean it. I'm a philosopher and when we philosophers use the term "argue," we usually mean "to provide rational reasons for or against an idea or action."

**Tiffany:** So why would a philosopher like watching propaganda?

**Socrates:** Good question. We did get a bit off of the track there, didn't we? I like to watch propaganda because it provides a good opportunity to evaluate arguments. You see, whenever someone tries to get you to do

**What Is Logic?**
Dialogue on Logic . . . and Propaganda

anything, they are trying to persuade. Usually, when someone is trying to persuade, they give reasons, and whenever they do, they are making an argument.

**Tiffany:** That's all that it takes to make an argument? You just have to give a reason for something?

**Socrates:** That's basically it. The reasons that you give are called the premises, and the thing for which you are giving the reasons is called the conclusion.

**Tiffany:** But . . . not all propaganda makes an argument. Take this one with the frogs and lizards that is trying to sell beer, for example. What kind of argument is it making?

**Socrates:** That is another good question. Here's an idea: Perhaps it is making an implied argument that goes something like this: "We make clever, funny commercials about frogs and lizards that entertain millions. You should buy our beer to show your appreciation for this public service."

**Tiffany:** That doesn't have anything at all to do with whether or not it is a good product.

**Socrates:** You are absolutely right once again. This brings to mind the first of the three great principles of critical thinking: relevance. Do the premises really "bear upon," or provide some support for, the conclusion? If not, the argument is just a distraction from the real issue.

**Tiffany:** Aren't you reading an awful lot into this commercial, though?

**Socrates:** Well, you're right. I was only being facetious. That commercial might be better explained as a form of "non-argumentative persuasion"—an attempt to convince you without making an open argument at all. That is something for which we need to be especially careful. After all, if someone wants to convince you to do something without giving you a single rational reason . . . Oh, but here is a perfect example of an irrelevant argument now. What reasons are they giving you to buy that soft drink?

**Tiffany:** Well, they seem to be saying that since Grant Hill likes the soda, you should go and buy it as well.

**Socrates:** Exactly. That is called an argument from illegitimate authority, and since there is no good reason to accept the authority of Grant Hill on the subject of soft drink desirability, it commits a very important fallacy.

**Tiffany:** What, exactly, is a "fallacy"?

**Socrates:** A fallacy is a commonly recognized type of bad argument.

**Tiffany:** Commonly recognized by whom?

**Socrates:** Good point. Unfortunately, the study of logic isn't exactly at its highest ebb these days and these fallacies aren't as commonly recognized as they ought to be. What I really mean by "commonly recognized" is that it is commonly recognized by those who have studied philosophy or logic.

**Tiffany:** So what type of fallacy does that commercial make?

**Socrates:** It's called the appeal to illegitimate authority. It is one of many fallacies of relevance.

**Tiffany:** So that's why you like commercials. You like to analyze them.

**Socrates:** Absolutely. Every commercial contains an attempt at persuasion. In almost every case, it will be one of three types: 1) a reasonable argument; 2) a bad type of argument, called a fallacy; or, perhaps worst of all, 3) an attempt to persuade without an argument, which is called non-argumentative persuasion.

**Tiffany:** Somehow, I thought that all of you philosopher types just sat around and asked dumb questions, like "how do I know that I really exist?"

**Socrates:** Well, there are many things that I like to question, but my existence is not one of them. Do you know how I generally respond to people who ask me how they can really know they exist?

**Tiffany:** How is that?

**Socrates:** I simply ask them, "Who wants to know?"

**Tiffany:** Well, that settles it for me.

**Socrates:** As it does for me. I must be off, but something tells me we will speak more later.

**What Is Logic?**
Dialogue on Logic . . . and Propaganda

## A. DEFINE THE FOLLOWING TERMS:

**1. Fallacy:**

A commonly recognized bad argument failing to meet the requirements of relevance, clarity, or presumption.

**2. Relevance:**

One of the three principles of critical thinking in which the premises of an argument provide some support for the conclusion.

**3. Persuasion:**

The art of convincing others.

**4. Propaganda:**

Techniques used to influence the opinions of others to do or believe something that they otherwise might not.

## B. FURTHER RESEARCH:

Write a short essay answering each of the following questions. Use available classroom resources, Internet sites, newspapers, or magazines.

1. How would you define the principle of relevance? Socrates has given you a few ideas. Give an example of an argument that is relevant and one that is not.

   The principle of relevance requires a person making an argument to relate that argument to the issue at hand and not stray from the issue by introducing evidence and arguments that, no matter how compelling, are not relevant to the issue at hand. Fallacies of this type may include celebrity endorsements for products for which they have no expertise or experts speaking authoritatively on topics unrelated to their fields of expertise.

2. Find three examples of non-argumentative persuasion from newspapers, magazines, or books.
   Answers will vary.
3. Create your own example of non-argumentative persuasion.
   Answers will vary. See the dialogue on page 22 for examples of non-argumentative persuasion.

# Unit 1: Relevance
## Definitions Summary

FALLACIES OF RELEVANCE: These arguments have premises that do not "bear upon" the truth of the conclusions. In other words, they introduce an irrelevancy into the argument.

It is quite easy in a debate for someone to slip off-subject, leave behind the real issue, and begin arguing about something else. Sometimes we do this without meaning to because new subjects come up in a discussion and we want to address each subject. Sometimes, however, we start arguing about something besides the real issue because we sense that our argument for the real issue is weak. When we argue "around" the real issue we are committing a fallacy of relevance—we are veering off-topic and not staying relevant to the real issue.

There are three basic ways we "avoid the issue" and commit a fallacy of relevance: 1) We can criticize the source of an argument instead of the argument itself, 2) we can appeal to an emotion of some kind instead of addressing the real issue, and 3) we can make another argument (even a good one) but not address the issue that is at hand. The three basic groups of fallacies are listed below. You will be studying them throughout this unit.

**A. *AD FONTEM* ARGUMENTS:** (Arguments against the source)
This subgroup consists of arguments that focus on the source of the argument, rather than on the issue itself.

1. ***Ad Hominem* Abusive:** In this most obvious of all personal attacks, the speaker assaults his rival with a great deal of abusive language in an attempt to avoid the issue. ***Ad Hominem*** means "to the man" in Latin.

2. ***Ad Hominem* Circumstantial:** Somewhat more subtle, this type of argument says, or implies, that the speaker's rival should not be trusted in making his argument because of various circumstances regarding his rival. The most common version includes an implication that a person's argument should be discounted because of his self-interest in the matter.

3. ***Tu Quoque:*** The person committing this fallacy assumes his rival's recommendation should be discounted because he does not always follow it himself. ***Tu Quoque*** means "you also" in Latin.

4. **Genetic Fallacy:** This most generic version of an *ad fontem* argument states that an idea should be discounted simply because of its source or origin. In a sense, all of the arguments in this group are genetic fallacies, but the genetic fallacy label is generally used when the source being attacked isn't a specific person, but a people group or institution.

## B. APPEALS TO EMOTION:

All fallacies appeal to our emotions in some form or another, but the following fallacies do it in a particularly obvious way.

1. **Appeal to Fear (*ad baculum*):** Without making a clear causal connection, a person committing this fallacy references the potential for bad consequences to occur if the person to whom they are speaking does not agree with them. ***Ad baculum*** means "to the stick" in Latin.

2. **Appeal to Pity (*ad misericordiam*):** Using this type of argument, the speaker tries to convince others of his point of view by making them feel sorry for him or for other people. ***Ad misericordiam*** means "to pity" in Latin.

3. **Mob Appeal (*ad populum*):** To make up for a lack of solid evidence and sound reason, this tool, often used by demagogues,[1] appeals to the emotions of the crowd or to the "common man." ***Ad populum*** means "to the people" in Latin.

4. **Snob Appeal:** This is an appeal to a sense of elitism or to those of "discriminating taste."

5. **Appeal to Illegitimate Authority (*ad verecundiam*):** This is an attempt to shame the listener into agreement by citing an illegitimate authority. ***Ad verecundiam*** means "to shame" in Latin.

6. **Chronological Snobbery:** This is an appeal to something's age to justify either accepting or rejecting it.

## C. RED HERRINGS:

This category includes types of proofs that don't necessarily play on our emotions, but are nevertheless irrelevant to the situation.

1. **Appeal to Ignorance:** This argument makes the mistake of saying that because a proposition cannot be disproved, it must, therefore, be likely.

2. **Irrelevant Goals or Functions:** This is an argument that assumes a goal or function of a certain practice or policy is either unrealistic or irrelevant. Therefore, the practice or policy is not acceptable.

3. **Irrelevant Thesis:** This type of argument may make a fairly sound case for what it is trying to prove. However, what it is trying to prove is irrelevant to the case at hand.

4. **The Straw Man Fallacy:** This is an attempt to disprove an opponent's beliefs by presenting those beliefs in an inaccurate light.

---

1. A demagogue is a leader who obtains power by means of impassioned appeals to the emotions and prejudices of a population.

# Finding the Main Issue . . . and Asking the Right Questions

DEFINITION: Fallacies of relevance have premises that do not "bear upon" the truth of the conclusions, and therefore they introduce an irrelevancy into the argument.

Now, it is time to start a valuable project—the mastery of twenty-eight different fallacies. You will learn them so well that you will be able to recognize them in arguments, commercials, books, and conversations! The best way to remember them is to keep in mind which of the three great principles they violate. The first group of fallacies we are going to cover are the fallacies of relevance, which are those that violate the principle of relevance. We will start with a study of relevance because it is important to be able to determine the real issue in an argument and know when someone is trying to distract you from that issue. When you're about to engage someone in an argument, the first thing you should be thinking about is the question of what is and what is not the real issue.

Fallacies of relevance have premises that, as the logician would put it, do not "bear upon" the conclusion. In other words, the premises do not have much to do with the issue at hand. While these fallacies all bring some irrelevant issue to the forefront, they sometimes can seem convincing. Usually, this is because they play upon our emotions. If we allow the speaker to get us stirred up emotionally, we are likely to miss the fact that his argument fails to provide good evidence for what he is trying to prove. Sometimes, what is being asserted in one of these fallacies is outrageous and unfair. At other times, it may be perfectly true and reasonable, yet it is still not relevant. The best response in this case is to simply say, "true, perhaps, but irrelevant."

During the course of this book, you will learn to ask four key questions of any argument you encounter. These questions will help you detect and identify fallacies of relevance, presumption, and clarity. You should master the following questions:

> **First Question: What is the issue at hand?**
>
> **Next Questions:**
> Relevance    ⟶    Is the argument relevant to the issue at hand?
> Presumption  ⟶    Is the argument assuming something illegitimate?
> Clarity       ⟶    Is the argument clear?

# Dialogue on Winning an Argument . . . Sort of, While Losing a Friend

*Socrates is sitting under a tree on campus when Tiffany suddenly comes up to him.*

**Tiffany:** Socrates! Boy am I glad to see you. Oooh . . . I'm so mad!

**Socrates:** Not at me, I hope. Perhaps I should make good my escape before it is too late.

**Tiffany:** No, no, not at you! I'm mad at my friend Mary. She's so argumentative.

**Socrates:** So Mary is quite contrary?

**Tiffany:** Yes, but it's not just that she likes to argue, but *how* she likes to argue.

**Socrates:** How is that?

**Tiffany:** She always makes me feel like I have absolutely no business having any views at all. When the issue of welfare reform comes up, she implies that I couldn't possibly know what I'm talking about, since I've never been poor. When the issue of race comes up, she says that I couldn't possibly have anything useful to add, since I'm a member of the dominant ethnic group. Once, we were talking about abortion, and she told my boyfriend he shouldn't be allowed to comment because he's a man!

**Socrates:** So, how does this make you feel?

**Tiffany:** Well, I guess sometimes it makes me feel a little intimidated and off-balance.

**Socrates:** Does it make you want to exploring the issue further with her?

**Tiffany:** Certainly not! It makes me feel as though I don't want to talk with her at all.

**Socrates:** But does it help her win arguments?

**Tiffany:** Well . . . sort of. I guess that depends on what you mean by winning.

**Socrates:** Well, how would you define the term "winning"?

**Tiffany:** Hmm . . . I've never really thought about what it means to win an argument before. What do you think it means? Oh, here's my boyfriend, Nate. Nate, meet my good friend, Socrates!

**Nate:** Pleased to meet you.

**Socrates:** The pleasure is all mine.

**Nate:** I overheard your conversation. Suppose you tell us what your definition of victory in argument is.

**Socrates:** Why, certainly. There are different ways of looking at this, I suppose. Let's try on a couple for size and see how they fit, shall we?

**Tiffany:** Sure.

**Socrates:** First, let's start by comparing arguments to battles. Do you know what the traditional definition of victory in battle is?

**Tiffany:** No. What is it?

**Socrates:** Traditionally, victory in battle is said to be won by whoever is left in command of the battlefield afterward. In my day, for example, we would all line up in a big, long shield wall and charge straight at each other. We did this until one group proved weaker, or lost their nerve and fled. The winner would lose very few men and the loser would take enormous casualties.

**Nate:** That sounds like a stupid way to wage war. Why didn't you just hunker down behind your city walls, or make use of all those steep mountains and thick forests to wage a never ending guerilla war like America did in its war for independence? The Greek terrain would have been perfect for it!

**Socrates:** Well, yes, I guess it was a little unsubtle of us, but, hey, your style of waging warfare would have made it hard to get home in time for harvest season.

**Tiffany:** *Touché*.

**Socrates:** Anyway, as I was saying, the losers would humiliate themselves by having to ask for permission to bury their dead. That's the difference between defeat and victory: whether or not you maintain control of the battlefield. So the next question is, "Does your friend Contrary Mary consistently find herself in command of the battlefield?" If that is so, then she obviously wins arguments.

**Nate:** I don't know about that. While I guess whoever has control of the battlefield has won a technical victory, I don't know whether that is really always the best measure. One could win a "Pyrrhic victory," for example.

**Socrates:** A "Pyrrhic victory"? I don't believe that I'm familiar with that term.

**Nate:** Well, it comes from a famous general who lived after your time. His name was Pyrrhus of Epirus, and he was known as the finest tactician of his age. He beat the Romans twice, at least technically, but lost so many men that he had to withdraw to friendlier territory. In fact, when his generals tried to congratulate him on his victory, he is reported to have said, "Another such victory and I shall be finished." When Mary cows and intimidates others into backing down, she may be displaying her command of argumentative techniques, but is she really succeeding in getting others to appreciate her point of view?

**Tiffany:** Yeah, that makes me wonder what the purpose of arguing for your ideas with people is in the first place. If it's to "maintain control of the battlefield," then sure, any old sophism[1] will do. But if it's to actually convince others that you are right in your ideas, then you have to fight fair.

**Nate:** The whole warfare analogy just doesn't fit here, anyway. After all, "all's fair in love and war," but I certainly think that Mary's argumentative tactics are unfair.

**Socrates:** But, then, is all really fair in both war and love?

**Nate** *(looking sheepishly at Tiffany)*: OK, I guess all isn't really fair in love, now that you mention it. But, look, my point is that while the goal in warfare is to control and coerce others, the goal of arguing is to convince others to accept your ideas of their own free will by presenting to them good reasons for accepting your ideas.

_____

1. A sophism is a plausible but fallacious argument. This kind of argumentation is called sophistry.

**Socrates:** Spoken like a true philosopher! I'm beginning to like this friend of yours, Tiffany. That was precisely the point to which I was hoping to bring this little dialectical exercise. So that brings us back to your friend Contrary Mary's approach. If the goal is to get others to want to change their minds and accept a new point of view, does she succeed?

**Tiffany:** Certainly not! It makes my resistance to her ideas stiffen.

**Socrates:** Which brings us back full circle to the question of how arguing with Mary makes you feel. Her argument fails at a rhetorical level, because it alienates her audience. It makes them not want to listen. But that isn't even the worst of it. It also fails on a logical level. Can you think of the great principle of critical thinking that we talked about the other day that her arguing approach violates?

**Tiffany:** That's easy. It fails the test of relevance. Just because Nate is a man, that doesn't mean his argument about whether or not a fetus is a person is wrong. When she tried to shove Nate's argument aside just because he is a man, she was really just putting up a smokescreen to hide behind.

**Socrates:** Absolutely! In fact, in all three of the examples you mentioned, she was committing the *ad hominem* circumstantial fallacy.

**Nate:** *Ad hominem* . . . doesn't that mean "to the man" in Latin?

**Socrates:** Precisely! The *ad hominem* fallacies are a group of fallacies that are committed when the arguer distracts his listeners from what should be the main issue by attacking, or deflecting attention to, his opponent and avoiding the real issue. In the *ad hominem* circumstantial fallacy, someone tries to say that someone with whom they disagree should be ignored because of the circumstances surrounding them.

**Nate:** But aren't there times when the **credibility** of the messenger matters?

**Socrates:** Well, yes, there are such times. But the general rule is that you are to avoid making your argument center around the man, and stick to the issue. After all, attacking the person rather than tackling the issue is a good way to "win" the argument and lose a friend.

**Nate:** Sounds like sage advice to me. We need to get going now, but it's been great getting to talk to you!

**Socrates:** The feeling is mutual, I assure you.

# Chapter 1

## The *Ad Fontem* Arguments (Arguments Against the Source)

DEFINITION: A subgroup of the fallacies of relevance, these arguments distract by focusing attention on the source of the argument, rather than on the issue itself.

Due to the large number of relevance fallacies, they are divided into subgroups. We will start with the subgroup of *ad fontem* arguments (sometimes referred to as "personal attacks") because they are some of the easier ones to spot.

The Latin phrase *ad fontem* can be translated as "to the source." (Literally, it means "to the fountain," or "the source of a stream.") Distracting your audience's attention to the source of an argument, and away from the real issue, is a very common debater's trick. Most of these fallacies can also be referred to as *ad hominem* arguments or "personal attacks." However, not all of these arguments are aimed at a specific person. Therefore, it is important to recognize these sorts of fallacies regardless of whether they are aimed at one specific person, a group of people, or even a broader set of ideas.

### Vocabulary:

- *Ad Fontem* Arguments
- *Ad Hominem*
- *Ad Hominem* Abusive
- *Ad Hominem* Circumstantial
- *Tu Quoque*
- Genetic Fallacy

*Ad hominem* can be translated as either "to the man" or "against the man." In either case, it refers to arguments that distract from the issue at hand by attacking one of the parties that are arguing. A speaker may be self-interested, not completely informed, or even a downright bad person, but that does not change the fact that his argument needs to be weighed on its own merits. Most of the time, an *ad hominem* argument is in some way unfair to whom it attacks. After all, an *ad hominem* argument is one of the "dirtiest" tricks in the debater's book. However, even if it is perfectly fair and accurate, it is still irrelevant. There are several different types of *ad fontem* arguments, but in this book we will cover just four.

# Fallacy 1:
## *Ad Hominem* Abusive

DEFINITION: Arguments that attempt to avoid the issue by insulting an opponent with abusive language.

The *ad hominem* abusive fallacy is easy to spot. You likely have this fallacy on your hands whenever a speaker talks about his opponent, saying bad things about him that have nothing to do with his opponent's argument.

*Ad hominem* means "to the man" in Latin. When a person commits this fallacy, he criticizes his opponent—the man himself—but not his opponent's argument. People committing this fallacy often make use of name-calling or other emotional language that reduces the possibility of rational debate and discussion.

In most cases, in order to avoid committing this fallacy, you must disregard who your opponent is and instead focus on his argument. For example, your opponent could be a convicted thief and still have a good argument for what computer to buy, what movie to see, or what policies will ensure public safety. In other words, even people with significant personal flaws can make good arguments. Simply pointing out a flaw in someone does not make his or her argument bad—"bad people" can make good arguments. In fact, if we are honest, we must admit that we have our own flaws, but hopefully we can make good arguments despite them.

Consider the following examples of the *ad hominem* abusive fallacy.

**Example 1**

Mr. Johnson is a drunk and has been convicted multiple times for driving under the influence of alcohol. Why would we consider his recommendation to install a stoplight at this intersection?

**Example 2**

Sharon, you are a lazy slacker. No one is going to listen to your advice on how to study for the exam.

Mr. Johnson may have been convicted for DUI (driving under the influence), but does this have anything to do with the argument he is proposing? Rather than dismissing his argument because of his flaws, let's hear the argument and judge it on its own merits. Sharon may be habitually late turning in homework, but what is her argument for how to study? It could be excellent. Regarding her character flaw, we can respond, "It may be true, but it's irrelevant."

We must keep in mind, however, that occasionally a personal flaw actually may be very relevant to an argument, especially in cases in which personal integrity and character matter. For example, we might justly criticize the character of a convicted felon who was running a campaign to become our town's sheriff.

## *Ad Hominem* Abusive

**Genus (general class):** An argument to the source.
**Difference (specific trait):** An argument involving obviously abusive language aimed at a rival.

Throughout this book we will include a key point box after each fallacy that restates the fallacy using different words. The box will also distinguish between the genus and difference of each fallacy. The **genus** represents the general class of fallacy (such as *ad fontem* fallacies) and the **difference** represents the specific example (such as *ad hominem* abusive) from that class. This approach will help you deepen your understanding of each *class* of fallacy and the *specific* examples contained in each class. It will also aid you in memorizing the key aspects of each fallacy in a class, which will help you to detect and identify fallacies accurately.

## *Ad Hominem* Abusive

| | |
|---|---|
| FALLACIES OF RELEVANCE | Arguments that are really distractions from the main point. |
| *Ad Fontem* Arguments *(Arguments against the source)* | Arguments that distract by focusing on the source of the argument rather than the issue itself. |
| *Ad Hominem* Abusive | *Ad hominem* arguments that insult or abuse an opponent. |

Do you really want a computer that is named after a fruit?

Buy a computer you'll use, not eat. Buy IBN.

## *Ad Hominem* Abusive

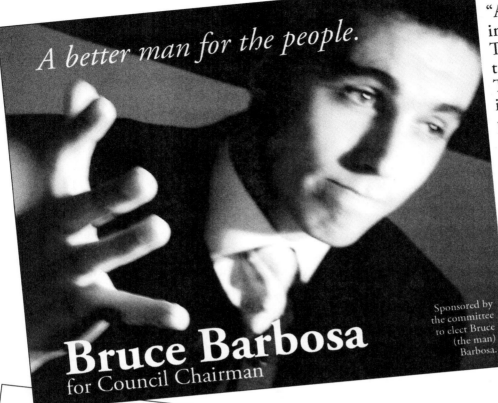

*A better man for the people.*

# Bruce Barbosa
## for Council Chairman

Sponsored by the committee to elect Bruce (the man) Barbosa.

"A vote for incumbent Sam Turnpaugh is a tragic mistake. That dirty dog isn't worth putting back in office much less the dog house he deserves . . .

. . . [Sam] acts like he's still in kindergarten. Why would we reelect him?"

Bruce Barbosa
Independent

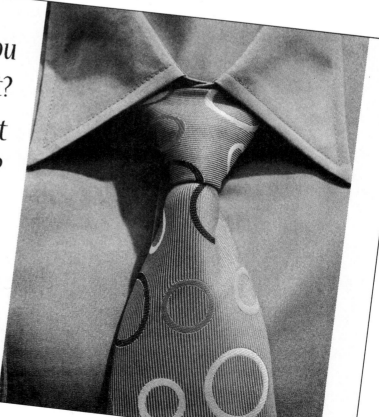

Um . . . where did you find your shirt?
The lukewarm rack at Hot·Stuff Central™?

**Buzz Rack**®
*The clothes you really want.*

# Fallacy Discussion on *Ad Hominem* Abusive

**Socrates:** Hello again, student philosophers! From time to time, I'm going to address you with some questions. While you won't be able to discuss your ideas with me, you can practice with each other the way that Tiffany and I do. Here's your first assignment: compare the following two arguments, which address the controversial issue of the credibility of President George W. Bush as commander-in-chief of the war with Iraq.

1. George Bush is a habitual liar. Surely you must see that it was useless to expect him to properly lead us into the war in Iraq or manage the war properly, since he is utterly untrustworthy.

2. Prior to the invasion of Iraq, President Bush told us that Iraq had weapons of mass destruction that it could use against the United States. As it turned out, this was false—Iraq had no weapons of mass destruction. There are certainly grounds for questioning whether Bush properly led the United States into this war.

Which one of the statements above do you think commits the fallacy of *ad hominem* abusive? Explain why and then compare your answer with one on the next page.

Example 1 is committing an *ad hominem* abusive fallacy. It attacks the character of

George Bush by calling him a "habitual liar." Whether he is or is not a liar is not directly

relevant to whether the war was justifiable. See the following page for further explanation.

**Socrates:** If you reasoned that the first example committed the fallacy of *ad hominem* abusive, then you were right! In both of the previous examples, the speaker is intending to show that the past behavior of President Bush may be evidence for the argument that Bush is untrustworthy. The second example, however, focuses on real evidence rather than simply making a general charge that Bush is a "habitual liar." If you followed the events leading up to the Iraq war, you know that Bush's claim that Iraq had weapons of mass destruction has become a highly controversial issue, in which there are many disagreements about the facts and the interpretations of those facts. While the argument given in the second example may not give conclusive proof that Bush improperly led the United States into the Iraq war (for there were several other reasons that Bush urged the invasion of Iraq, and Bush may have been reporting the facts as they truly appeared to be at the time), it is at least a reasonable position, with one piece of supporting evidence given. The first example not only contains unnecessary emotional language, but also places its emphasis on a personal attack, rather than on the issue of whether or not Bush properly led the United States to war. Emotive language and personal attacks are great for propaganda and browbeating those with whom one disagrees, but they are not useful for really solving problems and conflicts.

**Chapter 1: *Ad Fontem* Arguments**
Fallacy Discussion on *Ad Hominem* Abusive

# Fallacy 2:
## *Ad Hominem* Circumstantial

DEFINITION: Arguments that try to discredit an opponent because of his background, affiliations, or self-interest in the matter at hand.

The *ad hominem* circumstantial fallacy does not abuse the personal character of an opponent as the *ad hominem* abusive fallacy does. Instead, it criticizes something about the circumstances of an opponent—things such as the opponent's place of birth, educational background, job experience, family, friends, and the associations and organizations to which he belongs. For example, does it make sense to reject a person's argument because she is from the northern part of the country? Should we reject the argument of a person because he did not attend college or because he did attend college?

Consider the following examples of the *ad hominem* circumstantial fallacy.

**Example 1**

You can't accept her argument against abortion—she is a Catholic and the Catholic Church opposes abortion.

**Example 2**

You can't accept his argument favoring legalized abortion—he is a member of the American Civil Liberties Union, which supports legalized abortion.

**Example 3**

That is a typical argument from someone who was raised in a wealthy family—of course you want to reduce taxes for the rich!

**Example 4**

He worked for thirty years as a prison guard—that's why he wants the government to build ten more prisons we can't afford.

Whether someone is a Catholic or a member of the American Civil Liberties Union, as in examples 1 and 2, should not be a cause for rejecting that person's argument about abortion. The argument itself needs to be heard and stand or fall on its own merits. Notice that in examples 3 and 4, the critic seems to think that the person whose argument is in question is seeking his own personal benefit. In other words, the man raised in a wealthy family is accused of making an argument to reduce taxes for the wealthy only because he and his wealthy family members would benefit from such a reduction. The prison guard seems to be accused of supporting the construction of more prisons only because it would benefit other prison guards such as himself. In these cases, we would do well to separate the argument from any benefits that may come to the person arguing. Simply because you are interested in, and will benefit from, the thing for which you argue does not automatically discredit your argument. These people may have strong arguments, so let's hear them.

### *Ad Hominem* Circumstantial

**Genus (general class):** An argument to the source.
**Difference (specific trait):** An argument directed against the circumstances of the speaker's rival. (Not necessarily or obviously abusive.)

## *Ad Hominem* Circumstantial

| | |
|---|---|
| FALLACIES OF RELEVANCE | Arguments that are really distractions from the main point. |
| *Ad Fontem* Arguments *(Arguments against the source)* | Arguments that distract by focusing on the source of the argument rather than the issue itself. |
| *Ad Hominem* Circumstantial | *Ad hominem* arguments that try to discredit an opponent because of his situation. |

EVER FIND THAT THOSE BIG BANKS DON'T UNDERSTAND ANYTHING BUT BIG?

BANKING SMALL ENOUGH FOR EVERYONE

**Cornwall Community Bank**
member FDIU

Don't TRUST your hair to just any brunette

Nobody knows blondes like we know BLONDES

Enriches as it beatifies,
**Bomb Blondy** does your hair like no other.

## *Ad Hominem* Circumstantial

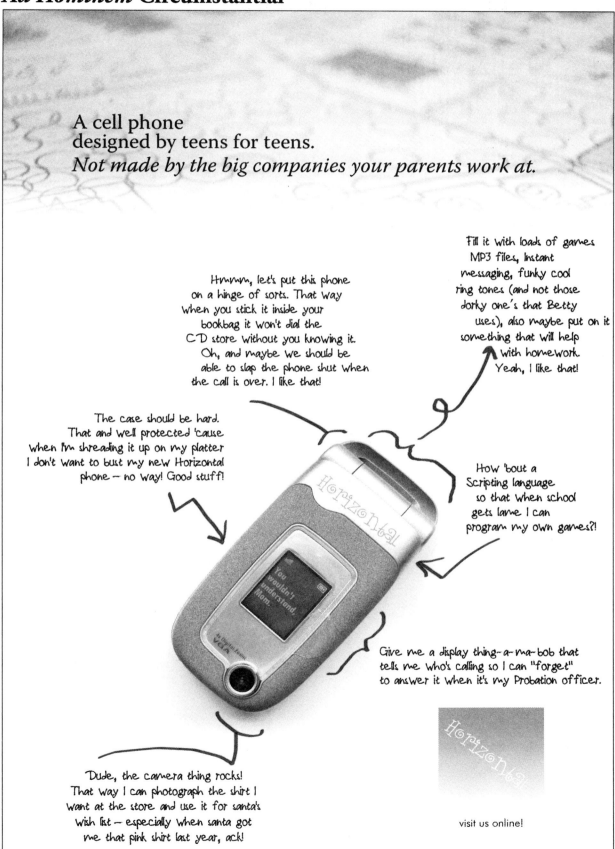

A cell phone
designed by teens for teens.
*Not made by the big companies your parents work at.*

# Fallacy Discussion on *Ad Hominem* Circumstantial

**Socrates:** Here's another exercise for you to try: discuss whether or not the following argument is an example of an *ad hominem* circumstantial fallacy.

*One should never trust a military man who wants an increase in military spending, since it is in his interest to use that money to create a larger military. The only reason why he wants to have a large military is because it makes him more important!*

How do you think this argument might or might not be fair and relevant? Is a fallacy being committed?

An answer appears on the next page, but don't look until you've thought about it yourself and written down your own answer.

This example is committing an *ad hominem* circumstantial fallacy by implying that any argument that benefits the presenter should automatically be discounted. The speaker judges the opponent's argument because of his situation and assumes that the military man is only motivated by increasing his own importance. Further discussion follows on the next page.

**Socrates:** If you answered that the example was, indeed, committing a fallacy, you were right! This sort of approach is actually quite common in the public sphere. When listening to arguments relating to politics and policy, one frequently hears a speaker attempting to refute his opponent's argument on the grounds that his opponent has some sort of self-interest involved. This line of argument fails on more than one level.

First, it unfairly imputes motives to the person involved. Because of this, it fails as an explanation for why the person is making the argument that he is making. Remember that it is always a tricky business to judge someone else's motives because no one can judge the heart. After all, it could be that the military man involved has dedicated his life to the military precisely because he has always been convinced of its vital importance from the beginning. (Thus there could be a "common cause" for both his being in the military and his thinking that we need a larger one.)

Of course, even if his motives for wanting a larger military are entirely noble, it still doesn't necessarily follow that a larger one would be better. However, explaining the speaker's motives for advocating a course of action is never the main point of an argument at all! That's why these sort of arguments are so misplaced; even to allow ourselves to be drawn into the tricky quagmire of ascertaining someone else's motivations is allowing ourselves to be drawn into the wrong debate. The best response is to return to our old standard response to all fallacies of relevance: "true or not, it's irrelevant."

# Fallacy 3:

## *Tu Quoque*

DEFINITION: Arguments that assume that a rival's recommendation should be discounted because the rival does not always follow it himself.

In Latin, *tu quoque* means "you too" or "you also." The person committing this fallacy accuses his opponent of having the same flaw that his opponent is pointing out in his argument. In effect, he says to his opponent, "But you also (*tu quoque*) do the same thing you are arguing against!" Take, for example, the classic case of an old man with a cigarette saying to a younger man, "Don't smoke. It's a filthy habit and will shorten your life." The younger man may reply, "But you are a smoker yourself. You can't argue that I shouldn't smoke!"

As you can see, the *tu quoque* fallacy charges a person with a kind of inconsistency regarding the argument being made. That inconsistency is often made out to be a character flaw.

Consider the following examples of the *tu quoque* fallacy.

**Example 1**

**John:** Slow down, you are going 10 mph over the speed limit.

**Mark:** You're telling me to drive more slowly, but you're the one with four speeding tickets this year! I may drive over the speed limit sometimes, but I don't drive nearly as fast as you do.

**Example 2**

**Former Governor:** The new governor should propose a balanced budget that won't increase our state deficit.

**Governor:** Last year, my predecessor spent $100 million more than the government collected, thereby adding another $100 million to our state debt. My budget is far more realistic and should only increase the debt by $15 million. This is a responsible budget. It is ridiculous that my predecessor should dare to offer any criticism of this budget given his previous spending policies.

Note that in each case above, the speaker is pointing out a flaw in his opponent—a flaw of inconsistency—while at the same time comparing himself favorably to the opponent. It as if the speaker is saying, "I may have a problem, but look how much worse you are. You, too, have a flaw, and a worse one than I do, so your argument doesn't count." In truth, John and the former governor may have strong arguments, despite their own flaws. The old man with the cigarette may have a strong argument for not smoking precisely *because* he has smoked for years. John, with four speeding tickets, may have learned a lesson or two about speeding that Mark should heed. The personal flaws of these people are not relevant to the argument they are making. Judge the argument, not the person making it.

As well, people with flaws and inconsistencies do sometimes change their views over time. In other words, just because someone had flaws and made mistakes in the past, does not necessarily mean that the flaws are still present or that the same mistakes continue. People often learn from their mistakes and change their views. For instance, the economist John Maynard Keynes was once asked by a reporter why he changed his view about regulating money during the Great Depression. He replied, "When the facts change, I change my mind. What do you do, sir?"[1]

---

1. Keynes' reply to a criticism during the Great Depression of having changed his position on monetary policy, as quoted in Alfred L. Malabre's *Lost Prophets: An Insider's History of the Modern Economists* (Boston: Harvard Business Press, 1995), 220.

**Tu Quoque Fallacy**
**Genus (general class):** An argument to the source.
**Difference (specific trait):** An argument centered entirely on the inconsistencies exhibited by the speaker's rival.

# Tu Quoque

| | |
|---|---|
| FALLACIES OF RELEVANCE | Arguments that are really distractions from the main point. |
| *Ad Fontem* Arguments *(Arguments Against the Source)* | Arguments that distract by focusing on the source of the argument rather than the issue itself. |
| *Tu Quoque* | Arguments that claim that because the opposing speaker is flawed, his argument can't be true: "We might be bad, but they're worse, so go with us instead." |

**Kids go crazy over Sugar Dump!**

And Moms, just remember, we don't have as much sugar as Sugar-Bombs® does and we cost less!

*Binner Cereals*

Only 128 grams of sugar per serving

SUGAR DUMP

SAVE 25¢

Buy up to 6 boxes with this coupon. Not valid with any other offer. Good at participating grocery stores. Valid through 6/12/14. Coupon value = $.00001

# Fallacy Discussion on *Tu Quoque*

**Socrates:** There is nothing like a *tu quoque* fallacy to start a good quarrel or to distract from the issue at hand. Consider the following dialogues and discuss how they are examples of a *tu quoque* fallacy. Further explanation of these examples is provided on the next page.

> **Ann:** Susan, you wore my new red sweater last night without asking me if you could! You can't wear it anymore.

> **Susan:** How can you say that? Just last week you wore my sweatshirt to the gym without asking!

Susan commits a *tu quoque* fallacy because whether or not Ann did the same thing to her in the past, it does not make it right for her to wear Ann's clothes without asking her first. Two wrongs do not make a right. This is a case of a fallacy fueling a quarrel.

**Socrates:** The following is a political example of a *tu quoque* fallacy.

> **Republican Senator:** Now that you Democrats are in control of the House and Senate, your party is spending the American people's money left and right on stimulating the economy and big government social programs!

> **Democratic Senator:** You should remember back a few years to the spending that your party did on the war! You have no ground to stand on if you are accusing us of being big spenders.

This is a *tu quoque* fallacy, since there are many different issues that a government can spend money on, and whether or not one party spent money in the past is irrelevant to whether money should be spent on something else in the present. In this case, the fallacy is likely being used to persuade a listening voter to continue to support a political party.

Socrates: Here is a third example on an issue many students encounter.

> **Father:** I know that you love cartooning, but it is tough to make a living selling artwork for comics. Perhaps you could consider a college major that would use many of your talents but would still provide you with marketable skills so that you can get a job that will support you.

> **Son:** Dad, I know you studied writing in college and wanted to be a novelist, but that's not what you're doing now. I don't see why I shouldn't get the chance to try to follow my dreams just because it didn't work out for you!

This son commits a tu quoque fallacy in the sense that simply because his father failed at becoming a novelist does not mean that his recommendation that his son change his major is discredited. The father may have made a misstep he fears his son will also make.

**Socrates:** These examples all commit the *tu quoque* fallacy, though they are quite different in character. Considering the first example, you can see how a *tu quoque* fallacy is very commonly found in small quarrels.

In the political example, it may be good to point out when there are inconsistencies in a political party or in a politician. It is wise to consider whether it is a sign of changing a position to fit popular opinions or of having a double standard when one is promoting one's own agenda. However, the past actions of a party or politician do not necessarily bear on the issue at hand, and it is important to keep your eye on the real issue. It is also likely that these arguments are being made to try to persuade voters to support one party or another. The Democrat's response does not address the issue of whether Congress is spending money wisely, but distracts the other side by causing the Republican to defend past actions rather than focusing on the issues at hand.

In the third example, the son commits a *tu quoque* fallacy by choosing to ignore advice on the grounds that his father chose to do something similar and failing when he was his son's age, rather than considering the wisdom that his father may have gained through his decisions. We can probably assume that the father has his son's best interests at heart and is lovingly trying to direct him. The son may well end up being successful at a comic career, but is certainly committing a fallacy by dismissing his father's advice by saying "you too," or *tu quoque*.

# Fallacy 4:
## Genetic Fallacy

DEFINITION: Arguments that state that an idea should be discounted simply because of its source or origin.

A genetic fallacy is the *ad fontem* fallacy that is most clearly an attack on the "fountain" (*fontem*) or source of an argument. The genetic fallacy ignores the argument it opposes and instead focuses on the source from which the argument came.

The word "genetic" comes from the Greek word *genesis*, which means "beginning." A person committing this fallacy thinks that if she can point out and discredit where the argument began, she can discredit the argument itself. That is almost like saying that because a computer was made in Mexico, it must be bad.

Consider the following examples of the genetic fallacy.

**Example 1**

Did you know that Greg believes in life in outer space? I think it started with that movie he watched last year about aliens. He believes in extraterrestrial life because of a Hollywood film!

**Example 2**

Of course Julie argues that car companies should build their cars to stricter standards of safety. Her brother works for the Automobile Safety Commission. His entire life is dedicated to car safety!

Greg may have become interested in the possibility of extraterrestrial life as a result of watching a movie on the subject. The movie may have presented some interesting evidence for the possibility of extraterrestrial life, but that has nothing to do with whether his argument is a good one or not. Let's hear Greg's argument for life in outer space and judge it, not its source. It is no surprise that Julie might be interested in car safety because of her brother's work and influence. Even if her argument does come from her brother, that is no reason to dismiss it. Her argument may be quite good regardless of where it came from, so judge it on its own merits.

**Example 3**

What causes belief in God? The famous psychologist Sigmund Freud proposed that sometimes when people do not have a good experience or relationship with their own fathers, they wish for and imagine a God who is a great, cosmic father figure who offers the things they missed in their relationships with their own fathers. Freud called this "wish projection," and his argument was that if belief in God was simply created out of people's wishes, God must not exist.

While this theory might have some validity in explaining the nature of people's perceptions of God, it actually does not bear on the issue of whether God exists or not. Many people may believe in God's existence for reasons other than a wish for a cosmic father figure. You can quickly see that a theist could also fall into the same fallacy by arguing that atheists don't believe in God only because of their desire to be free from any divine accountability—so they can live their lives without the worry or threat of the judgment of God (or gods). While it may be true that some atheists adopt atheism for this reason, it does not bear on the issue of whether there is a God or not. Many atheists do not believe in the existence of God (or gods) for reasons other than a desire to be free from divine accountability.

Note that the genetic fallacy is the least "personal" of all the *ad fontem* fallacies. The *ad hominem* abusive and *ad hominem* circumstantial fallacies both touch on the man (*hominem*). The *tu quoque* fallacy also features a flaw (of inconsistency) in one's opponent, which makes it a personal fallacy as well. The genetic fallacy, however, focuses on the source of a person's argument, making it a less personal attack. We might even call the genetic fallacy an *impersonal* attack. For instance, in example 1, it was the movie that Greg saw that led him to believe in extraterrestrial life, rather than a personal flaw in Greg himself. As with all the *ad fontem* fallacies, we can legitimately say of the attack on the source for Greg's argument that it is true, perhaps, but irrelevant—it is true that the movie gave rise to Greg's position, but that is irrelevant to the validity of his argument. Judge the argument, not its source.

**Genetic Fallacy**

**Genus:** An argument to the source.
**Difference:** An argument that isn't directed at an individual person: an "impersonal attack."

Eeeeeech!
I bet it tastes like mud
or dead beetles . . .

# Genetic Fallacy

| | |
|---|---|
| FALLACIES OF RELEVANCE | Arguments that are really distractions from the main point. |
| *Ad Fontem* Arguments *(Arguments against the source)* | Arguments that distract by focusing on the source of the argument rather than on the issue itself. |
| Genetic Fallacy | *Ad fontem* argument that distracts by focusing attention on an **impersonal** source of an opposing argument. |

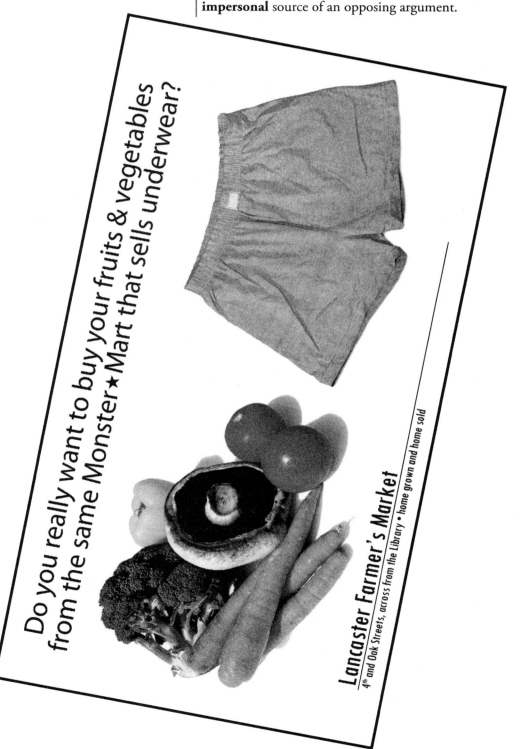

Do you really want to buy your fruits & vegetables from the same Monster★Mart that sells underwear?

**Lancaster Farmer's Market**
4ᵗʰ and Oak Streets, across from the Library • home grown and home sold

# Genetic Fallacy

**Chapter 1:** *Ad Fontem* **Arguments**
Fallacy 4: Genetic Fallacy

# Chapter 1 Review

**A. DEFINE: Include English translations for Latin terms.**

1. *Ad Fontem* Arguments:

 A subgroup of the fallacies of relevance consisting of arguments that focus on the source

 of the argument, rather than on the issue itself. Translation: "to the source or fountain."

2. *Ad Hominem* Abusive:

 An *ad fontem* argument that attempts to avoid the issue by insulting an opponent with

 abusive language. Translation: "to the man."

3. *Ad Hominem* Circumstantial:

 An *ad fontem* argument that tries to discredit an opponent because of his background,

 affiliations, or self-interest in the matter at hand. Translation: "to the man."

4. *Tu Quoque*:

 An *ad fontem* argument that assumes that a rival's recommendation should be discounted

 because the rival does not always follow it himself. Translation: "you also."

5. Genetic Fallacy:

 An *ad fontem* argument that states that an idea should be discounted simply because of its

 source or origin.

**B. IDENTIFICATION:**

Which *ad fontem* argument is being described in each instance below?

1. An argument directed against the circumstances of the speaker's rival.

 *ad hominem* circumstantial

2. An argument implementing obviously abusive language.

 *ad hominem* abusive

3. An argument centered entirely on the inconsistencies exhibited by the speaker's rival.

 *tu quoque*

4. An argument that isn't directed at a person; an impersonal attack.

 genetic fallacy

**C. APPLICATION:**

Find or write two examples of an *ad fontem* argument. You may use Internet sites, books, newspapers, or magazines as resources.

 See examples included in the fallacy descriptions for the first four fallacies in the text.

# Chapter 2
## Appeals to Emotion

DEFINITION: A subgroup of the fallacies of relevance. These arguments attempt to sway the opinions of people by compelling them to feel emotions such as pity, anger, fear, joy, peer pressure, intimidation, etc.

Most of the informal fallacies probably appeal to emotion in one way or another, but this particular class of fallacies do it in the most straightforward manner. Each of these fallacies makes a play straight for the emotions of the audience.

Why do you think the appeals to emotion fallacies are fallacies of relevance?

An appeal to emotion fallacy distracts an audience from the issue at hand by introducing an emotional issue and persuades by inducing fear, pity, etc.

What does "makes a play straight for the emotions of the audience" mean?

It means that the person making an argument is purposely evoking the emotions of his audience in order to persuade them.

## Vocabulary

- Appeal to Emotion
- Appeal to Fear
- Appeal to Pity
- Mob Appeal
- Snob Appeal
- Appeal to Illegitimate Authority
- Chronological Snobbery
- Non-Argumentative Persuasion

Before we dive in and tackle the next set of fallacies, let's see what our friend Socrates is up to.

# Dialogue on Appeals to Emotion

*Nate is walking down the street when he sees Socrates standing on the sidewalk.*

**Nate:** Socrates! I didn't expect to see you here!

**Socrates:** Believe me, most people don't expect to see me anywhere.

**Nate:** What are you doing here?

**Socrates:** I'm just studying the world around me. I do that.

**Nate:** What are you looking for?

**Socrates:** Answers. I want to know the answers to questions.

**Nate:** Like what?

**Socrates:** What do you think?

**Nate:** Oh, I don't know . . ."What is the nature of wisdom?"

**Socrates:** Not today. Right now I'm thinking more along the lines of, "Why don't these people understand?"

**Nate:** Understand what?

**Socrates:** This society you live in knows nothing about reasoning.

**Nate:** Now, wait a minute. You can't be saying that everybody in America is illogical.

**Socrates:** No, I'm not. Then I would be committing the fallacy of the sweeping generalization. But I'm seeing many people fall for fallacies of a different sort. Take that billboard over there, for example.

**Nate:** "Vote Steven Reed for President . . . the fate of the nation depends on it." What about it?

**Socrates:** Why don't you answer your own question?

**Nate:** Oh, uh, sorry. Well, I guess the problem with it is that it doesn't explain enough. It implies that the country may have severe problems if Steven Reed isn't elected president. But, that could be true. His opponents could make a big mess out of the whole country.

**Socrates:** Yes, they could. But does the billboard really say what kinds of troubles will happen if he's not elected?

**Nate:** No, it doesn't. So that billboard is playing on people's emotions to make them think something horrible will happen if they don't vote for Steven Reed. Hey, that seems like a fallacy.

**Socrates:** What makes you say that?

**Nate:** Well, it doesn't really give you a valid reason to believe the argument.

**Socrates:** Excellent! It is, indeed, a fallacy. That fallacy is called the *argumentum ad baculum*, or simply, the "appeal to fear." It doesn't provide a valid reason to believe the "argument" it makes at all and uses your emotions to make a point. Do you think threats would fit into this category?

**Nate:** Um, well . . . threats don't really make arguments at all.

**Socrates:** That's correct. All-out threats aren't arguments. They're really a sort of non-argumentative persuasion. If a thug jumped out of this alley and pointed a knife at you, he obviously wouldn't be trying to make you see things from his angle. He would be forcing you to do something, not persuading you to believe something.

**Nate:** Yeah, and even if someone threatened you to believe something, I don't think you really would be convinced that his side is the best side.

**Socrates:** True. But back to the *argumentum ad baculum*. It's only one of several fallacies that play on our emotions. There are others, the main ones being the *argumentum ad populum* and *argumentum ad misericordiam*. I'll bet you can guess what they mean.

**Nate:** Populace and misery? OK . . . the first one tries to sway a large crowd, and the second one . . . um . . . makes you sad?

**Socrates:** Right again! Now, how would you manipulate somebody using a crowd?

**Nate:** I guess I would try to make him want to be part of the crowd. Maybe something like "everybody's doing it."

**Socrates:** Very good. An *ad populum* argument doesn't even have to convince a crowd—it can simply make you want to be part of a crowd. It's also known as mob appeal. For example, if that billboard read, "Vote Steven Reed—the American Choice," people reading it who want to be thought of as American might vote for him.

**Nate:** But that has nothing to do with whether or not the argument is valid. If making the right decision automatically makes you un-American, I still think it would be the better choice.

**Socrates:** That's basically the whole premise behind all of these fallacies: they distract the audience from the point. They're not relevant.

**Nate:** You said that *ad populum* arguments can persuade a crowd, too. Let me think . . . would an example be if somebody in a speech said that his plan would be good for farmers and there were a lot of farmers in the audience?

**Socrates:** Not exactly. That would be more of an appeal to self-interest. *Ad populum* arguments are more along the lines of stirring up the crowd. There's a certain mentality when a group is involved, and the speakers can manipulate this and rouse the crowd into a frenzy. Often we find after a major social upheaval that many people are drawn into violent behavior by the "group think" of a mob. Naturally, I believe the crowd cannot be a lover of wisdom.

**Nate:** And a "lover of wisdom" is a philosopher, so a crowd cannot be a philosopher.

**Socrates:** Right. I also think that demagogues should be jailed immediately.

**Nate:** Why? What's a demagogue?

**Socrates:** One who makes these types of fallacious arguments and persuades the crowd by their emotions.

**Nate:** Like Brutus and Marc Antony?

**Socrates:** Now that you'll have to explain to me.

**Nate:** In the days of the Roman Empire, which you weren't around for, there was a powerful ruler named Julius Cæsar. Some members of the Roman Senate thought he was a little too powerful, so they killed him. As the good friend of Caesar, Brutus gave a speech to the public explaining why he helped kill Cæsar, using the *argumentum ad baculum* fallacy to gain the people's support. He argued that Caesar's great power threatened their liberty and peace. Next, Marc Antony addressed the crowd and used the same tactics to turn the crowd against Brutus and the other conspirators. Well, at least that's what happened according to Shakespeare. I don't know if he got the details right, but we all know who succeeded Julius Caesar as emperor . . . and it wasn't Brutus.

**Socrates:** Marc Antony . . . Marc Antony . . .

**Nate:** His girlfriend was Cleopatra, if that helps.

**Socrates:** Oh yes, I've heard of her. She was the Queen of Denial.

**Nate:** Huh?

**Socrates:** Great example. There are other fallacies that deal with emotions.

**Nate:** You mentioned one other; did you say it was . . . *ad misericordiam?*

**Socrates:** Yes, that was it. Why don't you tell me what it's about?

**Nate:** Hey, you're the philosopher here, not me.

**Socrates:** That's no reason not to make a guess.

**Nate:** OK, OK. Um . . . I guess it would target your misery. It would try to persuade you by making you feel sorry for somebody.

**Socrates:** Perhaps there is hope for this country after all. *Ad misericordiam,* or the appeal to pity, targets our emotion of compassion. You've probably seen an ad for an animal shelter showing pictures of helpless little animals just waiting for your help. Our instinctual response is to donate money. Do we know what they are really doing with the money? We'd better make sure that we aren't just swayed by our emotions, but that we are thinking clearly. What larger category do these sorts of arguments fit into?

**Nate:** You mean the ones that aren't relevant?

**Socrates:** That's right. This is another example of a fallacy of relevance. This argument relies on our human qualities to get us to believe even without really thinking. Can you think of an example?

**Nate:** Maybe campaigns for ending world hunger. The campaigns are not at all a bad thing, even though they may try to get us to give money. However, their methods for solving the problem could be completely ineffective, which would mean that we've wasted our money and our time. We need to make sure that the group we're giving money to not only sees a problem, but also has a solution in mind.

**Socrates:** Yes. Demagogues like to persuade us without letting us think, but people should know better.

**Nate:** Is there really much of a difference between the appeals to pity and fear? Can't you do something out of fear for the "other guy"?

**Socrates:** Yes, you can, although that really falls into the category of pity. Generally, pity is directed at the "other guy," but fear is a concern for oneself.

**Nate:** Oh, OK. Well, I guess I have no more questions.

**Socrates:** I still do, but I'm a philosopher. That's just me.

**Nate:** I guess I'll see you later, then. I have to watch a biography on Cleopatra, Queen of the Nile.

**Socrates:** Why?

**Nate:** Otherwise, I'll get a poor grade in Ancient History.

**Socrates:** *(shaking his head)* After all that, he goes and appeals to fear.

# Fallacy 5:
## Appeal to Fear
### (*Argumentum Ad Baculum*)

DEFINITION: Arguments that distract by making the audience afraid of the consequences of disagreeing with the speaker. This fallacy seeks to arouse a fear of harm that is not realistic or related to the issue at hand.

In Latin, *baculum* means "stick" or "club," so the fallacy of appeal to fear, or *argumentum ad baculum*, is sometimes called "waving a big stick." A person using this fallacy seeks to persuade others by arousing their fears. This fallacy is also sometimes called "an appeal to force."

It is clear that if someone threatens you with force if you don't agree with his argument, you might understandably become fearful. In other words, there is a clear relationship between the threat of force and fear. Still, an outright and straightforward threat of force does not involve an argument at all. For instance, imagine someone said to you, "You better buy this car or I am going to hit you with this club!" This is really just a demand that you do something with no attempt to engage you in conversation and no attempt to change your thinking or beliefs. This attempt at persuasion would be considered a form of **non-argumentative persuasion**. The club may be persuasive, but it is not an argument.

> **NON-ARGUMENTATIVE PERSUASION:**
> An argument is not made, but the audience is persuaded by force or rhetorical tricks, often ones which stir up the emotions.

Throughout history, people have sought to change behavior through an outright threat of force. Some totalitarian governments have threatened and used force against people in an attempt to change and control the way people think and in order to compel them to change their behavior. Note that force need not be in the form of a club or gun. Other types of force include imprisonment, exile, and the removal of rights.

There are several ways in which we can appeal to fear in an argument and commit this fallacy. Any time we seek to create an unrealistic fear of harm in an argument, we are appealing to fear. Keep in mind, however, that there are times when pointing out potential harm is not a fallacy at all, when such harm is realistic and related to the issue at hand. For example, your driving instructor may tell you that you should always wear your seat belt because if you don't, your risk of serious injury in an accident is quite high. When real danger is at hand, it is no fallacy to appeal to fear. When there is no real danger, however, then it is a fallacy to appeal to fear. For example, a dandruff commercial that shows an attractive woman being rebuffed by a man because of a flake on her shoulder is portraying an unrealistic danger. You won't likely lose the love of your life because of a flake of dandruff.

Consider the following examples of the fallacy of appeal to fear.

**Example 1**

What if cell phones cause brain cancer? It is better to do without a cell phone and preserve your health.

**Example 2**

Don't be just another student that can't get into a decent college because of mediocre SAT scores. Use the Acme SAT Super Study Course! You don't have to settle for mediocrity.

These two examples make use of scare tactics—they seek to create or arouse fear that is unrealistic. If there is no good evidence that cell phones cause brain cancer, it is not a realistic threat. If you are a hard-working student, there is no realistic danger that you will be unable to get into a decent college.

## *Argumentum Ad Baculum* (Appeal to Fear)

**Genus:** An argument that avoids the issue by appealing to the listener's emotions.
**Difference:** An argument appealing to the emotion of fear.

**ANSWER:**

1. Why is the Latin phrase *ad baculum* ("to the stick") an appropriate phrase for a fallacy that appeals to fear?

   The name implies that you will be hurt (beaten by some variety of stick) if you do not accept the argument being given.

2. What is the difference between the appeal to fear and the appeal to force?

   An appeal to force may involve fear but technically it is not an attempt to change beliefs but rather a blatant attempt to change one's behavior. As such, an appeal to force is not really even an argument but a form of compulsion.

3. Cite or create an example of non-argumentative persuasion.

   Answers will vary.

4. Cite or create an example of an *ad baculum* (appeal to fear) fallacy.

   Answers will vary. For examples, see examples 1 and 2 in the text on this page.

5. Can you cite a commercial that uses the *ad baculum* fallacy?

   Answers will vary.

# Appeal to Fear

| | |
|---|---|
| FALLACIES OF RELEVANCE | Arguments that are really distractions from the main point. |
| Appeals to Emotion | Arguments that distract by deliberately arousing our emotions. |
| Appeal to Fear (*Argumentum Ad Baculum*) | An argument that distracts by making the audience afraid of the consequences of disagreeing with the speaker. |

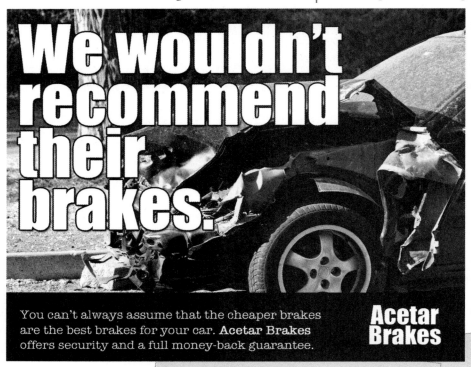

# Appeal to Fear

23 million years ago, this would have been a bad place to vacation.

**Mainard Travel Insurance**
You never know when nature may strike.

The marlin were biting, but not as much as the sharks.

**Mainard Travel Insurance**
You never know when nature may bite back.

# Fallacy Discussion on Appeal to Fear

**Socrates:** Often advertisers will appeal to fear as a way of persuading you to purchase their products or services. Explain why the television advertisement described below is an appeal to fear. What is the real issue the advertisers are trying to get at? Have they argued successfully?

People are emptying bins of dollar bills out of windows on the eighth floor of an apartment building. The bills flutter down to the street below.
**Narrator:** Are you throwing your money away? If you're not using Levera Auto Insurance, then you are probably spending more money than you need to on your car insurance, which means you are throwing your money away! Levera: we cost less.

### The following points could be made:

1. The real issue for the advertiser is to persuade the viewer to buy its auto insurance.

2. By showing money being thrown away, the advertiser is appealing to the fear its audience has of simply taking hard-earned money and throwing it out the window.

3. Then the advertiser connects this fear of waste to the money the audience is currently spending on auto insurance, suggesting that with Levera the audience would pay less, thus not "throwing" money away.

4. The image of money being thrown out the window is gripping and evokes an emotional response: Why would anyone throw money out into the street?

5. As an argument, however, the advertisement is not successful. Even if Levera insurance does cost less, consumers often get what they pay for. The advertisement says nothing about the quality of the insurance offered by Levera. Maybe Levera insurance only pays for a relatively small portion of the damages if an accident occurs. In that case, Levera might be cheaper, but only until an accident occurs. This advertisement is simply trying to scare the audience into considering purchasing the product by presenting the painful prospect that the audience is throwing its money away.

# Fallacy 6:
## Appeal to Pity
## (*Argumentum Ad Misericordiam*)

DEFINITION: Arguments that distract by making the audience feel sorry for the speaker or someone on behalf of whom the speaker is arguing. This fallacy appeals to our sense of compassion. Like the other appeals to emotion, it tries to get us to accept certain views or courses of action by causing us to sympathize with the speaker rather than by providing good and careful reasoning.

This should be a very familiar fallacy. We have all made appeals to pity, and we regularly receive such appeals. Of course, there are many times when appealing to pity is a very appropriate thing to do. When a hunger-relief organization appeals to your pity for support of people in great need of food, is that organization committing a fallacy? No. In fact, it is quite right to be moved with pity for those in need, and appealing to that pity need not be a fallacy.

So when is an appeal to our pity a fallacy? An appeal to pity becomes a fallacy when we are distracted by our pity from other important issues that we should consider. For example, someone who wishes to steal your money may pretend to be helping the needy as he solicits donations for his "organization." Should you give money to an unknown organization that comes knocking on your door asking you to help starving children in Africa? We should not let our pity be stirred to the point of ignoring other important questions about the legitimacy of the need and the legitimacy of the organization or person seeking to meet that need. We should remember that even if the need is quite real, such as relieving hunger in Africa, it does not necessarily follow that the specific plan or organization someone is advocating will really meet this need or meet it well.

Consider the following examples of appeals to pity.

**Example 1**
   **Defense Lawyer:** My client, Mr. Jones, may have taken the money from the bank as these witnesses have testified, but as you know, he was out of work and trying to find the means to buy his children presents for Christmas. He was filled with anguish at the thought of not being able to give his children a happy holiday experience, and it was with these troubled thoughts running through his mind that he held up the bank, fully intending to repay the bank after he found work. I encourage the jury not to send Mr. Jones to jail, but to give him the chance to resume his life as he seeks to personally remedy what he has done.

Mr. Jones may, indeed, have been out of work and wanting desperately to buy presents for his children, but does that justify taking other people's money? The jury must not be distracted from the law by pity for the man's circumstances. The judge would have charged them—according to the law—to find him guilty or innocent based upon the evidence showing whether he committed the crime or not.

### Example 2

**Susan:** Mom, if we don't take this injured squirrel to the vet, he will die! We can't let it die!

What Susan says is probably true. We have all seen injured animals and often we want to help. However, it simply cannot be the job of every mother to rescue every injured squirrel or bird by taking them to the vet and paying for their care. Susan's mom likely has other important tasks from which the injured squirrel should not distract her. Susan's mom will likely say to her daughter, "You are right that the squirrel will probably die, but we still cannot try to rescue it."

### Example 3

**Government official:** If we don't get more funding for this program, there will be more jobless people out on the streets. I urge the legislature to vote to increase funding for this program as soon as possible.

Obviously the legislators will want to know a lot more about this program before voting to give it more money. Has the program worked well in the past? Is the money being used well? Are there other ways of addressing the problem besides this program? An appeal to pity should not distract us from asking the hard questions.

Note that sometimes the appeal to pity can also be merged with an appeal to fear, especially when the speaker suggests not only that we have pity but also that if we don't act something really bad will happen—even to us. For example, the government official mentioned above could say, "If we don't get more funding for this program, these poor prisoners won't be properly educated in prison and may well return to a life of crime in our own communities when they are released." This argument appeals to our pity (the prisoners not being properly educated) and our fear (they could end up committing crimes in our towns).

You will know that you are hearing an appeal to pity in an argument if it refers to a problem that already exists (e.g., the prisoners are not being properly educated). You will know that you are hearing an appeal to fear if it refers to a problem that is yet to come (e.g., released prisoners committing crimes in your town).

## *Argumentum Ad Misericordiam* (Appeal to Pity)

**Genus:** An argument that avoids the issue by appealing to the listener's emotions.

**Difference:** An argument appealing to the emotion of pity.

**Chapter 2: Appeals to Emotion**
Fallacy 6: Appeal to Pity (*Argumentum Ad Misericordiam*)

# Appeal to Pity

| | |
|---|---|
| FALLACIES OF RELEVANCE | Arguments that are really distractions from the main point. |
| Appeals to Emotion | Arguments that distract by deliberately arousing our emotions. |
| Appeal to Pity (*Argumentum Ad Misericordiam*) | An argument that distracts by making the audience feel sorry for the speaker or someone on behalf of whom he's arguing. |

## Appeal to Pity

# Fallacy Discussion on Appeal to Pity

**Socrates:** Consider the scenarios below and see if you can spot the appeal to pity fallacy.

Imagine that you just got a job as a checkout clerk at your local grocery store. You are trying to save money for college, and your parents just informed you that you must pay for your own car insurance now that you have a job. While you check out groceries for customers, you start to think about how much money the store is making and the fact that they are only paying you minimum wage! Then you consider that your coworker is a single mom with only a high-school diploma who could get no other job. She is also making minimum wage, and she has to get food stamps in order to feed herself and her daughter, even though she is working for a grocery store that makes thousands of dollars a day! You hear that Congress is considering a raise to the minimum wage, and you think of your coworker (and your future college tuition!). You are thinking of writing a letter to your congressman telling him how much a raise in the minimum wage is truly needed.

How do you think a letter like this could set up an appeal to pity?

The letter could easily become an appeal to pity because it is attempting to persuade by

making one feel pity for the poor who are not making enough money to live on.

Now imagine that the grocery store owner is also composing a letter to Congress. He considers the higher prices he has to pay to food manufacturers and the price he is able to sell the food for in his store, which results in smaller profits. He looks at his payroll costs, which are his greatest single cost and then adds up the cost of lighting and heating a huge grocery store. He is afraid that if the cost of minimum wage goes up, he will not be able to maintain the business as it is. Though he does not want to let any of his employees go, he may need to run his store with fewer employees and reduce the size of his business.

How do you think that his letter to his congressman could also end up making an appeal to pity?

This letter could also easily become an appeal to pity because it is attempting to persuade

by making one feel pity for small-business owners and for people who would become

unemployed. Further discussion follows on the next page.

**Socrates:** Well, this is a great issue to debate, and we can see appeals to pity everywhere. Here is a bit more of the story of the US minimum wage for you to ponder yourself.

> "No business which depends for existence on paying less than living wages to its workers has any right to continue in this country."
>
> —President Franklin D. Roosevelt[1]

In the midst of the Great Depression, a young girl slipped a note into the hand of an aide to President Roosevelt. She asked for his help because her wages had been reduced by half, even though she was working many long hours a day, six days a week. In time, the president responded to her and the cries of many workers whose wages were not enough to live on. In 1938 he signed into law the first federal minimum wage, guaranteeing that a worker could be paid no less than $.25 per hour, which was at that time a living wage. Certainly the plight of poor workers who are not paid enough to make a living is a thing to consider with great compassion. The reason given for the claim that the government should regulate wages is that, if left to themselves, big corporations will pay meager wages and take advantage of cheap, unskilled labor. There are also arguments about how much the minimum wage should be, and when it should be raised. For example, the minimum wage has often been outpaced by inflation. In other words, though minimum wage earners today make much more than $.25 per hour, they may still be below the poverty line if the minimum wage is not raised along with the rising cost of living. Also, some economists believe that if people have more money to spend, it will help the economy and end up being better for everyone.

> "The enactment of this legislation will further increase unemployment, not reduce it. It is bound to increase unemployment unless all human experience is reversed."
>
> —Representative Carl Mapes, just after the legislation was passed in 1938[2]

On the other side of the story, more financially conservative economists believe that because businesses need to be able to stay profitable, raising the minimum wage causes one of two things to happen. Either people will lose their jobs, because if a business pays its employees more, it may not be able to afford to keep all of them. Or, a business will need to raise prices to pay the higher wages, and then the people who just got the raise will pay more for the items that they need. So in the end, some people believe that poor workers may still be oppressed even if wages increase. It is also believed that teens have the hardest time finding a job when the minimum wage is raised.

The clash of interests between employees and business owners results in a difficult dilemma because we want employees to be paid fairly, and we want business owners to stay in business and keep people employed. It is still very important to remember that there are many valid appeals to show mercy and be generous, and it may often be the right thing to do. A fallacy occurs when an appeal to pity is an irrelevant distraction from the real issue.

In this case of a proposed increase in minimum wage, what is the real issue that the government must try to address?

The real issue can most likely be viewed as a question of how the government can best protect

the rights and liberty of all parties and all its citizens—both business owners and employees.

---

1. G.H. Bennett, *Roosevelt's Peacetime Administrations, 1933-1941: A Documentary History of the New Deal Years* (New York: Manchester University Press, 2004), 99.
2. Irving J. Sloan, *American Landmark Legislation Labor Laws*, 2nd ser., vol. 4 (New York: Oceana Publications, 1984), 319.

**Chapter 2: Appeals to Emotion**
Fallacy Discussion on Appeal to Pity

# Fallacy 7:
## Mob Appeal
### (*Argumentum Ad Populum*)

DEFINITION: Arguments that distract by making the audience want to be part of the crowd or one of the "common people." To make up for a lack of solid evidence and sound reason, this argument appeals to the emotions of a crowd, the desire to be part of the majority, or the interests of the "common man."

The Latin phrase *ad populum* means "to the people." People committing this fallacy seek to convince you of a belief or course of action by suggesting that their view is the popular one, that "the people" side with their view.

We have all felt the pressure to do something or buy something because "everyone is doing it" or "everyone has one." Generally, we want to feel as though we are part of the crowd, rather than a lonely outsider. If "everyone" has a cell phone, that may be reason enough to get one, right? If "everyone" is going to the beach this summer, shouldn't we go, too?

In a debate or argument, the application of mob appeal would usually be an obvious exaggeration that "everyone" is doing something. Make note, however, that when people fall into this fallacy, they don't usually make use of the word "everyone." Instead they will find other ways of suggesting that most people or large numbers of people take their side of the argument.

Consider the following examples of mob appeal.

**Example 1**
> **Senator Green:** The American people don't want Congress to endlessly debate this health-care bill. They want sensible health-care reform now, and I say it is about time.

Many politicians will make references to what "the people" want or think. It is an easy claim to make, but hard to prove. Do the American people really want the health-care debate to end? How would you find out what 300 million people might really want? Senator Green is seeking to make his argument look better by suggesting that a large majority of Americans—perhaps even *all* Americans—want what he wants.

In politics, we will find many examples of mob appeal. It is an ancient technique used by a long list of charismatic manipulators traditionally called "demagogues" who have manipulated "the masses" to accept one course of action or another. Any educated citizen should be on his guard for political mob appeal, for it can find expression in any political party at almost any time.

**Example 2**

**Car Salesman:** Droves of people have been coming in to look at these new Z-1 cars and get a fantastic deal. Hurry! Act now! These cars won't be here long!

This is an oh-so-familiar method of selling cars, isn't it? The impression we get is that there is a rush of humanity overwhelming the poor car salesman, who is doing you a favor by letting you know what is happening so that you can get there ahead of some other guy and actually get one of those remarkable Z-1 cars. Isn't he nice? Shouldn't we join the mad rush? After all, those "droves of people" must be on to something.

Mob appeal is frequently used in many kinds of commercials. Here are a couple of examples that you may recall: A Verizon wireless commercial shows an employee out installing Verizon wireless Internet service. He runs into a man from a cable Internet company, whose customer is canceling his cable service. It is discovered that the customer canceling the cable service is having Verizon wireless installed. This implies that "everyone" is switching, suggesting that the viewers should switch as well.

Truck commercials commonly portray their truck as the truck preferred by the "working man." In one Chevrolet truck commercial, we see the truck either "out on the range" among cowboys or in the midst of a steel plant. Suddenly the action stops and we hear the strong tones of the popular song "Like a Rock," while our heroes, the great American working men, drop everything and come gaze with awe at the shining truck. The argument is clear: The great working men (the "common man") of America love this truck—shouldn't you?

## Argumentum Ad Populum (Mob Appeal)

**Genus:** An argument that avoids the issue by appealing to the listener's emotions.

**Difference:** It appeals to the emotions by making us want to be a part of the "crowd" or to identify with the "common man."

# Mob Appeal

| | |
|---|---|
| FALLACIES OF RELEVANCE | Arguments that are really distractions from the main point. |
| Appeals to Emotion | Arguments that distract by deliberately arousing our emotions. |
| Mob Appeal (*Argumentum Ad Populum*) | An argument that distracts by making the audience want to be a part of the crowd or one of the "common men." |

"When the people march together hand-in-hand, you'll find us leading the crowd."

OBEY LANE SIGNALS

*Bradling & Templeton*

Attorneys at Law

232-555-6547

## Mob Appeal

# The common man's beer

Gruber
Beer

*since 1844*

Nothin'
Fru-fru
here

**Chapter 2: Appeals to Emotion**
Fallacy 7: Mob Appeal (*Argumentum Ad Populum*)

# Mob Appeal

**Salt of the earth**™

Everyday seasonings
for every meal.

**Salt is Life!**

**common condiments**™
Peppering your meals with flavor

make your own ad

# Mob Appeal

American as Mom, apple pie, & shih tzu

ASIAN™ CHEESE IMPORTS

Found in your grocer's cheese section

Chapter 2: Appeals to Emotion
Fallacy 7: Mob Appeal (*Argumentum Ad Populum*)

# Fallacy 8:
## Snob Appeal

DEFINITION: Arguments that distract by making a person want to feel "special." This is an emotional appeal to a sense of elitism or to those of "discriminating taste."

"Only the best for a distinguished gentleman like yourself," says the store clerk, handing a man a red silk tie for inspection. "Very nice," says the gentleman, "but I only wear Italian ties."

From time to time we all want to think of ourselves as people with a great sense of what makes something really good. You may want to have discriminating or even impeccable (faultless) taste. When someone appeals to this desire to be people of good taste, it is called snob appeal. It is usually a distraction from the real issue. Advertisements for luxury cars, fine clothes, jewelry, wine, and even coffee often appeal to our sense of "discriminating taste" and our desire to be part of an elite group. Beware: if you fall victim to this appeal, you may end up spending a lot of time and money pursuing some kind of illusory "status."

The word "snob" does not sound quite as good as "a person of discriminating taste," does it? We use the word "snob" when we want to criticize this tendency in others or ourselves. Here is how the *Random House Dictionary* defines "snob": "a person who believes himself or herself an expert or connoisseur in a given field and is condescending toward or disdainful of those who hold other opinions or have different tastes regarding this field: *a musical snob*."[1]

Note that this fallacy is almost the opposite of mob appeal, which appeals to our perception that "everyone" favors a certain belief or action. In the case of snob appeal, the fallacy appeals to our perception that just a "select few" favor a belief, style, or action. In the case of mob appeal, we want to be like the crowd. In the case of snob appeal, we want to be set apart from the crowd as part of a special, elite group. Consider the following examples of snob appeal.

### Example 1

People who know how a computer should work buy a Mac if they can afford it. Not everyone can appreciate just how great a Mac works, but those who do will not settle for any other kind of computer. If you are a serious computer user, you should definitely get a Mac.

---

1. *Dictionary.com*, s.v. "snob." <http://dictionary.reference.com/browse/SNOB>. Accessed March 10, 2010. Based on the *Random House Dictionary*.

**Example 2**

How can you drink that coffee? What if John saw you drinking coffee from a mini-mart? Come on, let's go to Starbucks and get some *real* coffee.

**Example 3**

I am definitely going to start supporting overseas adoption. A lot of cool movie stars are adopting children from Africa and Asia.

Some people really love their Macs, but should you pay significantly more for a Mac just to be considered "a serious computer user" who really knows how a computer works? Will people really think you are a serious computer user just because you bought a Mac? It may be possible that a Mac is a better purchase, but we need to hear an argument for why a more expensive Mac is a better purchase than other computer options. Also, will sporting about with a four-dollar Starbucks cup change the way John thinks of you? What kind of person is John, then? Finally, supporting overseas adoption may be a fine thing to do, but will you do that just to imitate movie celebrities? Let's hear the real argument for supporting overseas adoption.

### Snob Appeal

**Genus:** An argument that avoids the issue by appealing to the listener's emotions.

**Difference:** This is an appeal to elitism or to a desire to be part of a select group.

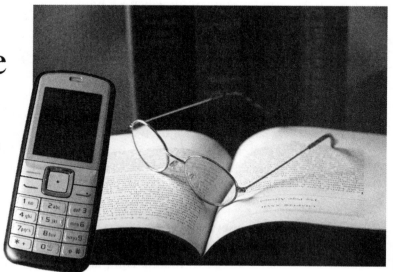

Introducing the new

# GeniusPhone

Now get a phone that automatically comes equipped with a global positioning system, a searchable encyclopedia, a dictionary of Greek and Latin roots, a personal language translator, historical timelines of the five largest countries, a graphing calculator, a combinatorics quiz game, and Tetris!

## Be the smartest person you know!

**Chapter 2: Appeals to Emotion**
Fallacy 8: Snob Appeal

# Snob Appeal

| | |
|---|---|
| FALLACIES OF RELEVANCE | Arguments that are really distractions from the main point. |
| Appeals to Emotion | Arguments that distract by arousing deliberately our emotions. |
| Snob Appeal | An argument that distracts by making the audience want to feel special and unique. |

*For distinguishing & discerning tastes . . .*

Silver Leaf Wines

**Bona Vidä!**

## No ordinary spring roll

You can always find Chinese takeout right around the corner. But to find an extraordinary spring roll takes something more . . . Bona Vidä!

# Cumulative Fallacy Worksheet

**DIRECTIONS:** Identify each fallacy.

1. It's time to take all of your money out of the stock market. This recession is going to cause stock prices to fall so dramatically that you will lose almost all your wealth if you don't pull your money out now. I know there are experts saying that the stock market will go up, but that's just what they said right before the Great Depression!

appeal to fear

2. Yesterday on *Fox News Sunday,* Brit Hume strongly argued that we should take military action against Iraq. You can't trust anything coming from that right-wing news organization.

genetic fallacy

3. Don't listen to that Harry Burns talk-radio show. He is a long-haired, bad-mouthed wise guy who needs to take a shower.

*ad hominem* abusive

4. If you elect those heartless Republicans to Congress, they'll leave all of the poor, underprivileged school children without a square meal because of all the cutbacks that Republicans advocate in school lunch funding.

appeal to pity

5. You shouldn't comment on the abortion issue because you're a man, and you couldn't possibly know what a woman dealing with an unwanted pregnancy goes through.

*ad hominem* circumstantial

6. Mr. Jones has no right to tell us to study hard, because he admits that he was a poor student when he was our age.

*tu quoque*

7. Vote for Harkin, champion of the working man!

mob appeal

8. **Teenager:** Mom, if my friends hear that I got my hair cut at Fantastic Cuts, I will be teased mercilessly. I have to get my hair cut at that upscale salon downtown—that's where my cool friends go. Even the mayor gets her hair cut there!

snob appeal

# Fallacy 9:
## Appeal to Illegitimate Authority
## (*Argumentum Ad Verecundiam*)

DEFINITION: Arguments that distract by attempting to shame the listener into agreement by citing an illegitimate authority.

We live in a world in which there is so much to know that no one can ever become an expert in every subject. Since this is true, we often need information and guidance from experts, people who are specialists in a certain field of knowledge. We all enjoy having access to experts to solve problems (for instance, to whom do you turn when you are having computer problems?). When we are seeking guidance or solutions to important problems, it is helpful to consult a person who really is a qualified expert. It is also helpful to know the ways in which your opponent in an argument may try to persuade you of a point of view by citing "experts" who turn out not to be legitimate experts after all.

The Latin name for the fallacy of appealing to an illegitimate authority or expert is *argumentum ad verecundiam*, which means "argument to shame." The name of the fallacy emphasizes how we may be "browbeaten into accepting an erroneous conclusion because we are ashamed to dispute the supposed authority."[1] After all, who would want to disagree with Michael Jordan, arguably the greatest basketball player of all time, whether he's talking about basketball or toothpaste?

In our current culture, there are at least four ways in which people make an appeal to an expert or authority that is illegitimate. First, it is common for people to make an appeal to an expert who actually is not an expert, or who is the wrong expert for the issue at hand. Second, it is common for people to appeal to an expert who is so prejudiced toward a viewpoint that the expert cannot be considered fair or trustworthy regarding the issue. Third, sometimes people appeal to an unnamed expert, which makes the appeal untrustworthy. Fourth, people often appeal to a celebrity as an expert, thinking that the fame of the celebrity will somehow grant the celebrity expert opinions. Let's look at each of these illegitimate appeals to authority.

## FOUR APPEALS TO ILLEGITIMATE AUTHORITY

1. **The Wrong or False Expert:** Suggesting that we accept the opinions of one who has no expertise in the field about which he is speaking

2. **The Biased Expert:** Suggesting we accept the opinions of one who has an unreasonable bias or prejudice

3. **The Unnamed Expert:** Suggesting we accept the opinions of an unnamed source, official, or spokesperson, therefore relying on secondhand information from unknown sources

4. **The Celebrity Expert:** Suggesting we accept the opinion of a celebrity who has no real expertise relating to the issue or product being promoted

1. S. Morris Engel, *With Good Reason*, 5th ed. (New York: St. Martin's Press, 1994), 220.

## 1. The Wrong or False Expert

We know that it is fine to appeal to an expert who truly is an expert for the question or problem before us. However, if your car won't start, it won't likely do you any good to consult Dr. Winklebean, who has a PhD in marine biology and published three books on marine life off the coast of the Hawaiian Islands. You would do better to talk to your auto mechanic or even that guy you know who rebuilds engines in his backyard shed. Dr. Winklebean is clearly an expert, but he is the wrong expert to consult to solve your car problems. Unfortunately, it is quite common for people to cite the wrong experts when making arguments. This appeal to the wrong expert usually involves a well-known scholar, professor, or author (this increases the potential "shame" you might experience if you reject the advice of the expert).

### Example

**John:** Climate change is caused by an irreversible cycle of the earth, as noted by several prominent scholars, such as Harold Johnson in his recent ground-breaking book.

**Bill:** What was the title of that book?

**John:** *Shakespeare for All of Life*

**Bill:** Isn't Johnson a famous English scholar?

**John:** Yes, one of the best.

Harold Johnson may, indeed, be an expert, but he is not a qualified expert on climate change!

## 2. The Biased Expert

First, we must point out that it is possible to legitimately appeal to an expert who may share with you a certain belief or course of action. If the expert truly does have the necessary training and background that relates to the issue for which you are arguing, then she can be a legitimate expert even if she shares your opinion on the issue. It also helps if the expert shows no unreasonable bias and does not imply that her expert opinion makes for a complete proof. Note that an appeal to an expert authority can be good evidence for an argument, but is almost never a complete proof. Even qualified experts can be wrong. If an expert is wrong it does not mean the appeal to that expert was a fallacy—it just shows that even experts can make mistakes. There are cases, however, in which the unreasonable bias of the expert calls his opinion into question. Here is an example of one such case described in T.E. Damer's *Attacking Faulty Reasoning*.

### Example

"Senator, if you think that the FBI has been engaging in illegal activities, why don't we get the director and his staff over here at this hearing and get to the bottom of this thing? Who would be in a better position to testify about FBI operations than the director and the division heads?"[2]

In this case, the senators might, indeed, want to speak to the director, but they should do so with some skepticism, since it would certainly not be in the best interest of the director to reveal any evidence that he was poorly managing the operations of the FBI. If there were additional evidence that the director was poorly managing the FBI, the senators would have even more skepticism about the "authority" of the director's opinions about FBI operations and would therefore ask a lot of hard questions of him.

You have to be careful about charging someone with being biased, and therefore an unqualified expert. If you don't have good reason for charging someone with being unreasonably biased, then our charge is another form of the *ad hominem* circumstantial fallacy. It is important, therefore, to really pay attention to the circumstances, or qualifications, of the expert. If the

---

2. T. Edward Damer, *Attacking Faulty Reasoning*, 2nd ed. (Belmont, CA: Wadsworth Publishing Co., 1987), 123.

circumstances show that the expert has appropriate background and training and is not showing unreasonable bias, then such a person can be a legitimate expert. You will have to use wisdom to determine how much bias is operating in the opinion of an expert.

### 3. THE UNNAMED EXPERT

Judging by their frequent appearance in media reports today, there are thousands of unnamed experts in the world. It is quite common for newspaper, radio, television, and Internet reports to cite "unnamed sources," "anonymous officials," and "unidentified spokespersons" who give important evidence in these reports. You can understand the dilemma of journalists: they need sources for the credibility of their stories and often their sources will only give information if the reporter promises not to use their name. Still, you have to treat these sources with a healthy dose of skepticism since you know nothing about them.

#### Example 1

Many are suggesting that President Obama should pull half of the US troops out of Afghanistan in the next six months, stop fighting the Taliban in the countryside, and use remaining troops to protect urban areas. An unidentified official at the Pentagon said that increasing corruption in the Afghan government was making it nearly impossible to believe that an ongoing military offensive by the United States would be successful.

#### Example 2

Buy gold now and invest in your future. Many experts agree that this may be the best time to buy gold in decades.

### 4. THE CELEBRITY EXPERT

Just as some might be tempted to "transfer" the authority of biology expert Dr. Winklebean to an auto-mechanical problem, so are many willing to seek the opinion of a celebrity as evidence for an argument in an area in which the celebrity has no expertise. The most common use of the "celebrity expert" is the widespread use of celebrity "testimonials" for almost every product under the sun. Often there is little or no connection between the product and the celebrity's career and life. When a famous baseball star endorses cologne, we can't assume any reasons he gives for using the cologne are expert reasons. He might, however, give a credible reason for buying a particular bat or baseball glove.

#### Example

Hi, I am Kent Strongarm, quarterback of the Big City Rams. Nothing gives a closer shave than the Rip Razor IV. When you want a shave that makes for a winning performance, choose Rip Razor IV!

Often today, movie stars, sports stars, and famous singers are sought for their opinions on social, cultural, and political issues. While we should carefully assess what the Surgeon General says about our nutritional health, there is no good reason why we should give serious attention to the nutritional opinions of a sixteen-year-old pop singer.

## *Ad Verecundiam* (Appeal to Illegitimate Authority)

**Genus:** An argument that avoids the issue by appealing to the listener's emotions.

**Difference:** This type of argument plays on the listener's sense of shame by appealing to an illegitimate authority.

# Appeal to Illegitimate Authority

| | |
|---|---|
| FALLACIES OF RELEVANCE | Arguments that are really distractions from the main point. |
| Appeals to Emotion | Arguments that distract by deliberately arousing our emotions. |
| Appeal to Illegitimate Authority (*Argumentum Ad Verecundiam*) | An argument that distracts by attempting to shame the listener into agreement by citing an illegitimate authority. |

## "When you have leg pain, I recommend Repcine."

### Doctor Bob

as seen on:

*Love in the Afternoon*

MADE WITH NATURAL OILS and compounds found in rare South American reptiles, **Repcine pain medicine** brings the power of modern medicine and the wisdom of ancient healing to all your aches and pains. After all, when Doctor Bob helped to nurse the lovely Laura Taylor back to health after her frightful abduction by her ex-boyfriend, Tommy McCollough, he used the power of Repcine to keep her from going nearly mad from the pain (episode 354). Don't you want that kind of help for your everyday aches and pains as well?

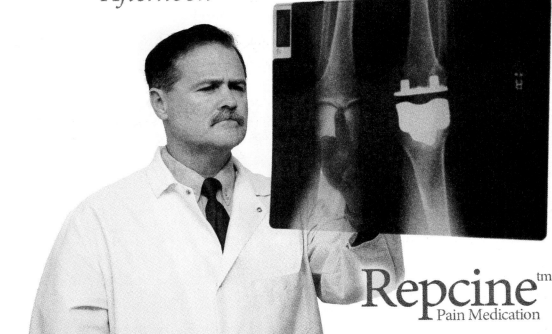

Repcine™ Pain Medication

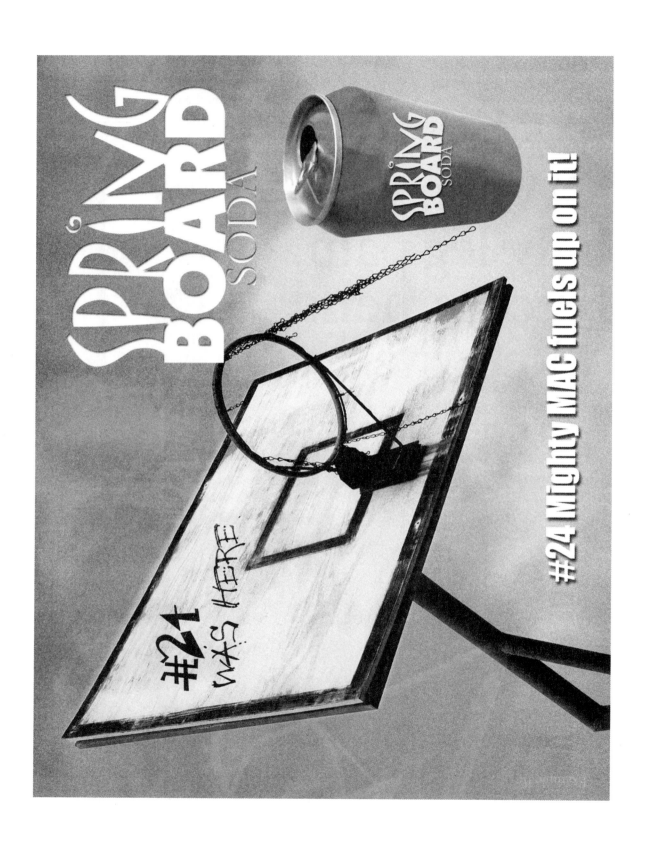

**Chapter 2: Appeals to Emotion**
Fallacy 9: Appeal to Illegitimate Authority (*Argumentum Ad Verecundiam*)

# Fallacy Discussion on
# Appeal to Illegitimate Authority

**Socrates:** Hello again, young philosopher! Let's listen in on a fictional news broadcast.

**Anchor:** Now, let's head to the Olympic stadium where our chief sports correspondent is standing by with breaking news about alleged performance-enhancing drug use among members of the American hockey team.

**Correspondent:** The American hockey team was just awarded the gold medal last night, but this morning the International Olympic Committee received a letter from a source close to the team accusing several players of taking performance-enhancing drugs. The letter claims that one of the team physicians has been supplying the illegal drugs to the team for the last six months. It is a new type of drug that is untraceable by current Olympic drug tests. The players in question have denied using any illegal drugs, but the International Olympic Committee, committed to its zero-tolerance position on performance-enhancing drugs is still in discussion about how to proceed. Back to you.

Students, do you think that this is a case of appeal to illegitimate authority? How?

This example is committing the fallacy of appeal to illegitimate authority because it is
citing an anonymous authority. Further discussion follows on the next page.

**Socrates:** Ahh, sports scandals. We even had them back in our day now and then. Oh, yes! You are waiting for my analysis of the news report. Well, in this case, there appears to be an appeal to illegitimate authority. Let's consider the letter the committee received. Note that the sender of the letter is called "a source close to the team." Why is the source anonymous? It could be because the writer was someone on the American hockey team and did not want to get in trouble with his teammates. Or, the person cold have been concerned about getting in trouble with the doctor himself. Or, of course, it could have been sent by a bitter member of an opposing team whose motive was to undercut a winning opponent. Or it could be just a terrible prank! In any case, we have no actual evidence that the claim made in the letter is valid. It is just difficult to trust an anonymous authority. Until supported by more substantial evidence, patience and a healthy dose of skepticism is probably a good idea.

**Further Discussion**

1. Scan the newspaper or news magazines for examples of unnamed sources who are cited as authorities. Find an example that you think justifies "a healthy dose of skepticism" and explain why.

2. Look for examples of print advertisements that make use of the *argumentum ad verecundiam.*

3. Can you think of any television commercials that make use of this fallacy?

**Chapter 2: Appeals to Emotion**
Fallacy Discussion on Appeal to Illegitimate Authority

# Fallacy 10:
## Chronological Snobbery

DEFINITION: Arguments that distract by making the audience want to either be part of an old tradition or part of the latest cool, new thing. In other words, this fallacy distracts by rejecting or accepting something merely on the basis of its age, making an appeal to tradition or to novelty.

Sometimes the age of something—its oldness or newness—is relevant to an argument. For example, some things can be "better with age," such as wine, cheese, and violins. On the other hand, some things are often better because they are newer, such as computers, phones, televisions, and other kinds of digital technologies. Furthermore, we can legitimately reject some things because they are old, such as a ten-year old racehorse or a fifty-eight-year-old NFL quarterback.

Often, however, the age of something is not at all relevant to the issue at hand, especially when the issue involves a belief or practice. An old idea is not automatically bad, nor is a new idea automatically good. For that matter, an old idea is not automatically good, nor is a new idea automatically bad. Let's consider first how people commit the fallacy of chronological snobbery by appealing to something old, such as tradition.

### THE APPEAL TO TRADITION

Is a traditional belief, practice, or institution good or bad simply because it is old? Consider the following examples.

**Example 1**
"The institution of marriage is as old as human history, and thus should be considered sacred."[1]

**Example 2**
Prostitution has been practiced for thousands of years, and thus should be considered an acceptable human institution.

**Example 3**
Prisoners of war have been tortured for centuries as a common means of acquiring information about one's enemy, and such torture should be employed to help us ensure victory over our enemies.

To all of these examples, we can respond, "That may be true, but it is irrelevant." If we are arguing for marriage, prostitution, or torture, we must present some compelling reasons for them besides their age. After all, bad practices can persist throughout history as well as good ones. There are other good reasons for considering marriage as sacred, besides its age (the propagation of the race, the nurture and education of children, etc.).

---

1. Engel, 226.

There are even reasons that could be presented for and against prostitution and torture. Just because something is old does not make it necessarily good or bad. What about when that something is new? Let's consider the appeal to novelty.

### THE APPEAL TO NOVELTY

Here in the twenty-first century, we are often excited by the "latest thing." We have been conditioned by the accelerating advance of technology to expect and want new and improved computers, phones, cars, watches, or other gadgets. This makes us especially prone to the appeal to newness or novelty. Is new always better? When it comes to technology, new often is better. When it comes to beliefs and practices, however, new is not automatically better. Consider the following examples.

**Example 1**

> The latest research suggests that students learning to read in phonics-based programs do not acquire reading comprehension skills as quickly as their peers in whole-language reading programs.

**Example 2**

> Don't be caught wearing clothing that is out of style! At Cool Topics clothing outlets, we update our clothing inventory on a weekly basis, so you can wear the very latest coolest styles.

**Example 3**

> Professor Standish has just published a new, groundbreaking book advocating an Internet political system in which all Americans would vote online and Congress would meet only in giant online "Webinars." This book represents the latest development in the quickly growing field of "virtual" political theory.

The latest research does not automatically mean the best research. In fact, some of the best research on a topic may have been done in the past, and may need to be given more weight than the latest study. The same is true of Professor Standish's new book. Because it is new, this by no means makes it the best. We should evaluate his arguments in the book and not accept his theory simply because it is new or "groundbreaking." When it comes to the weekly fashions offered by Cool Topics, we should ask if we should spend money on a regular basis simply to stay abreast of constantly changing fashion styles. We should also ask whether Cool Topics is actually following styles or trying to create "styles" weekly to encourage weekly buying. The principle remains: just because something is the latest thing does not make it the best thing.

## Chronological Snobbery

**Genus:** Chronological Snobbery is a fallacy that plays on our emotions.
**Difference:** More specifically, it plays on our emotions by getting us to approve or disapprove of something merely because of its age.

# Chronological Snobbery

| | |
|---|---|
| FALLACIES OF RELEVANCE | Arguments that are really distractions from the main point. |
| Appeals to Emotion | Arguments that distract by deliberately arousing our emotions. |
| Chronological Snobbery | An argument that distracts by making the audience want to either be part of an old tradition or the latest "cool" new thing. |

# Chronological Snobbery

## Old equipment won't provide a new education

Each of our students receive a brand-new wireless GeniusPhone, iComputer, SmartBook, and GPS!

## Au Courant Prep School

At *Au Courant Prep School*, everything is new and shiny! Only the latest, greatest, and most progressive materials will give your child the best education.

**THEY DON'T BUILD 'EM LIKE THEY USED TO**

**ROCKPORT RADIOS**

THE WARMTH OF RADIO RETURNS

# Chapter 2 Review

**A. DEFINE:** Define each fallacy. Include the English translations for the Latin terms.

1. Appeals to Emotion:

 Arguments that attempt to sway the opinions of people by compelling them to feel

 emotions such as pity, anger, fear, joy, peer pressure, intimidation, etc.

2. *Argumentum Ad Populum*:

 An argument that distracts by making the audience want to be part of the crowd or one

 of the "common people." Translation: mob appeal.

3. *Argumentum Ad Baculum*:

 An argument that distracts by making the audience afraid of the consequences of

 disagreeing with the speaker. Translation: appeal to fear.

4. *Argumentum Ad Misericordiam*:

 An argument that distracts by making the audience feel sorry for the speaker or someone

 on behalf of whom the speaker is arguing. Translation: appeal to pity.

5. Snob Appeal:

 An argument that distracts by making a person want to feel "special." This is an

 emotional appeal to a sense of elitism or to those of "discriminating taste."

6. *Argumentum Ad Verecundiam*:

 An argument that distracts by attempting to shame the listener into agreement by citing

 an illegitimate authority. Translation: appeal to illegitimate authority.

7. Chronological Snobbery:

 An argument that distracts by making the audience want to either be part of an old

 tradition or part of the latest cool, new thing.

**B. CHRONOLOGICAL SNOBBERY REVIEW:**

All of the examples below are cases of chronological snobbery. Identify the examples that emphasize tradition by putting a *T* in the blank and those that rely on novelty by putting an *N* in the blank.

T Yuengling Lager: brewed by America's oldest brewery.

N Come down to the Bon-Ton sales event and pick up this summer's latest fashions before they're all gone!

| N | Don't tell me you're reading H.D.F. Kitto's, *The Greeks*! That book was written a generation ago! You should pick up something that reflects the latest research.

| N | Don't tell me that you oppose bill 3129! Mark my words, you cannot oppose the March of Progress.

| T | We can't change now. We've always done it that way.

**C. IDENTIFICATION**: Which appeal to emotion argument is being described below? Explain your answer.

Mark suspected his company was involved in some illegal activities. He decided to resign, and on his last day, he stole a file containing incriminating evidence from a co-worker. He had plans to take the file to a lawyer. The company executives found out about the missing file and sent a message to Mark in a very unconventional way. They leaked the story to a reporter at a local television station, omitting the details about the contents of the file, of course.

The next morning, Mark watched the news in amazement as the reporter recounted the details relayed to her by the company. Mark's picture flashed on the screen as the reporter named him as the prime suspect in the case.

That afternoon, Mark received a call from one of the executives, informing him that the smear campaign would last as long as he was in possession of the file. The executive reminded Mark that he was unemployed and looking for a job. The executive asked him questions about his future. How did he expect to find work if employers suspected him of being a thief, a whistle-blower, and a criminal? The executive encouraged Mark to think about his actions and return the file immediately.

Answers may vary, but it's clearly an appeal to fear because, as an attempt to persuade Mark to change his course of action, the employers were pointing out several painful consequences that Mark would experience if he continued in his present course of action.

**D. APPLICATION:** Name all four types of appeal to illegitimate authority. Then create or find two examples of each.

See pages 80–82 for examples of each kind of appeal to illegitimate authority.

1.  The Wrong or False Expert

    Example A:

    Example B:

2.  The Biased Expert

    Example A:

    Example B:

3.  The Unnamed Expert

    Example A:

    Example B:

4.  The Celebrity Expert

    Example A:

    Example B:

# Cumulative Fallacy Worksheet

**DIRECTIONS:** Identify each fallacy. Provide the Latin names as applicable.

1. It's foolish to keep a gun in the house for self-defense. I read just the other day that more people are killed in accidents with guns than are killed by people breaking into their houses.

    appeal to fear (*argumentum ad baculum*)


2. There are certain people who demand more of their trucks than 99 percent of all truck owners. We call them the "one percenters." For them, we make GMC trucks.

    snob appeal


3. Even if it needs a lot of work and has no closets, my old farmhouse was built better than those McMansions that are built today!

    chronological snobbery


4. Buy a Ford truck, transportation for the American working man!

    mob appeal (*argumentum ad populum*)


5. Really, you don't believe in climate change? The vast majority of scientists believe that the earth's climate is quickly changing!

    mob appeal (*argumentum ad populum*) because it is relying on a majority opinion; snob

    appeal because scientists are a sort of elite within society; appeal to a false expert (appeal
    to illegitimate authority) because not all scientists are experts on climate change

6. You can't be serious that you don't own a bikini. All of the girls at the pool wear them.

    mob appeal (*argumentum ad populum*)

7. You really ought to take Jen to the prom, Jon. Just think of how sad and lonely she'll be if you don't.

  appeal to pity (*argumentum ad misericordiam*)

8. "Hi, I'm Dan Marino, former quarterback for the Miami Dolphins. If you need money, come see the friendly folks at the Money Store."

  appeal to illegitimate authority (*argumentum ad verecundiam*)

9. Senator Helm's argument concerning the tobacco bill ought to be discounted, since he is obviously not objective. The tobacco companies are his biggest campaign contributors.

  *ad hominem* circumstantial

# Chapter 3
## Red Herrings

DEFINITION: A subgroup of the fallacies of relevance. These arguments make a more subtle appeal to emotion, but include types of proofs that are irrelevant to the case at hand.

Sometimes an argument will make a very strong case, and yet be fallacious because it is arguing for something that is not the real issue. The speaker has, in effect, missed the point. In such a situation, the speaker is using an irrelevant proof, known in popular terminology as a "red herring." Of course, the argument itself might be a weak one as well. Weak or strong, if we respond directly to such irrelevancies, we will become distracted by peripheral issues. As we evaluate the arguments made around us, we need to cultivate a sharp eye for identifying the issue at hand. Then, whenever one side strays from that key issue, even if what the speaker says sounds good, we can respond by saying, "true, perhaps, but irrelevant."

A note about the term "red herring" is in order here. There are different, conflicting explanations on precisely how this term originated. The most commonly accepted explanation, however, is that criminal escapees would make use of herrings (which turn red or brown when spoiled) to throw pursuing dogs off the trail, either by throwing them onto the trail or by smearing themselves with them. Whatever its origin, the term in ordinary usage refers to any device or debating trick used to throw an opponent or an audience off track.

## Vocabulary

• Red Herring

• Appeal to Ignorance

• Irrelevant Goals or Functions

• Irrelevant Thesis

• Straw Man Fallacy

# Fallacy 11:
## Appeal to Ignorance

DEFINITION: **Arguments that claim that since a proposition cannot be disproven, it must therefore be true or likely.**

Normally, when we make a claim that something is true, right, or good, we are expected to offer some evidence or proof for that claim. For example, if someone claimed that there is life on Mars, you would expect her to present some evidence for that claim. We call the obligation to present evidence for such claims "the burden of proof"—and that burden of proof would be upon the person who made the claim, and she would need to produce evidence that there is life on Mars. But what if she argued this way:

**Example 1**

> There has to be life on Mars. I have never seen one shred of evidence that proves there is no life there.

While at first the argument may sound plausible, it is not. The person making this argument cannot assume there is life on Mars without any evidence nor can she shift the burden of proof to you, asking you to prove her assumption is wrong. Note that she would be asking you to "prove a universal negative," which is nearly impossible. In an infinite universe (or at least a very large one!), it is not possible to prove there is no "X." Can you prove there are no three-headed lizards or purple swans? Can you prove there are no fairies (they are very good at hiding)? To prove there are no purple swans, you would have to travel and search the entire universe.

Note that since this fallacy claims that the speaker is ignorant of evidence that could disprove his position, it earns the name "appeal to ignorance." Consider these additional examples of appeal to ignorance.

**Example 2**

> The ZX-4 sedan is a really safe car, even when traveling at over 100 mph. There are no road tests yet which have shown driving the car to be dangerous at these speeds.

**Example 3**

> Sending 50,000 more troops into this country will ensure that we win the war. No one has demonstrated that this won't work.

Such appeals to ignorance ("no road tests", "no one has demonstrated") are distractions from the issue. There's a good chance that we will be ignorant of things in regard to our opponent's argument, but the presenter making a case is the one with the burden to show us evidence for his proposition. To point out that we are ignorant of something does not prove his case. To point out that we cannot prove something that is impossible to prove (such as "there is no life on Mars") is a mere distraction and not relevant to the issue at hand.

**Appeal to Ignorance**

**Genus:** A red herring argument that distracts from the main issue.

**Difference:** An argument that distracts by insisting that the opponent disprove the speaker's point, while the speaker avoids giving any evidence for his point.

# Review Exercises

1. Can you find or create an example of a fallacy that appeals to ignorance?

Answers will vary. For examples of this fallacy, see page 97.

2. Why are the following advertisements examples of the appeal to ignorance?

Both advertisements shift the burden of proof to the customer, who would have great difficulty

proving that the advertised product is not the best.

THE VERY BEST IN DINING

Petit Pâture

BOSTON

PARIS

DILLSBURG

YOU ASK HOW WE CAN PROVE THAT WE'RE THE VERY BEST? WE ASK YOU TO TASTE OUR CREATIONS AND PROVE THAT WE'RE NOT.

**FRENCH CHEF: MONSIEUR TOAST**

# Appeal to Ignorance

| | |
|---|---|
| FALLACIES OF RELEVANCE | Arguments that are really distractions from the main point. |
| Red Herrings | This is basically a catchall category for other types of arguments of distraction. |
| Appeal to Ignorance | An argument that distracts by trying to get an opponent to disprove the speaker's point rather than to give real arguments *for* that point. |

Can you prove that your lung cancer comes from our cigarettes?

If not, here's a coupon.

**$1.00 OFF**

Not valid with any other promotional sale or offer. For use in the continental United States. Limit one coupon per family household. Good at participating grocery stores and gasoline stations. Valid until 04/09.

0 12345 67890 5

joe blow cigarettes

SURGEONS WARNING: some doctors have a hunch that cigarettes may be bad for you. But where is the hard proof—that's what we want to know. Smoke on, brother.

joe blow cigarettes

10 oz US (not to be sold individually)

# Fallacy Discussion
# on Appeal to Ignorance

**Socrates:** I see your entertainment industry often uses television shows and movies as forums to persuade viewers on current issues, much the way Athenian actors used the theater and plays in my day.

For instance, as Tiffany and I flipped through some television channels the other day, we found the popular movie *Contact*. In it, Jodie Foster, an actress, plays an astronomer who works tirelessly in the hope of contacting life on other planets. She, being a scientist, negates the possibility that there is a God due to the fact that she finds no empirical evidence of such a being. In one discussion, she asserts that she finds it impossible to believe that an all-powerful God created everything from the tiniest elements of an atom to the largest stars in the universe yet left no concrete evidence that it was His handiwork.

Tiffany asked me whether or not Jodie Foster's character committed the fallacy of an appeal to ignorance. What do you think? Why?

This example is, indeed, illustrating the fallacy of appeal to ignorance. The character

denies that God exists because she has not yet been presented with concrete evidence of

God's existence. She argues that because she is ignorant of such evidence, it must mean

that God does not exist.

As an extra exercise, try to argue the flip side of the character's argument without committing the fallacy yourself.

An opposite example would be for a person to say that she believes in the existence of

God since she is not aware of any proof that there is no God. Further discussion follows

on the next page.

**Socrates:** I think that the astronomer in the film did commit the fallacy of an appeal to ignorance. But how did she do so? Well, the fact that she has not found, or is ignorant of, any evidence for God's existence, does not prove that God does not exist. Theists also can commit this fallacy if they argue that since you can't prove God doesn't exist, then He must exist.

Later in the movie, the astronomer, whose father died when she was a young girl, has an enlightening conversation with a friend who does believe in God. When she insists he prove that there is such a being, he answers her with another scenario. He asks her whether or not her deceased father loved her. She answers, "Yes." He asks her to prove it. What evidence does she have that the relationship she had with her father existed? How could she prove her father's love for her?

She becomes frustrated, knowing she doesn't have proof of his love for her. She tells her friend how sure she is of her father's love. She asserts that the relationship they shared was very real, and that his love continues to influence her. Her friend argues from this example to show her that the same may be true with God, suggesting that there could be evidences of God's existence in life and the universe that she has not previously recognized.

Oh, nice argument.

# Fallacy 12:
## Irrelevant Goals or Functions

DEFINITION: Arguments that distract by measuring a plan or policy according to goals it wasn't intended to achieve.

We could possibly call this the fallacy of unintended goals or functions because a person committing this fallacy assigns an unintended goal or function to his opponent's proposal. The tactic works this way: First assign a goal or function to your opponent's proposal that he never intended or considered; and second, attack that goal or function, showing it to be flawed or unhelpful. Consider these examples of irrelevant goals or functions.

**Example 1**

You want me to run three times a day, but how will that help me to make new friends?

**Example 2**

If the Navy builds a new aircraft carrier, toy model companies will produce and sell many thousands of plastic models of the ship, thus increasing their revenues by millions of dollars. Do we really want to spend all this money on a new ship just to see the toy companies make millions?

**Example 3**

If you choose to go away to college, you will spend thousands of dollars on tuition. How will that affect the economy of our town? Our town needs people to spend their money here, building up our economy and improving our quality of life. Getting your education in our town helps us all.

**Example 4**

You want to study philosophy? John, be realistic—philosophy doesn't bake bread.

In all four examples, we see that the speaker has assigned an unrealistic and unintended goal to his listener and then criticized that goal. Running three times a day is not a recipe for making friends, but rather for getting into good physical condition. The Navy does not build aircraft carriers with toy companies in mind, and a student going off to college is not focused on the local economy, but on getting an education. (In fact, it may actually

## Irrelevant Goals or Functions

**Genus:** A red herring argument that distracts from the main argument.
**Difference:** The source of the distraction in this case is a faulty goal or function that the policy or practice was never intended to fulfill.
*(If an argument is an irrelevant goals or functions argument, you should be able to name the goal or function by which the policy or practice is being judged.)*

help the local economy when she returns to town with a college education.) Studying philosophy is not meant to provide training in practical, everyday skills (such as baking bread), but is instead a discipline that examines some of the most pivotal, deep, and profound questions in life. Surprisingly, studying the big questions often *does* help immensely with the practical issues of life. All of these examples become red herrings, or distractions from the real issue at hand.

# Irrelevant Goals or Functions

| | |
|---|---|
| FALLACIES OF RELEVANCE | Arguments that are really distractions from the main point. |
| Red Herrings | This is basically a catchall category for other types of arguments of distraction. |
| Irrelevant Goals or Functions | An argument that distracts by measuring the opponent's plan or policy according to things it wasn't intended to do. |

You've chewed their gum. And did you get more friends?

MR. MINT'S GUM
FLAVOR FRESH MINT CRYSTALS

The friendly gum!

# Irrelevant Goals or Functions

Does your investment firm make you smile?

We make you smile

Princeton & Plumber Financials, Inc.

# Fallacy 13:
## Irrelevant Thesis

DEFINITION: **Arguments that distract by making a case for the wrong point.**

Sometimes in an argument, as we give and take, we may be tempted to start arguing for something that is not related to the issue at hand. We may even argue very well and prove our point to everyone, but it's the wrong point. For example, someone may be arguing for why the United States should send more troops into a war and then end making the point that the Marines are a very highly trained fighting force. Or, someone may argue that a school should buy Macs for its computer system and end up arguing that Macintosh is a Scottish name. Just because the Marines are a formidable fighting force does not mean they should go and fight one place or another. And the fact that "Mac" comes from "Macintosh" which is of Scottish origin is hardly relevant to whether a school should buy several of them.

Consider the following additional examples of irrelevant theses.

**Example 1**
> **School Administrator:** Of course I think our school should start a football team. I have evidence right here that shows that students who participate in sports programs actually perform better academically.

**Example 2**
> **Senator:** I am in support of this bill to improve housing in our capital city. Everyone needs to live in decent housing. Here is a study showing that people who live in decent housing are healthier and more productive citizens.

**Example 3**
> **John:** Why do you think the Steelers will win the Super Bowl?
> **Luke:** I am quite sure the Steelers will win the Super Bowl. They have a great team and a great name. The name "Steelers" is really cool. They are called the Steelers because Pittsburgh used to be a large steel-producing city.

Like the other fallacies of relevance, we can respond to each of these examples, by saying that they are true perhaps, but irrelevant. It may be true that students who participate in sports do better academically, but that is not relevant to starting a *football* program rather than another sports program. The senator may convince us that decent housing is great for every citizen, but what does that have to do with the merits of the bill before the Senate? Will that bill actually provide decent housing in a responsible manner? Because no one is questioning that people should have decent housing, it has no bearing on the argument for the bill. Luke obviously likes the Steelers and he has shown us how they got their name. However, he has not given us any concrete reasons why he thinks they will win the Super Bowl.

### Irrelevant Thesis

**Genus:** A red herring argument that distracts from the main issue at hand.

**Difference:** This type of argument is arguing positively for something, but what it is arguing for is irrelevant to the issue.

*(Note: this is different from a "straw man" argument discussed later, because the straw man argument is arguing against something, not for it.)*

**Chapter 3: Red Herrings**
Fallacy 13: Irrelevant Thesis

# Irrelevant Thesis

| | |
|---|---|
| FALLACIES OF RELEVANCE | Arguments that are really distractions from the main point. |
| Red Herrings | This is basically a catchall category for other types of arguments of distraction. |
| Irrelevant Thesis | An argument that distracts by making a case for the wrong point. |

LIKE FLIES TO HONEY

Joey's Used Car Lot

South on I-43. On the Right.

Chicks dig these cars!

# Fallacy Discussion on Irrelevant Goals or Functions and Irrelevant Thesis

**Socrates:** Here is another example of a fallacy provided by fellow philosopher, S. Morris Engel. The fallacy is either an example of the irrelevant goals or functions fallacy or the irrelevant thesis fallacy. Restate the argument being made in your own words, determine which fallacy it is, and explain your answer.

"I fail to see how hunting can be cruel to animals when it gives great pleasure to so many people and employment to many others."[1]

The argument can be restated as:

Hunting is not cruel to animals because it gives pleasure to people (hunters) and

employment to people (gun stores, producers of hunting clothes, gear, etc.).

This argument contains an irrelevant thesis because it fails to address the charge that

hunting is cruel to animals. It dodges the question completely and instead argues that

hunting is pleasurable and provides employment.

    1. Perhaps it is true that hunting gives pleasure to hunters, but the pleasure hunters

        experience (or the employment it provides to others) has nothing to do with

        whether or not hunting is cruel to animals.

    2. What is pleasurable to hunters could still be cruel to animals.

    3. What gives employment to many could still be cruel to animals.

Hunting may not be cruel to animals, but this argument does not speak to that issue,

instead introducing a different and irrelevant point or thesis. Further discussions follows

on the next page.

---

1. Engel, 175.

**Socrates:** The speaker in this case is arguing that hunting is not cruel to animals. His stated reason is that it gives pleasure to hunters and employment to others. We could restate his argument to say that hunting animals is not cruel to animals because it gives pleasure to hunters (and provides jobs to others). Clearly his argument dodges the issue of whether or not hunting is cruel to animals by citing an irrelevant thesis: the pleasure it brings to hunters. It may be true that hunting brings pleasure to hunters, but that is not relevant to whether or not it is cruel to animals. Hunting could, indeed, be pleasurable to hunters and still be cruel to animals. We need to hear another argument that actually addresses the issue of whether or not hunting is cruel to animals. A defender of hunting might try to argue by some other means that hunting is not cruel to animals or he may argue that in some hunting situations it is OK to be cruel to animals. This argument, however, simply does not address the issue of cruelty—it is irrelevant to the issue at hand.

This argument is not an example of irrelevant goals or functions because it does not judge or assess hunting against any goal or function. Clearly, hunters do hunt for pleasure (that is one main reason why many hunt), so the pleasure of hunting is not an irrelevant goal at all.

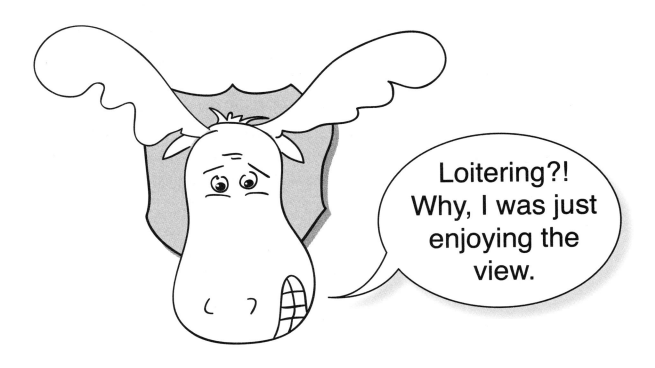

# Fallacy 14:
## Straw Man Fallacy

DEFINITION: Arguments that attempt to disprove an opponent's position by presenting it in an unfair, inaccurate light.

If we have to fight, we might prefer to fight against a dummy stuffed with straw than a real flesh and blood opponent who can strike back! Similarly, in arguments, we may be tempted to distort or exaggerate our opponent's position to make it easier to knock down. Whenever we distort, misrepresent, or cast our opponent's position in a poor light (making it look as bad as we can), we commit the straw man fallacy. It is likely that someone has done this to you before by making your position or viewpoint look silly and foolish.

Consider the following examples of the straw man fallacy.

**Example 1**

Mr. Jenkins does not think the school should build a new gym. He thinks the school should save all of its money as a miser would and never borrow money. He does not want the school to be in debt to anyone, ever.

**Example 2**

Linda's mom won't let her get her ears pierced. Her mom won't let Linda grow up; she wants to control her every move.

**Example 3**

Senator Johnson, you are against raising taxes to pay for increased health care services for the poor. What do you have against poor people? Have you no compassion for their difficult plight?

**Example 4**

Senator Richards, you want to raise taxes on the rich to pay for this bill. Why do you want to punish people simply for being successful?

In each example above, the speaker seeks to misrepresent and discredit his opponent's views and beliefs. Mr. Jenkins may have some compelling reasons that are not miserly at all for why the school should not borrow money. Linda's mom is not necessarily controlling just because she said "no" to her daughter's piercing request. Senator Johnson may have compassion for the poor and still oppose the tax hike for many good, unstated reasons. It is unfair to suggest that Senator Richards is punishing anyone by supporting a tax increase.

### WHAT ARE YOU AFRAID OF?

One additional example of creating a "straw man" in our current cultural setting is to charge your opponent with having a "phobia"—a psychological disorder characterized by an irrational fear of something. By saying that someone has a phobia, you characterize that person as being irrational and perhaps in need of some counseling help. For example, those in favor of gay marriage may characterize opponents as homophobes, or having homophobia, thus discrediting their reasons and arguments against homosexual marriage. This happened in 2009 when Miss California was called a homophobe by one of the judges in the Miss USA pageant because she expressed her opinion that marriage should only be between a man and a woman. Religious people may characterize non-religious people as suffering from theophobia (fear of God or gods), or christophobia if they reject Christianity. Non-religious people may characterize religious people as suffering from thanatophobia (the fear of death). Charging people with phobias is almost always a red herring that distracts from real discussion and debate about an issue.

## Straw Man Fallacy

**Genus:** A red herring argument that distracts from the main issue.
**Difference:** This type of argument argues against a position that is not really the position held by the opposition.
*(The speaker is, in effect, setting up a "straw man" only to knock it down again rather than doing battle with a flesh-and-blood opponent.)*

# Straw Man Fallacy

| | |
|---|---|
| FALLACIES OF RELEVANCE | Arguments that are really distractions from the main point. |
| Red Herrings | This is basically a catchall category for other types of arguments of distraction. |
| Straw Man Fallacy | An attempt to disprove an opponent's beliefs by presenting them in an unfair, inaccurate light. |

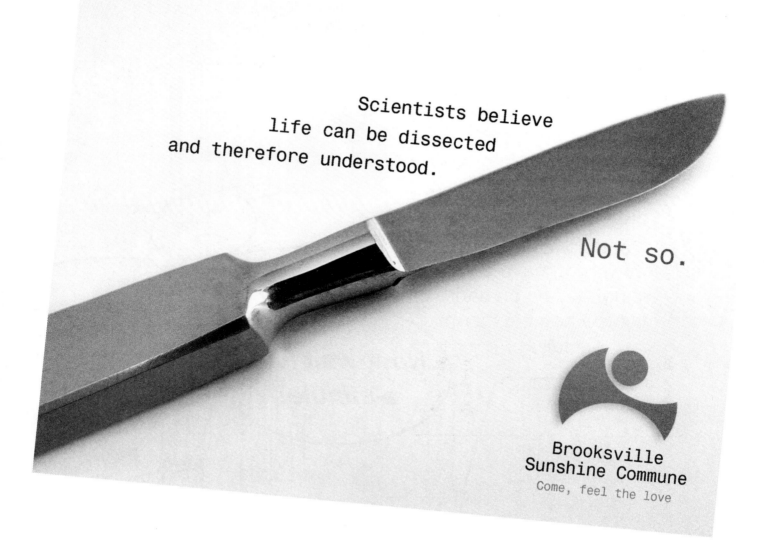

Scientists believe
life can be dissected
and therefore understood.

Not so.

Brooksville
Sunshine Commune
Come, feel the love

# Straw Man Fallacy

than a few humour bath-room jokes about snot that indeed were funny I can't recommend the film. Also, if the producers had bought one less cup of coffee they could have put that savings into the film's budget which sorely needed it. ■

## New Bridge Promised

The South Street bridge is making news again this week. Ever since the bridge was weakened in the winter 2003 ice-flow, the bridge has been an area of political tension. Mayor Jones commented, "The South Street bridge needs to be rebuilt. It's as simple as that. With the traffic congestion in and around the city, this project can not be ignored any longer." The mayor continued with, "All this talk about what color the new bridge should be after it's built—I don't care. There are better people out there than me to determine those aesthetic concerns. I'm afraid I'd just pick the wrong color and then get a truck load of mail on my desk the next week telling me what I already know." The South Street bridge project is slated to begin ber and cost the city construction

**"...I don't care."**
Mayor Jones

Isn't it time we had a mayor that DID care about the South Street Bridge? After all, isn't your safety and the safety of all Bainbridge at stake here?

# James R. Tublinsky

Mayoral Candidate 2010

*A man who genuinely cares*

# Chapter 3 Review

**A. DEFINE:** Define each of the following.

1. Red Herring:

An argument that abuses the "burden of proof" by making an opponent irrefutably prove

his position rather than making a sound argument for your own position.

2. Appeal to Ignorance:

An argument that claims that since a proposition cannot be disproven, it must therefore

be true or likely.

3. Irrelevant Goals or Functions:

An argument that distracts by measuring a plan or policy according to goals it wasn't

intended to achieve.

4. Irrelevant Thesis:

An argument that distracts by making a case for the wrong point.

5. Straw Man Fallacy:

An argument that attempts to disprove an opponent's position by presenting it in an

unfair, inaccurate light.

**B. IDENTIFICATION:** Which red herring argument is being described below? Explain your answer.

My parents have always told me to stay away from drugs and alcohol. They've pointed out that getting caught up in a lifestyle that includes drugs and alcohol usually hinders a person's ability to reach high standards and goals.

Now that I'm on my own and in college, I think it's time that I stop doing exactly what Mom and Dad tell me and start making my own decisions. If I rely on my parents to decide everything for me, I won't learn how to be a responsible adult. They shouldn't tell me what to do anymore.

So, the next time someone offers me something to drink or smoke, I won't automatically say "no" because my parents told me to. I'm going to wait and make my own decision when the time comes. I might accept the offer, but that's OK because I'm making my own decisions, and I'm going to learn responsibility by asserting independence.

This is an irrelevant thesis fallacy. The student attempts to make a case that as a college student he (or she) should start making his own decisions independently, rather than simply choosing a recommended course of action. This is true enough, but in this case he is dodging the issue raised by his parents. They are not asking him not to think for himself, but rather they are asking him to think about one particular idea or argument: Those who get caught up in a lifestyle of drugs and alcohol are less likely to reach high standards and goals; therefore don't adopt this lifestyle or you will be less likely to reach high standards and goals. The student does not even respond to the issue in this argument, but dodges it by making a case for independent decision making.

**C. APPLICATION:** Name all four types of red herring arguments. Then create or find two examples of each.

1.   Appeal to Ignorance

   Example A:   See fallacy 11 (page 97) for some examples of this fallacy.

   Example B:

2.   Irrelevant Goals or Functions

   Example A:   See fallacy 12 (page 102) for some examples of this fallacy.

   Example B:

3.   Irrelevant Thesis

   Example A:   See fallacy 13 (page 105) for some examples of this fallacy.

   Example B:

4.   Straw Man Fallacy

   Example A: See fallacy 14 (page 110) for some examples of this fallacy.

   Example B:

# Cumulative Fallacy Worksheet

**DIRECTIONS:** Identify each fallacy.

1. As far as I'm concerned, the Medicaid program is a total waste. There are still people in this country who go without care because they're uninsured.

   irrelevant goals or functions

2. You shouldn't put any stock in the accusations made against the president. They were only the result of the overzealousness of reporters who were out to make names for themselves.

   either *ad hominem* circumstantial (since it refers to the self-interest of the speakers) or

   irrelevant thesis (since it is likely that they are out to make names for themselves, but that is not the key issue)

3. **Senator Jones:** I support legislation banning abortion, or even a constitutional amendment if necessary. A civilized society simply cannot stomach the killing of so many innocent children.

   **Senator Smith:** If you're so concerned about the sanctity of life, why won't you join me in my opposition of the death penalty?

   irrelevant thesis

4. Representative Johnston has no grounds making any judgment about the president. It's been proven that he's an adulterer himself.

   *tu quoque*

5. I don't see how any good Christian can celebrate Christmas. It's nothing more than an attempt to Christianize the old pagan festivals of the winter solstice.

   genetic fallacy

6. **Scully:** So far you haven't presented me with any solid evidence of this government conspiracy that you're referring to.

   **Mulder:** And you haven't found anything to definitely disprove it.

   appeal to ignorance

7. Ladies and gentlemen, do you really want these bigoted fundamentalists to be running things? Don't let them bring their hillbilly religious agenda here to the Central School District. Vote against Jackson, Andrews, and Noll for school board.

   *ad hominem* abusive

8. Hindus don't believe in helping the poor. That's why Hinduism is a religion of callous inhumanity. All one has to do is walk the streets of India to see how little Hindus care about the plight of those less fortunate.

   straw man

9. **Reporter:** Mr. President, do you think that your age ought to be a factor in the voter's decision in November?

   **Mr. President:** No, I don't think age ought to be a factor. After all, I've never made an issue of my opponent's age and inexperience.

   irrelevant thesis

# Unit 2: Presumption
## Definitions Summary

In unit 1, we studied fallacies of relevance and learned three basic ways we can "avoid the subject": by attempting to discredit the source of an argument, by appealing to an emotion, or by making another irrelevant argument rather than addressing the real issue of the real argument. We called these fallacies *ad fontem* arguments, appeals to emotion, and red herrings.

In this unit, we are going to study fallacies of presumption. Fallacies of presumption can be broken into two classes: fallacies of presupposition and fallacies of induction.

In the midst of a debate, it is easy to make assumptions that seem correct but actually are not. For example, someone may say that we must choose to go to either a private or a public school. On further analysis, however, we realize that there is a third option—homeschooling. The assumption that there are only two educational choices turns out to be wrong. Sometimes, therefore, we presuppose (assume or suppose beforehand) that something is true when it is not. Sometimes we call these presuppositions "hidden assumptions" since they are not always obvious. We will call the group of fallacies that contain hidden assumptions fallacies of presupposition.

Sometimes we also make faulty assumptions about empirical facts or data (data verifiable to the five senses) or the way we reason with the facts or data. For example, it may be a verifiable fact that the power is out in your house, but that does not mean that it is out in your neighbor's house or in your entire neighborhood. A fallacy of this kind belongs to the group we call fallacies of induction, because induction is the kind of reasoning (good or bad) that moves from the particular to the general or from a single or few instances to a whole class (e.g., the red cars that I have seen are fast, therefore all red cars are fast!).

The following list contains all the fallacies of presumption (which are divided into fallacies of presupposition and induction)—eleven fallacies in all. You will study them all in this unit.

# FALLACIES OF PRESUMPTION: Fallacies that make unwarranted assumptions about either the data or the nature of a reasonable argument.

## A. FALLACIES OF PRESUPPOSITION:
These are fallacies that contain hidden assumptions that make the arguments unreasonable.

1. **Begging the Question:** This is an argument that assumes the very thing that one is trying to prove.

2. **Bifurcation (False Dilemma):** This is an attempt to frame the debate in such a way that only two options are possible, when, in fact, other possibilities may exist.

3. **Fallacy of Moderation:** This is an argument based on the assumption that the correct answer is always a middle ground between extremes.

4. **Is-Ought Fallacy:** This type of argument assumes that just because something is a certain way, it ought to be that way.

5. **Division:** This is an argument based on the assumption that individual parts of a collective whole will necessarily have all of the characteristics of the collective whole.

6. **Composition:** This is an argument based on the assumption that a collective whole will necessarily share all of the characteristics of its individual pieces.

## B. FALLACIES OF INDUCTION:
These are fallacies that make unnecessary assumptions about empirical data or inductive reasoning from that data.

1. **Sweeping Generalization (Accident):** This involves taking a generalization (that may be true) and applying it to cases that are legitimate exceptions to it.

2. **Hasty Generalization (Converse Accident):** This argument results in making a generalization about a class of things on the basis of too few examples.

3. **False Analogy:** This is an argument by analogy that fails, largely because the things being compared aren't similar enough to warrant the analogy.

4. **False Cause:** This argument uses any sort of weak, causal connection as the basis of the argument.

5. **Fake Precision:** This argument uses numbers in a way that is too precise to be justified by the situation.

# Fallacies of Presumption

**DEFINITION:** Arguments that make unwarranted assumptions about either the data or the nature of a reasonable argument.

Now we come to the second largest category of fallacies: the fallacies of presumption. While our classification of the fallacies of relevance was rather diverse, with three main categories (*ad fontem* arguments, appeals to emotion, and red herrings), the one for the fallacies of presumption is simpler with only two. The three categories under relevance (and more could have been added) reflect the various ways people introduce irrelevancies into an argument.

There are also various ways people introduce faulty assumptions into an argument which can be conveniently divided into two major categories. Each one reflects one of the two primary modes of reasoning: inductive or deductive. One of the categories, **fallacies of induction**, deals almost exclusively with inductive arguments. An inductive argument makes use of data that is gathered from the world and then used to give evidence for a conclusion. In these cases, either the evidence used, or the way in which it is used, is unsound, resulting in an extremely weak argument.

The relationship between deductive reasoning and the other category, **fallacies of presupposition**, is not quite as clear or simple. It's not so much that these fallacies can only be found in deductive arguments; it's more that they imply a certain premise that is unjustified. These unstated assumptions become essentially unstated **axioms**, or assumed general principles. Since every deductive argument is actually an application of an axiom or presupposition to a specific case, each of these fallacies is, in effect, a hidden deductive argument based on an unjustified general principle. A deductive argument with a hidden premise or assumption is known as an **enthymeme**. Therefore, in addition to the definition for each fallacy, each fallacy under the presupposition category will have a separate subcategory called "hidden assumption revealed" in which the enthymeme (with the hidden and faulty premise) is disclosed.

*(Note: There is another category of fallacies, formal fallacies, which deals exclusively with formal, deductive arguments. Each of these fallacies is derived from a problem in the form, or structure, of the argument. As already noted, this text concentrates on the informal fallacies, which deal with the rules of everyday language arguments, rather than formal, deductive ones. The formal fallacies are taught in our book on formal logic entitled* The Discovery of Deduction.*)*

# Chapter 4
## Fallacies of Presupposition

DEFINITION: A subgroup of the fallacies of presumption. These arguments contain hidden assumptions that make them unreasonable.

These fallacies all occur in arguments that may sound persuasive, but contain some sort of hidden assumption. If that assumption were spelled out in no uncertain terms, the suspect nature of the argument might be more obvious.

All the fallacies of presupposition presuppose something that is hidden—what we may call a hidden presupposition, premise, or assumption. With all of these kinds of fallacies, the trick will be to detect the hidden assumptions!

## Vocabulary
- Begging the Question
- Bifurcation (False Dilemma)
- Fallacy of Moderation
- Is-Ought Fallacy
- Fallacy of Composition
- Fallacy of Division

Can you find the hidden assumption in the following argument?

"I am determined to learn how to play a musical instrument. I can study the piano or the stand-up bass. However, a piano is too expensive and a stand-up bass is too big. Unfortunately, I guess I won't be able to learn a musical instrument as I had hoped."

### Analysis
Our aspiring musician seems to think that the piano or the stand-up bass are the only instrument options before him. The hidden assumption here is that the speaker must choose between the piano and the bass. But is this assumption reasonable? Why couldn't he choose a cheap guitar or a recorder? He is assuming a false dilemma, which you will study soon.

# Fallacy 15:
## Begging the Question
## (*Petitio Principii*)[1]

DEFINITION: **Arguments that assume the very thing that one is trying to prove.**

Just how can someone "beg a question"? In the case of this fallacy, you "beg the question" by asking that your conclusion just be granted to you without your having to build an argument to prove it. The "question" in the phrase "begging the question" refers to the issue that is subject to debate. In other words, when you "beg the question," you are seeking to keep the principal issue from really being proven—you are asking that it simply be assumed as true. We will consider several examples of "question begging" under four different categories.

### CIRCULAR REASONING

A circular argument may simply present a conclusion while trying to trick us into thinking that we are also being given a real premise that leads to this conclusion. What a circular argument actually does, however, is restate the conclusion in other words.

### Example 1
The sky is blue because the color perceived when we examine the sky in daylight is light blue.

### Example 2
Susan is having trouble writing because she has writer's block.

### Example 3
To use textbooks that contain profane or obscene language is not right because it is immoral for our children to hear vulgar, disrespectful words.[2]

In all of these examples, the argument simply restates the conclusion in another form. The first example essentially says that the sky is blue because the sky is blue. The second argument tells us that Susan can't write because she can't write (when someone has writer's block it means that he can't start writing). The third example uses a lot of words to say that it is not right to present children with bad words because it not right to do so. In each example, we are asked to assume the conclusion that is supposedly proven in the argument.

### THE LOADED QUESTION

When you ask a loaded question, you ask a question that is "loaded" with an assumption that you want others to simply accept without any evidence.

### Example 1
Have you stopped cheating on tests?

---

1. The Latin phrase *petitio principi* literally means "petitioning" (asking, requesting, demanding) "the principle" (beginning, foundation). In the context of this fallacy, what is being petitioned or requested is that the primary point of the argument simply be assumed without proof.
2. Damer, 38.

**Example 2**

When will Mark start taking his homework seriously?

**Example 3**

**Prosecutor:** Where did you hide the gun after you fired it at Mr. Johnson?
**Defendant:** I didn't hide it anywhere!
**Prosecutor:** So you still have it!
**Defendant:** No, I don't have any guns!
**Prosecutor:** But you just said you didn't hide it, so you must have it. May I remind you that you are under oath to tell the truth?

Note that in all three examples, the question is loaded with an assumption that we are "begged" to grant or simply accept without any reason or evidence. The first question assumes that you are, in fact, cheating. The second question assumes that Mark is not taking his homework seriously. The third question, asked by the prosecutor, assumes that the defendant fired a gun at Mr. Johnson and that is what the trial is probably about. Such an important fact can't be assumed, it must be proven.

### THE LOADED DEFINITION

This fallacy is also called a "question-begging definition." Sometimes a presenter will try to define terms in his argument in a way that assumes a conclusion that he is obligated to prove.

Consider the way that a "good critic" and "American" are defined in the following examples.

**Example 1**

Any good critic will tell you that Shakespeare was the greatest poet of the English language. How do you know if you are hearing from a good critic? She will be the one who acknowledges the superior talent of Shakespeare.

**Example 2**

**Senator Green:** No true American can support universal health care paid for by the government.
**Reporter:** But Senator Sanderson does support government-provided health care for all people.
**Senator Green:** Sadly, then, Senator Sanderson is not a true American.

In both examples, we are presented with a definition that "begs" us not to require evidence for a controversial definition. Why should a good critic only be the one who thinks that Shakespeare is the greatest English poet? We are not given any reason. Could you be a good critic and think that Milton was the greatest English poet? Why should a true American have to oppose universal health care? Shouldn't there be an argument for that, or should we just assume it to be true? When presented with a controversial, question-begging definition, it is always appropriate to ask the presenter to give a reason why his definition should be accepted or to prove that which his definition assumes.

### THE LOADED LABEL

This fallacy is also called the question-begging epithet (epithet is another name for label) and occurs when someone labels another person or thing in a way that assumes a conclusion

**Begging the Question**

**Genus:** Arguments that are based on unwarranted assumptions.
**Difference:** These arguments either assume their conclusions or include a highly questionable and hidden premise.

without offering any evidence for that conclusion. This frequently occurs when we use a label that assumes what we are trying to argue.

**Example 1**

**Prosecutor:** Ladies and gentleman of the jury, this thief that sits before you is a man that you must judge according to the clear requirements of the law.

**Defense Attorney:** Objection, Your Honor! Prosecution cannot refer to Mr. Harrison as a thief—that is what he is obligated to prove!

**Example 2**

**Senator Brown:** This do-nothing immigration bill is not worthy of our consideration.

**Example 3**

**Teacher:** Lucas, you did not hand in your homework this morning.

**Lucas:** Mrs. Cruz, I chose not to do this unrealistic homework assignment.

We should be careful about using in our arguments labels that assume a conclusion that we are obligated to prove. A prosecutor is prohibited from calling a defendant a thief or murderer in a trial in which he must prove these things beyond a reasonable doubt. Senator Brown is obligated to show how the immigration bill does nothing helpful rather than just labeling it as such. In order for Lucas to explain why he did not hand in his homework, he must show how the assignment was unrealistic, not just label it so.

RadWheelz

Cool dudes ride RadWheelz
Obviously!

**Chapter 4: Fallacies of Presupposition**
Fallacy 15: Begging the Question (*Petitio Principii*)

# Begging the Question

| | |
|---|---|
| FALLACIES OF PRESUMPTION | Arguments that make unwarranted assumptions about either the data or the nature of a reasonable argument. |
| Fallacies of Presupposition | Arguments that contain hidden assumptions that make them unreasonable. |
| Begging the Question | An argument that contains an important, hidden, and unjustified assumption. |

We know quality

After all, we built it.

W
Wolfgang
Furniture

CHAPTER

4

# Fallacy Discussion on Begging the Question

Can you detect the way in which the following argument "begs the question" to remain hidden?

> People of good literary taste have established that Shakespeare is the best poet to have ever written in the English language. To find a person of good literary taste, all you need to confirm is that he recognizes Shakespeare as the greatest English poet the world has ever seen.

This argument assumes what it sets out to prove—that people of good literary taste think Shakespeare is the best English poet. Is it possible that someone with good literary taste will not think Shakespeare is the best English poet? Not if you assume that such a person must think Shakespeare is the best English poet to be considered a person of good literary taste!




Create two arguments of your own that "beg the question."

1.   Answers will vary. For examples, see pages 122-124.




2.   Answers will vary.

**Hidden Question:**
Isn't more always better?

# Fallacy 16:

## Bifurcation (False Dilemma)

DEFINITION: Arguments that frame the debate in such a way that only two options are possible, when other possibilities may exist.

**Hidden Assumption Revealed:**

> Either A or B.
> Not A.
> Therefore B.
>
> Either the cat is brown or the cat is white.
> The cat is not brown.
> Therefore the cat is white.

In the above example, note what is being assumed. The speaker assumes that there are only two color options for the cat—he must be either brown or white. But can't a cat also be black, gray, or a combination of colors? The first statement, or premise (either the cat is brown or the cat is white), makes a false assumption—it assumes only two options are possible when, in fact, there are other options.

This kind of fallacy has several names. It is often called the fallacy of false dilemma (or false dichotomy), because it proposes a dilemma between only two options when, in fact, those two options are not the only ones possible. This fallacy is also known as the fallacy of bifurcation. The word "bifurcate" comes from the Latin *bi + furca* (fork), which means "to split or divide." A person using this fallacy seeks to split the issue into only two possible options. Try to detect the false dilemma (or illegitimate "split") in the following argument.

### Example 1

> You've got to do something about that junky cell phone of yours! Get a new GeniusPhone or you'll be teased by everyone.

OK, so your cell phone may be a bit old, but do you have to get the GeniusPhone to avoid being teased? Why not get the new zPhone2 that so many people like? Why not get rid of your phone altogether and save the money? Is it really true that you will be teased by *everyone*? There are obviously other alternatives to be considered here.

Sometimes in a debate a speaker will seek to put her opponent "on the horns of a dilemma," with each horn (think of a bull) representing one of only two difficult options. Consider this example.

**Example 2**

> John just got a big pay increase at work. That must be because his grandfather owns
> the business or because he does the manager special favors, such as bringing him coffee
> in the mornings.

Do you see the "horns" of this dilemma? This argument is saying that John got the raise for
one of two questionable circumstances—either his grandfather gave him a raise simply because
John is his grandson or the manager gave him the raise because John performs some special
favors for him. It is possible, however, that John got the raise for his excellent work. It is possible
to "go between the horns" of this dilemma.

Sometimes, however, a dilemma can be proposed that is not false. Consider the following example.

**Example 3**

> Either the war in Afghanistan can be won or lost. If we win, it will cost the United States
> billions of dollars we don't have and take us further into debt. If we lose, terrorism will
> likely increase in the Middle East and around the world.

Do you see the "horns" of this dilemma? If we win the war, the country goes into great debt;
if we lose, terrorism spreads. Either alternative (winning the war or losing it) will be costly. This
qualifies as a true dilemma.

When evaluating arguments that propose an "either-or" dilemma, ask yourself whether or not
there is a possible third option, or a fourth or fifth option! If you can find other options, then
you know you have detected a false dilemma.

### Bifurcation (False Dilemma)
**Genus:** Arguments that are based on unwarranted assumptions.
**Difference:** This type of argument is built on a false dilemma.

Create two arguments that contain a false dilemma:

1. Answers will vary. _____

_____

_____


2. Answers will vary. _____

_____

_____


After studying the following advertisements, try to create one of your own that makes use of a
false dilemma.

# Bifurcation (False Dilemma)

| FALLACIES OF PRESUMPTION | Arguments that make unwarranted assumptions about either the data or the nature of a reasonable argument. |
|---|---|
| Fallacies of Presupposition | Arguments that contain hidden assumptions that make them unreasonable. |
| Bifurcation | An argument that frames the debate in such a way that only two options are possible, when, in fact, other possibilities may exist. |

**Chapter 4: Fallacies of Presupposition**
Fallacy 16: Bifurcation (False Dilemma)

# Bifurcation (False Dilemma)

Get Fix-it or don't go out!

Fix-it!
Acne cleansers

# Dialogue on Presumption

As you read the following dialogue, underline the fallacies of presumption as the characters discuss them. Socrates is going to invite you to join in the discussion, so look for the fallacy discussion on bifurcation near the end of this section.

*Socrates approaches Nate and Tiffany, who are sitting under a tree. Nate is reading a book and Tiffany is reading a news magazine.*

**Socrates:** Good morning! You both must be reading something interesting, since you didn't notice my approach until I was right on top of you!

**Tiffany:** Oh, sorry, Socrates. I guess we were rather engrossed. We're both reading about the hot topic of our times, Islamic terrorism.

**Socrates:** It must be very interesting.

**Nate:** It is interesting, but I am questioning some of the author's reasoning.

**Socrates:** Well, give me an example, and let's see if we can diagnose the problem.

**Nate:** OK, here's an example. He's trying to argue that there is no true obstacle to Islamic countries achieving a process of economic modernization. The reason he gives is that "other traditional" societies, such as Japan, had no trouble doing it.

**Socrates:** So what is wrong with that argument?

**Nate:** Well, I don't see how Japan is any more similar to Islamic countries than it is to Western countries.

**Socrates:** So, what you're saying is that the author's argument rests on an <u>analogy, a comparison between two things, but that the things being compared are just too different.</u>

**Nate:** Exactly. <u>So it's not really a good analogy, and therefore the argument that it rests on is a false analogy.</u> Isn't that some sort of fallacy?

**Socrates:** As a matter of fact, it is, and it's one of the most common fallacies. We tend to make a lot of arguments on the basis of analogies. It's also one of the main ways that we learn. If we do something a certain way, for example, and get a good result, we often draw the conclusion that we will get a good result the next time if we do it the same way. Analogies are something that one must be very careful with, though, because if the things being compared aren't enough alike in the right ways, it can lead to all the wrong conclusions.

**Nate:** I think there's something else wrong with this, too. There are a bunch of hidden assumptions, here. For example, the author is assuming that Japan is a "traditional" society and that its "modernization" is a recent thing, but Japan started making extraordinary efforts to modernize its economy as early as the 1860s. You don't find too many Islamic states that have been trying to modernize for that long. Many, such as Saudi Arabia, have been attempting to retain their traditions and avoid Western ideologies by fighting all forms of modernization.

**Socrates:** I see your point. On the one hand, the argument has some unnecessary hidden assumptions and thus commits a fallacy of presupposition, a fallacy in which there is an unspoken and unjustified assumption. On the other hand, since it makes use of false analogies, it also commits a fallacy of induction.

**Nate:** Induction? As in "inductive reasoning"?

**Socrates:** That's right. Do you know what inductive reasoning is?

**Nate:** I always heard that it was reasoning from the particular to the universal, whereas deductive reasoning is going from the universal to the particular.

**Socrates:** Well, it's sometimes portrayed as that, but I don't think that is the best way to describe it. Take that false analogy comparing Saudi Arabia to Japan, for example. What is the universal and what is the particular in that argument?

**Nate:** I guess there is no universal in that argument. It is comparing one country to another— one particular to another particular.

**Socrates:** Precisely. Inductive reasoning is better understood as reasoning on the basis of experience or evidence collected from sense perceptions. Sometimes, we use this evidence to create a "generalization," a statement about how things tend to be. This is reasoning from the particular to the universal. Sometimes, though, we only use it to draw an analogy, a statement about what will likely be the case in one particular instance. You have to be really careful, though, when you reason on the basis of evidence, because you probably will never have *all* of the evidence. That is why we usually say that an inductive argument is either strong or weak, but we usually don't say that it is valid or invalid because we reserve that term for deductive arguments.

**Nate:** So, how are deductive arguments different?

**Socrates:** Deductive arguments start with premises, which are "givens" or "axioms"—things we accept as being true from the beginning of an argument, foundational principles upon which an argument rests. On the basis of these, we create an argument—like table legs holding up a table top. If put together correctly, the conclusion will follow from its premises and the argument will stand and be valid.

**Nate:** So what if a deductive argument isn't put together correctly and doesn't really follow from its premises?

**Socrates:** Well, that would make it fallacious. The fallacies that can be committed by a deductive argument are usually referred to as "formal" fallacies, since they all have to do with the form or structure of the argument. But, let's get back to the presupposition fallacy that you mentioned. I would say that the argument might also commit the fallacy of begging the question.

**Nate:** Is that because it contains the unproven assumption that Saudi Arabia and Japan are able to develop the same way simply because they are both traditional societies?

**Socrates:** Precisely. Like a table missing one leg, if the justification for a conclusion needs even more proving than the conclusion itself, what good is it? You could say that "begging the question" is sort of a catchall term for all sorts of fallacies that are caused because of assumptions that need to be proven first. There are several other presupposition fallacies that are more specific. They usually get their names from the sort of assumption they utilize.

**Nate:** Give us an example.

**Socrates:** Well, there's the fallacy of bifurcation, or false dilemma, which is also sometimes referred to as the "either-or fallacy." That happens when an argument assumes that there are only two possibilities, when, in fact, there could be others.

**Tiffany** (*who has been listening intently up to now*): Oh, I think I just read a good example of such a fallacy in this magazine. Here's the passage:

Shortly after the September 11 terrorist attacks in 2001, President Bush was scheduled to deliver the State of the Union Address. He delivered an eloquent speech. It was passionate, encouraging, and it gave hope to millions of people around the world. Speaking to Americans and to those listening abroad, he called on the nations of the world to unite under the common purpose of eradicating organized terrorism across the globe. President Bush promised to fight the terrorists wherever they were, saying, "We will not tire. We will not falter. And, we will not fail." He went on to say, "Either you are with us, or you are with the terrorists."

Strong words! And it was a very important and well-delivered speech, but it's pretty easy to guess that many nations around the world don't want to align themselves with terrorists or the United States. Those nations would just prefer to stay out of it. Iran's religious leader, Ayatollah Ali Khamenei, summed it up best when he responded, "No. We are not with you, and we are not terrorists."

It sounds to me as though Khamenei is accusing the president of committing the fallacy of bifurcation, and it sounds to me like he's right.

**Socrates:** I think you're right about that, but why?

**Tiffany:** Well, other nations don't have to be pro-American to be antiterrorist.

**Nate:** Wait, not so fast! I'm not sure that is what the president was doing. I think that President Bush was trying to persuade the nations of the world to stand up against evil, do their part, and wipe out terrorism . . .

**Socrates:** Excuse me, Nate, but I think I know where you're going with this. Let's ask the class for their opinion before we continue . . . (*See the fallacy discussion on the following page.*)

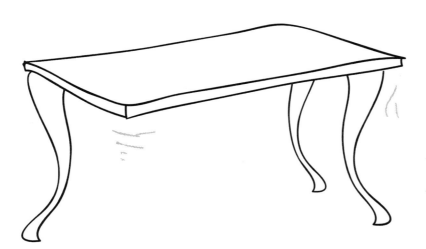

# Fallacy Discussion on Bifurcation (False Dilemma)

**Socrates:** Class, what do you think? Are nations that refuse to fight terror really aiding the advancement of terrorist organizations, or are they just refusing to be pigeonholed by a bifurcation fallacy? Make sure you think through your argument before reading on to find out what Nate and Tiffany think.

What do you think of the statement, "You are either with us, or with the terrorists"?

The example does commit the bifurcation fallacy. It is presenting only two options in

a complex situation in which there are likely many other reasonable options. Further

discussion follows on the next page.

**Nate:** Think of it this way: prior to and during World War II, European Jews were being murdered by the millions. When it was all said and done, nearly 6 million Jews died at Hitler's command. In the midst of the war, world leaders became aware of the crisis, but few of them rallied to try to save the Jews. You could argue that by refusing to stop Hitler, the nations of the world were really helping him by allowing him to continue his campaign against Jews. So, in the same vein, President Bush crafted his argument such that if a nation refused to assist the United States in its fight against terror, that nation would be viewed as aiding the terrorists. He tried to offer the nations of the world just two options for how to proceed. He's not saying they have to side with the United States on every issue that has divided us from other nations in the past or else they are pro-terrorism. He's saying that when thousands of innocent people are being killed, it's just wrong to stand on the sidelines and say that it's none of your business and that it's even worse to harbor, shelter, and fund those who are doing the killing.

**Socrates:** Well, that's an interesting argument, and by the way you just made an analogy! Whether it is a strong or weak one, we won't debate here, but I will say that there may be limitations to this stance of "for" or "against." Surely one person or nation can't be blamed for not stopping all of the evil in the world.

**Tiffany:** I see what you mean, Socrates. What if I see someone being held up at gun point? Do I have a responsibility to charge right on in and get myself shot? That wouldn't accomplish anything.

**Nate:** Well, OK, I see your point. But I do think that you have the responsibility to try to find a way to call the police and help them in their investigation and maybe try your best to help out the victim if he gets shot. And you certainly would be culpable if you helped the perpetrator escape justice.

**Socrates:** So, I guess the whole argument about whether or not the president was committing a fallacy actually revolves around what he really meant by "with us." Does "with us" mean fighting alongside or supporting the cause and not hindering?

**Tiffany:** Great question! Hey, we need to be getting back to class now, Nate. Good to see you again, Socrates.

**Socrates:** Always a pleasure.

# Fallacy 17:
## Fallacy of Moderation

DEFINITION: Arguments that assume the correct answer is always the middle ground or a compromise between two extremes.

As with all fallacies of presumption, this fallacy presumes or assumes something illegitimate. The fallacy of moderation presumes that the correct way of addressing two conflicting or opposite viewpoints is to find a compromise position between them. This fallacy can appear reasonable, since there are indeed times when a compromise between two extremes is wise.

Consider the following reasonable examples of moderation.

**Example 1**
> Not hot weather, not cold weather, but warm weather.

**Example 2**
> Not reckless, not cowardly, but courageous.

**Example 3**
> John wants a high-end, $1,500 desktop computer. His dad wants to buy him a $400 cheap computer. They compromise and agree to buy a decent computer for $800.

These three examples show that sometimes a compromise is reasonable. Most of us prefer warm weather to very hot or very cold weather (the same with showers!). However, most of us prefer hot chocolate over warm chocolate. We even have words for an undesirable kind of warm—lukewarm, tepid. Aristotle said that courage was the "golden mean" between recklessness on one extreme and cowardice on the other. In the third example, John and his dad seem to work out a reasonable compromise. We often have to make compromises when buying things and there is often wisdom in buying a moderately priced item rather than the cheapest or most expensive.

While there are certainly reasonable compromises, there are also fallacious ones. The choice between two extremes is not automatically the best choice, as the examples below show.

**Example 4**
> Not a black sweater, not a white sweater, but a black and white sweater!

**Example 5**
> John never wants to go to school. His mother wants him to go to school every day. As a compromise, John agrees to go to school half of the time.

**Example 6**
> John wants to keep his hair long. His dad wants him to get a buzz cut. They compromise and John gets a buzz cut on the left side of his head and keeps his hair long on the right side.

**Example 7**

The Democrats think the governor of the state should be removed from office for lying to the people. The Republicans suggest a compromise in which he is merely criticized for his bad behavior.

**Example 8**

Many are suggesting that we do not send any additional troops to Afghanistan. The general wants an additional 50,000 troops. Senator Wilkins wisely suggests that we send 25,000 troops.

The first three of these examples show that a compromise between extremes can sometimes be absurd. Getting a black and white sweater will not likely impress advocates of the black or white varieties. Going to school half of the time is not a reasonable solution, nor are two haircuts on one head. Example 7, however, is not as obviously unreasonable. In politics, making compromises is a regular exercise, but a political position should be justified not because it stands between two extremes, but because it stands on its own merits. Is criticizing the governor the fitting response for his actions or merely the compromise between doing nothing and removing him from office? In the case of example 8, does Senator Wilkins have legitimate reasons for why 25,000 troops is a justifiable number, or is he simply choosing the number between 0 and 50,000? If so, then his "moderate" position is not a very thoughtful one.

In political situations, we should be careful not to assume "everyone is wrong" and "just compromise." On the other hand, sometimes we must give up something we would like in order to achieve an ultimate good—even if it is not the *best* solution. Sometimes we will have to settle for the best we can achieve, even if that solution is not the best possible.[1]

## The Fallacy of Moderation

**Genus:** Arguments that are based on unwarranted assumptions.
**Difference:** These arguments make the assumption that compromise is always best.

1. Study the following advertisements that feature the fallacy of moderation. Can you see how the fallacy operates in each ad?

Both advertisements assume that a compromise between two extremes is best. The first advertisement

proposes that a political group that is a compromise of Republican and Democratic policies is best. The

second advertisement proposes that the best bread is a compromise between fluffy and gritty bread.

2. Create your own advertisement that features the fallacy of moderation.

Answers will vary.

---

1. Damer says the following about political compromise: "A compromise may be the best way to resolve a difficult situation; for example, it may prevent continued economic deprivation, bloodshed, or mental anguish. However, it may not be 'best' in the sense of being the most accurate, justifiable, or morally responsible solution to a problem. Nonetheless, you may have to accept the compromise without granting that it is the most justifiable solution. In order to maintain your logical integrity and protect yourself against charges of inconsistency or betrayal in the future, it might be wise to make it clear which of the 'bests' you are accepting" (Damer, 63).

# Moderation

| | |
|---|---|
| FALLACIES OF PRESUMPTION | Arguments that make unwarranted assumptions about either the data or the nature of a reasonable argument. |
| Fallacies of Presupposition | Arguments that contain hidden assumptions that make them unreasonable. |
| Moderation | An argument that assumes that the correct answer is always a middle ground between extremes. |

Republicans favor big business. Democrats favor big government. The **Cumberland County Independents' League** wants a moderate-sized government supporting average-sized businesses . . . just what the county needs!

Sponsored by the Cumberland County Independents' League

**Chapter 4: Fallacies of Presupposition**
Fallacy 17: Fallacy of Moderation

# Moderation

Too fluffy

Too gritty

Brite Bread™
**Just right!**

Brown & White Mixed:
Brite Bread

Try it today!

# Fallacy 18:
## Is-Ought Fallacy

DEFINITION: Arguments that assume that just because something *is* a certain way, it *ought* to be that way.

Many of us have a tendency to accept things the way we find them, such as approving of the practices, customs, and laws that we encounter in society. There are many things that we don't question, such as speed limits, the use of paper money, and singing "Happy Birthday" to friends on the day of their birth. There is nothing unreasonable about accepting and approving of various traditions, practices, customs, and laws, but our approval of them should be based upon more than the mere fact of their existence. There ought to be a reason for speed limits beyond the fact of their existence. In other words, we should not uncritically accept various practices simply because they exist. For example, for many years, many Americans accepted the institution of slavery as a common practice simply because it was just that, a common practice.

Occasionally, people will argue that their position should be accepted because it is a position that exists. Consider the following examples.

### Example 1
There has always been a lower caste in India that has been impoverished and there always will be. We must accept this fact.

### Example 2
How can you criticize people for gambling at the casinos? Gambling is a legal activity in this state.

### Example 3
Why do you want to pay lower taxes? Tax rates are set by Congress, and they are the law of the land.

In each of these examples, the presenter illegitimately assumes that because a practice exists, it should exist—in other words, it is justified simply because it exists. Just because there has been an impoverished lower caste in India for centuries does not mean it should continue, or that we should not seek to change this fact. Simply because an activity such as gambling has been declared legal does not mean that it should continue to be legal. In American history, many previously legal activities have been declared illegal (e.g., slavery, prohibition of alcohol sales, prohibition of female and black voting). It is true that Congress sets our tax rates, but if Congress has set our tax rates, Congress can lower them as well, and citizens can argue that they should lower them. Our tax rates need not stay high just because they are high.

### Is-Ought Fallacy
**Genus:** Arguments that are based on unwarranted assumptions.
**Difference:** These arguments assume that something is right or preferable simply because it's the way things are at the moment.

# Is-Ought Fallacy

| | |
|---|---|
| FALLACIES OF PRESUMPTION | Arguments that make unwarranted assumptions about either the data or the nature of a reasonable argument. |
| Fallacies of Presupposition | Arguments that contain hidden assumptions that make them unreasonable. |
| Is-Ought Fallacy | An argument that assumes that just because something **is** a certain way, it *ought* to be that way. |

# If God . . . ◆

...didn't want us to eat animals, why did He make them out of meat?

Bulgarian Beef Growers Association

# Is-Ought Fallacy

Why ask why?

BEETHOVEN: SONATAS
VLADIMIR HOROWITZ

tm

Gold Edition Audio Cassettes
"Music is better with the fuzz"

Make your own ad.

**Chapter 4: Fallacies of Presupposition**
Fallacy 18: Is-Ought Fallacy

# Fallacy Discussion on the Is-Ought Fallacy

**Socrates:** See if you can detect the is-ought fallacy in this exchange.

**Student Council President:** Students should have a greater voice in the decision-making process of this school!

**Principal:** Well, a school is not really a democratic organization, and we are not going to try to change the governmental structure. There are many other important issues on which we should focus.

Do you think the principal has committed the is-ought fallacy? Explain your answer.

The principal has, indeed, committed the is-ought fallacy. Just because the governmental structure of the school is a certain way does not necessarily mean that it should be that way. Further discussion follows on the next page.

**Socrates:** As many of you know, back in my day, I was considered by many to be a teacher. I engaged young men in philosophical discussions. Democracy was one of my favorite topics. Just *how* democratic a school ought to be is precisely the issue in the above example. The point is that we shouldn't accept things simply because they are as they are. When a speaker tries to argue in this way, ask for a better reason.

**Chapter 4: Fallacies of Presupposition**
Fallacy Discussion on the Is-Ought Fallacy

# Fallacy 19:
## Fallacy of Composition

DEFINITION: Arguments based on a hidden assumption that the properties of the whole will be the same as the properties of the parts.

It might seem logical to assume that what is true of a part must be true of something that contains that part. Is it not true that if a single diamond is expensive then a necklace made of many diamonds will be expensive? If one flower smells good, won't an arrangement of many of those flowers smell good? While sometimes what is true of a part is true of the whole, that is not always the case. For example, if a new movie trailer is really excellent does that mean that movie will be excellent? We all know better than that. Does a great cover guarantee a great book? Not necessarily. To think that way is to fall into the fallacy of composition—when we assume what is true of a part of must be true of the thing that contains that part (or is composed of one or more of those parts).

Consider the following examples of the fallacy of composition.

**Example 1**
> Boy, this feather is light. That feather pillow must be light, too.

**Example 2**
> This test was not hard at all! This is going to be an easy class.

**Example 3**
> Why is this metal chain so flexible? It is made up of so many hard, rigid links!

**Example 4**
> I don't get it. The National Hockey League All-Star team got beat by the team that won the Stanley Cup. How could a team of the best hockey players not be the very best team in existence?

These examples should make it clear that the quality of a part does not ensure that the whole will have that same quality.

The box below represents the fallacious flow of thought contained in this fallacy. Such thought assumes that what is true of one part will be true of the collective whole.

### Fallacy of Composition
**Genus:** Arguments that are based on unwarranted assumptions.
**Difference:** An argument that assumes that a collective whole will have the same properties as its individual parts.

## Fallacy of Composition

One part $\longrightarrow$ Collection of parts (collective whole)

A feather is light $\longrightarrow$ A feather pillow must be light

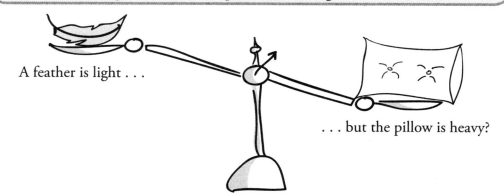

A feather is light . . .

. . . but the pillow is heavy?

The artist dream team!

# Many Hands Portraiture Studio

Our portraits are compilations created by a team of the best artists! From graphic artists and medieval painters to abstract sculptors and poets, we have the very best!

"Johnny came out looking like I never expected!"

"The artists... are... creative."

"Everyone talked about my portrait!"

# Composition Fallacy

| | |
|---|---|
| FALLACIES OF PRESUMPTION | Arguments that make unwarranted assumptions about either the data or the nature of a reasonable argument. |
| Fallacies of Presupposition | Arguments that contain hidden assumptions that make them unreasonable. |
| Composition | An argument that assumes that a collective whole will be like its individual parts. |

# Fallacy 20:
## Fallacy of Division

DEFINITION: Arguments that are based on the hidden assumption that a collective whole determines that all of its parts will be like the whole.

It seems logical to assume that what is true of a collection of parts will be true of each part, don't you think? For example, is it not true that if a cake is sweet, then a piece of that cake will be sweet? Is it not true that if pot of stew is hot then a bowl of that soup will be hot? Sometimes a characteristic of a collection of parts will be true of each part, but sometimes not. For example, you probably don't think that because an airplane can fly then all of its parts can fly. You also probably don't think that because the earth is round then everything that comes from the earth is round. To think that way is to fall into the fallacy of division, which is when we assume that what is true of a collection of parts (or collective whole) must be true of each (divided) part.

Consider the following examples of the fallacy of division.

**Example 1**

Boy, this feather pillow is heavy. Each feather that makes up the pillow must be heavy, too.

**Example 2**

The Department of Transportation is always slow at getting things done. Since this official works for the Department of Transportation, he won't get his work done for a good, long while.

**Example 3**

A helium blimp can soar up into the sky—they say it is lighter than air. Does that mean that all of its parts are lighter than air?

These examples should make it clear that the quality of a whole does not ensure that the parts of that whole will share that quality.

The box below represents the fallacious flow of thought contained in this fallacy. Such thought assumes that what is true of the collective whole will be true of each individual part.

---

### Fallacy of Division

Collection of parts (collective whole) ⟶ Every part
A feather pillow is heavy ⟶ Each feather must be heavy

---

## Division Fallacy

**Genus:** Arguments that are based on unwarranted assumptions.

**Difference:** An argument that assumes that the parts will have the same properties as the collective whole.

Bath & Shower makes the best products for your skin-care needs.

If you liked our Aloe-fresh bar soap, then you'll like our Aloe-fresh shower gel, body butter, hydrating face wash, exfoliating face wash, day creme, facial serum, night creme, baby oil, toner, body spray, deodorant, shave gel, and sunscreen!

Bath & Shower

# Division Fallacy

| | |
|---|---|
| FALLACIES OF PRESUMPTION | Arguments that make unwarranted assumptions about either the data or the nature of a reasonable argument. |
| Fallacies of Presupposition | Arguments that contain hidden assumptions that make them unreasonable. |
| Division | An argument that assumes that individual parts of a collective whole will be like the collective whole. |

You've enjoyed the fine dining at restaurant bon dinant. Now try our new table seasonings in your own home!

bon dinant

**Chapter 4: Fallacies of Presupposition**
Fallacy 20: Fallacy of Division

# Fallacy Discussion on Composition and Division

**Socrates:** When your historians study the ancient Greeks and Romans, they very often focus on the military history. In fact, many of you might know a thing or two about the men who made up the Greek and Roman armies. You might be able to tell me about the armor they wore or the battles they fought. You might even be able to relay some examples of bravery by a specific man or men.

Some claim the Roman and Greek cultures fielded the most proficient militaries in ancient history. But, were their successes due primarily to the prowess of the individual soldiers or to their military strategies and formations?

Tell what you think.

If an argument was made that the strength and success of the Greek and Roman armies

was because of the skill of each soldier, it would be committing the fallacy of composition

and ignoring the role that military strategies, discipline, command, and formations played.

Further discussion follows on the next page.

**Socrates:** The military success of the Greeks and Romans was not due primarily to the proficiency and expertise of the individual soldiers, but rather to the fact that they had **a tactical system** that required the individuals to master only a limited battery of skills and to be brave. The armies of ancient Greece and Rome were truly greater than the sum of their parts! (Take it from me; I have plenty of experience in the front lines of the Athenian phalanx.)

**Chapter 4: Fallacies of Presupposition**
Fallacy Discussion on Composition and Division

# Chapter 4 Review

**A. DEFINE:**

1. Fallacies of Presupposition:

Arguments that contain hidden assumptions that make them unreasonable.

2. Fallacies of Presumption:

Arguments that make unwarranted assumptions about either the data or the nature of a reasonable argument.

3. Axioms:

Foundational principles upon which an argument rests.

4. Enthymeme (Hidden Assumption):

An argument in which at least one statement (premise or conclusion) is assumed rather than explicitly stated.

5. Begging the Question:

An argument that assumes the very thing that one is trying to prove.

6. Bifurcation (False Dilemma):

An argument that frames the debate in such a way that only two options are possible, when other possibilities may exist. Also called a false dichotomy.

7. Dilemma:

A situation in which one must choose between two unpleasant alternatives.

8. Fallacy of Moderation:

An argument that assumes the correct answer is always the middle ground or a compromise between two extremes.

9. Is-Ought Fallacy:

An argument that assumes that just because something *is* a certain way, it *ought* to be that way.

10. Fallacy of Composition:

Arguments based on a hidden assumption that the properties of the whole will be the same as the properties of the parts.

11. Fallacy of Division:

Arguments based on the hidden assumption that a collective whole determines that all of its parts will be like the whole.

**B. IDENTIFICATION:** Determine which fallacy is being used in each of the following examples.

1. The speaker makes the assumption that the parts will have the same properties as a collective whole.

   division

2. The speaker is either just restating the conclusion in other words or uses a justification that is more controversial than the original conclusion.

   begging the question

3. The speaker assumes that a collective whole will have the properties of each of its parts.

   composition

4. The speaker assumes that something is the right thing simply because it is the way that things are.

   is-ought

5. The speaker assumes that the best solution to a problem is necessarily a compromise between extremes.

   moderation

6. The speaker assumes that only two possibilities exist when there may actually be others.

   bifurcation (false dilemma)

**C. IN DEPTH:** Name which fallacy of presumption is being committed in the following examples. Explain your answers.

1. Now, you think the problem is mostly your wife's fault, and your wife thinks it is mostly your fault. Let's just start out by admitting that there's probably an equal amount of blame on each side.

   Moderation: Starting with an assumption that both the husband and the wife must share equally in the problem they are experiencing is unjustified, particularly before exploring the issue. Sometimes two people do share the blame more or less equally for a problem they are having, but not always. Without any evidence, there is no justification for assuming the blame must be shared equally.

2. Look, either you accept that we need full funding for the V-22 Osprey, or you admit that you don't have the best interests of our national defense at heart.

Bifurcation: It is quite possible for someone to oppose funding the Osprey and still have the best

interests of the national defense at heart. For example, a person may wish to see the funding

directed to another airplane that he or she thinks would better serve to protect the country.

3. Veritas School is the finest school in the Chattanooga area! You ask how I can state this with such confidence? Easy: Each of our teachers have won teaching awards.

Composition: Just because every teacher has won an award does not mean they work together well

to make the school excellent. Individual teachers must collaborate, share information and insight,

and work together on curriculum and student needs in order to achieve school-wide excellence.

4. Luc Longley is just the ingredient that the Phoenix Suns need to win a championship. Everyone conceded that the center position has been their Achilles' heel since time immemorial, and Luc has started at center for all six championship seasons of the incomparable Chicago Bulls.

Division: Just because the Bulls were a great team doesn't mean they had a great center.

5. Failure to support our public schools is a failure to support education, because that is how America is educated!

Is-ought fallacy: Just because Americans are generally educated that way doesn't mean they

ought to be.

6. Of course I can't support public education. It's nothing more than a big-government monopoly.

Begging the question: The assertion that big-government monopolies are a bad way to educate

must first be argued.

# Cumulative Fallacy Worksheet

**DIRECTIONS:** Identify each fallacy. (Hint: Some examples may commit more than one.)

1. What do you mean the Palestinians should have their own state? They've never had a state before, they don't have one now, and that's how things ought to be.

   is-ought (the speaker is confusing the way that a situation is for the way that it should be; it could also possibly be called an appeal to tradition)

2. **James:** Surely you must see that life inexorably follows the principle of "survival of the fittest."

   **Bryan:** Well, in that case, how do we know which are the fittest?

   **James:** Why, they are the species that survive.

   **Bryan:** Well, what do you mean by "fittest?"

   **James:** Why, I mean the set of qualities which best enable one to survive.

   begging the question (this is a classic case of a circular argument; since it also concerns the definition of the term "fittest" it is also begging the question; note that, used in this way by Darwinists, the term "fittest" is often equivocated on)

3. **Volkswagen commercial:** On the road of life, there are passengers and there are drivers. Drivers wanted.

   bifurcation (false dilemma) and snob appeal

4. We can't possibly believe that the vice president's energy program is in the best interests of the country. He's a former executive for a prominent energy company.

   _ad hominem_ circumstantial

5. The US Marines did a great job in Afghanistan. They're a great organization. We need to hire a marine for our security company.

 _division (just because the US Marines as a whole are very effective doesn't mean that an_

 _individual marine is going to be the best man for the job)_

6. The best and brightest always read *The New York Times*.

 _snob appeal_

7. Look, the Palestinians want all of the land and the Israelis want all of the land, so let's just compromise and give each group exactly half.

 _moderation (a fifty-fifty split isn't always the most just solution)_

8. How can you oppose this bill? Either you support this bill or you do not have the safety of the American people at heart.

 _bifurcation (false dilemma)_

9. Create a lighter-than-air vehicle? That's impossible! What part of any vehicle is lighter than air?

 _composition (the vehicle as a whole can be lighter than air even if individual pieces aren't)_

10. How can you support Senator Jones's bill? He's nothing but a debauched, drunken idiot!

 _ad hominem abusive_

11. How can Senator Bruce support this bill against drunk driving? He's been convicted of drunk driving himself.

 _tu quoque_

# Chapter 5
## Fallacies of Induction

DEFINITION: Arguments that misuse empirical data or don't follow proper methods of inductive reasoning.

You may remember that we discussed the difference between inductive and deductive reasoning near the beginning of this book. Whereas deductive reasoning is based on premises that must necessarily lead to a conclusion and moves from the whole to the part, inductive reasoning moves from the part to the whole. **Inductive reasoning seeks to begin with particular facts and tries to prove a general conclusion.** If such a general conclusion is considered proven, then it could be used in a deductive argument as a premise. For example, if we reason from many particular facts that the law of gravity exists, then we can argue this way: Since all objects fall toward the center of the earth (the law of gravity), then if I let go of my pen it will fall toward the center of the earth. The particular facts are just other names for **empirical data**—data that comes to us by observation or experience.

You can probably guess that science makes significant use of inductive reasoning. Newton was reflecting on his observations that apples (and other objects) always fall to the ground when he formulated the law of gravity. The movement in his mind was clearly from part to whole—from the apple to the universe, one might say.

Since I'm clearly a quality apple . . . the best fruit must be those on the ground!

Whenever we arrive at general conclusions on the basis of our various observations, we are engaged in inductive reasoning, whether we are doing scientific work or not. **Inductive reasoning is essentially the process of working back from things we observe in order to arrive at accurate generalizations.** When we do this, we put our observations together and mentally organize them into bits of information we call evidence. Because of the limitations of being human, however, our conclusions based on inductive reasoning are never absolutely, 100 percent certain. With our limits as humans (limited knowledge, limited observations, the capacity for making mistakes) we never know and study *all* the evidence—we can never achieve omniscience. Therefore, **the conclusions of an inductive argument can never be certain, but can only follow with more or less probability**. While the argument for the law of gravity is very strong, indeed, it is still only probable. Has anyone observed a pen float upwards?

Since inductive arguments are built on evidence (or empirical data), it is the body of evidence that may likely be a weak link in these arguments. The two most common reasons why the evidence could be weak are: 1) the evidence could be incomplete, lacking one or more critical facts, or 2) the evidence could be distorted, causing the argument to be deceptively weak. We will study five types of inductive fallacies that will fit into one of these two categories. These fallacies are: **sweeping generalization**, **hasty generalization**, **false analogy**, **false cause**, and **fake precision**.

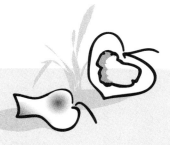

Draw your own ad with
your favorite fallacy so far
on the billboard below.

You're selling what?!

**Chapter 5: Fallacies of Induction**

# Fallacy 21:
## Sweeping Generalization (Accident)

DEFINITION: Arguments that overextend a generalization to include facts or cases that are exceptions to it.

Just what is a generalization? Well, we all make generalizations—or generalize—on a regular basis. We generalize when we make observations and assumptions about how things are for an entire class of facts. When we say that "all SUVs are gas-guzzlers" or "all bees sting," we are making generalizations. There is nothing wrong with making general statements about facts and affairs based on our observations and study. There is a problem, however, when we make unwarranted generalizations—when we make a generalization that does not pay attention to facts that simply don't fit into the generalization we are making.

For example, it is true that many (probably most) SUVs use a lot more gas than the average car. They are bigger cars, and they come with bigger engines that use more gas. There are some SUVs, however, that get pretty good gas mileage, like a hybrid SUV that employs electric and gasoline power.

It is one thing to make a generalization as a part of everyday conversation; it is another thing to make a generalization when we are arguing or debating. In an argument, generalizations should be accurate, especially when a point that is important to the argument is a generalization. For example, to make a passing comment about SUVs being gas guzzlers may pass unchallenged as a part of a casual conversation, but if you were to argue that SUVs should be banned because "all SUVs are gas guzzlers," your opponent could charge you with making a sweeping generalization that does not take into consideration that there are some SUVs that don't guzzle gas.

Here are some other examples of sweeping generalizations that could be challenged in an argument.

### Example 1
**Joe:** Don't get a PC. They crash at least once a week. Get a Mac. They don't crash!

**Bob:** I have owned a PC that crashed far less than once a week. I have a Mac and it has crashed.

### Example 2
**Carrie:** You have got to move to Southern California—it never rains there, and everyone is so laid back and relaxed.

**Juliette:** I know several uptight Southern Californians who have been caught in the rain.

The sweeping generalization fallacy is also called the fallacy of accident. In philosophic terms, an "accident" is a trait or quality that a thing or class of things can have. For example, we could say that "snow is white," and "snow" would be the **substance** and "white" would be an **accident** (a particular quality of snow relating to color). Another accident of snow would be "cold." Well, what if you said, "All clouds are white"? Can you think of another trait, or accident, that would show this to be untrue? It's likely that you have seen gray clouds. Gray would be an accident that proves that the statement "all clouds are white" is false, or a sweeping generalization. Therefore, a fallacy of accident is a fallacy in which the accident that is being proposed (e.g., all clouds are white) turns out not to be true, since clouds can also be gray (or pink, or orange, or red-orange, etc.).

The box below represents the fallacious flow of thought contained in this fallacy. Such thought assumes that an entire class of things has one quality, with the result that every member of that class must also have that quality, without exception.

---

### Sweeping Generalization

Whole class $\longrightarrow$ Every fact/quality

All clouds are white $\longrightarrow$ Every cloud must be white, with no exceptions

---

### Sweeping Generalization
**Genus:** Fallacies relating to problems in inductive reasoning.
**Difference:** These arguments extend generalizations more than they should be extended.

---

**ANSWER:**
How can inductive arguments be weak?

1. The evidence could be incomplete, lacking one or more critical facts.

2. The evidence could be distorted, causing the argument to be deceptively weak.

Create two sweeping generalizations of your own:

1. Answers will vary. See the examples on page 163 for fallacy ideas. Here is an additional example: The roads in Pennsylvania are terrible. If you drive in Pennsylvania you can count on hitting a pothole every time you drive.

2. Answers will vary.

# Sweeping Generalization

| | |
|---|---|
| FALLACIES OF PRESUMPTION | Arguments that make unwarranted assumptions about either the data or the nature of a reasonable argument. |
| Fallacies of Induction | Arguments that misuse empirical data or don't follow proper methods of inductive reasoning. |
| Sweeping Generalization (Accident) | An argument that takes a generalization and applies it to cases that are legitimate exceptions to it. |

Protect Yourself

FACT: Carpenters hit their thumbs with hammers. Protect yourself with Binder's Steel-Tipped Utility Gloves.

One size fits all.
Real leather.
Made in America.

Binder's Utility

# Sweeping Generalization

# THE CHOICE IS YOURS

Most airline travelers prefer another bag
of peanuts over the dinner provided.
With Chesterfield Peanuts, you will, too!

CHESTERFIELD PEANUTS
*Cracking a better nut*

**Chapter 5: Fallacies of Induction**
Fallacy 21: Sweeping Generalization (Accident)

# Fallacy 22:
## Hasty Generalization (Converse Accident)

DEFINITION: Arguments that make an unwarranted generalization on the basis of too few samples.

We have seen that we can make an unwarranted conclusion by overextending a generalization to include facts that are exceptions to it (e.g., all clouds are white). We can also generalize when we assume that what we observe about one particular fact must be true for a whole class. For example, you might notice that all the school buses you see in your town are yellow, and then generalize that all school buses everywhere are yellow. Or, you might notice that the two coffee shops in your town roast their coffee beans right in the store and then generalize that all coffee shops everywhere roast coffee beans in their stores.

It is sometimes humorous to watch little children exercise their ability to generalize. To a two-year-old child, anything round that you can hold in your hand may qualify as a "ball"—even a round, glass Christmas ornament! And watch out, because any stick could be a "bat." It is wise for a parent to teach a two year old about this fallacy—"No, Johnny, that's not a ball, and that is not a bat."

A generalization becomes a hasty generalization (and thus a fallacy) when we "jump to a conclusion" based on only a small sample of evidence. If every school bus you have ever seen for fifteen years has been yellow, you would not be "hasty" in proclaiming that school buses are yellow. If your first school bus driver was a 250-pound grandfather of two, you would be hasty to announce that all bus drivers are large grandfathers. As we stated before, it is important to use generalizations accurately in debate and argument, especially when a point that is important to the argument is a generalization.

Here are some additional examples of hasty generalizations.

**Example 1**
My dad's laptop battery started smoking last night and ruined his laptop. Don't ever buy an Acme laptop—they're junk!

**Example 2**
Matt Damon is such a limited actor! In *The Bourne Supremacy* all he did was fight scenes and car chases.

The hasty generalization fallacy is also called the fallacy of reverse (or converse) accident. Remember that the fallacy of accident generalizes that a whole class is characterized by certain accidents (or traits) and ignores exceptions to it (e.g., all clouds are white; but what about gray clouds?). The fallacy of reverse accident starts with the observation of one accident (or trait) and then concludes that the trait characterizes a whole class (e.g., this cloud is white—therefore all clouds are white).

---

### Hasty Generalization

One fact (or few facts) $\longrightarrow$ Whole class

This cloud is white $\longrightarrow$ All clouds are white

---

**COMPARING THE FALLACY OF SWEEPING GENERALIZATION TO THE FALLACY OF DIVISION**

These two fallacies are similar in that they move from whole to part. But note that the generalization fallacy deals with a class (which can include many qualities) whereas the division fallacy deals with a collective (which is really one thing that can include many parts).

Whole ⟶ Part

**Sweeping Generalization**
Class ⟶ Every fact/quality
All clouds are white ⟶ Every cloud must be white with no exceptions

**Division**
Collective whole ⟶ Every part
A feather pillow is heavy ⟶ Each feather must be heavy

Clouds are a class of things and white is a quality of that class. A feather pillow is not a class of things, but a thing itself, though a thing that is made up of parts (including feathers).

**COMPARING THE FALLACY OF HASTY GENERALIZATION TO THE FALLACY OF COMPOSITION**

These two fallacies are similar in that they move from part to whole. But note that the hasty generalization fallacy deals with one individual fact and then projects a quality of that fact to a whole class, whereas the composition fallacy deals with one part of a collection of parts and then projects the quality of that part to the collection.

Part ⟶ Whole

**Hasty Generalization**
One fact/quality (or few) ⟶ Whole class
This cloud is white ⟶ All clouds are white

**Composition**
One part ⟶ Every part (collective whole)
A feather is light ⟶ A feather pillow must be light

## Hasty Generalization

**Genus:** Fallacies relating to problems in inductive reasoning.
**Difference:** These arguments are hasty generalizations based on too few samples.

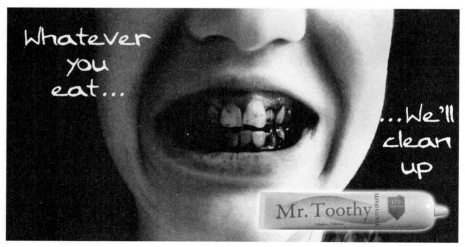

# Hasty Generalization

| | |
|---|---|
| FALLACIES OF PRESUMPTION | Arguments that make unwarranted assumptions about either the data or the nature of a reasonable argument. |
| Fallacies of Induction | Arguments that misuse empirical data or don't follow proper methods of inductive reasoning. |
| Hasty Generalization (Converse Accident) | An argument that makes a generalization on the basis of too few examples. |

# Fallacy 23:
## False Analogy

**DEFINITION:** Arguments that fail because they create an analogy between two things that are not similar enough to warrant an analogy.

An analogy is a comparison of two different things that are alike in some way. For example, we might say that a heart is like a pump. Even though a heart is a very different thing from a pump, it is like a pump in at least one important aspect—the heart pumps blood through the body. An analogy becomes false or weak when the two things compared are not really that similar, making the comparison unconvincing.

Consider the following examples of strong and weak analogies.

**Example 1 (Strong Analogy)**
   **Mohammed Ali (famous boxer):** I float like a butterfly and sting like a bee.

The famous boxing champion Mohammed Ali did, in fact, make the boast written above. His descriptive words aptly compared his boxing to both a butterfly and a bee. The fast footwork that moved him quickly and smoothly around the boxing ring made it seem as if he was floating like a butterfly. His opponents could surely attest to his punch being like a bee sting—quick and painful. As you can see, it is easy to understand the similarity between the bee's sting and Ali's punch and the movements of a butterfly and Ali's footwork. However, what if Ali had said, "I float like a cloud and sting like the air"? The floating of a cloud is aimless, not purposeful. Can the air sting? These comparisons aren't similar enough to persuade us of Ali's boxing skill.

If we wish to argue using an analogy, we should use an analogy that compares two things that are fairly similar. If the two things we compare are not very similar, the analogy will not be persuasive and we will commit the fallacy of weak or false analogy.

**Example 2 (Strong Analogy)**
   Just as a car will stop running unless you refuel it with gas, so too an army will stop fighting unless it is fed.

**Example 3 (Weak Analogy)**
   Just as a car will stop running without gas, so too a student will stop studying without good grades.

### False Analogy
**Genus:** Fallacies relating to problems in inductive reasoning.
**Difference:** These arguments are based on weak analogies between two cases.

Example 2 holds up quite well since cars and humans are similar enough in this respect: they both need their own kinds of fuel to keep functioning. In example 3, however, the two things being compared are not similar enough to be persuasive: gas is not similar enough to good grades to make the analogy work. In fact, there are many students who aren't getting good grades who are studying very hard and will likely be getting good grades in the future!

Remember that analogies will come in either stronger or weaker varieties, depending on the similarity of the two things being compared in the analogy. As with all inductive arguments, an analogy can be strong or weak, but it cannot prove something with certainty.

**TANKER MOTOR OIL**

Don't Smoke, kids

EAT @ JOES

EFFERVÉ SCENT CANDLES

Buck's Crab Shack

Little Timmy's Cheap Tires

**BOBBY DUGAN**

Our motor oil helped Bobby Dugan win the Indy SpringBoard 640.
*Drive like a winner!*

ALL WEATHER MIX

DRIVE LIKE A WINNER!

TANKER MOTOR 1030 W OIL
>>>
32 fluid oz., 1.33 liter

# False Analogy

FALLACIES OF PRESUMPTION | Arguments that make unwarranted assumptions about either the data or the nature of a reasonable argument.

Fallacies of Induction | Arguments that misuse empirical data or don't follow proper methods of inductive reasoning.

False Analogy | An argument that rests on an analogy that fails, usually because the things being compared aren't really similar enough to be analogous.

Actress *Diane Gilbert* looked great in our wedding gown

Look just as good

Maxfield P.
Bridal Designs

# Fallacy Discussion on False Analogy

**Socrates:** Let's discuss an example of false analogy that might be a bit more clear.

Tiffany argues that just as it is impossible for a human being to be in two places at one time, it is also impossible for a person to laugh and cry at the same time. How might this be a false analogy?

This argument is committing the fallacy of false analogy because it is comparing two

situations that are very different. Further discussion follows on the next page.

**Socrates:** A human is a physical body that exists in time and space. It can clearly only be in one place at one time, and otherwise would be breaking the laws of physics. Laughing and crying express human emotions and emotions are not governed by the laws of physics. We have all laughed so hard that tears start coming from our eyes, and sometimes, we are so happy that we express it with "tears of joy." Tiffany is making a comparison of two things that are just not comparable.

**Further Discussion:**

**Identify each analogy below as either a good or bad analogy, and explain your answer.**

1. Providing a laptop to every college student is a bad idea. That would be like giving them a free pass to an arcade.

   Bad analogy—computers, while they do have games on them, are not similar to arcades.


2. Giving a laptop to every college freshman is an excellent idea. Every workman performs better with the best tools.

   Good analogy—a computer is very much like a workman's tool.


3. Reading a great book is like making a new friend.

   Good analogy—books are often the presentation of a person in written form.


4. We shouldn't cut anyone from the basketball team any more than we should excuse students from P.E. class.

   Bad analogy—P.E. is usually a required class, and being on the basketball team is not.


5. Getting a summer job to save money to pay for college is no different than doing household chores as a child. All that work and you don't even get any money to spend.

   Bad analogy—one does get paid for a summer job, and one does get to spend the money—on college!

# Fallacy 24:
## False Cause

DEFINITION: Arguments that are based on a weak cause-and-effect connection.

One of the most difficult and important tasks of scientists and historians is establishing the cause of something. If every effect has a cause, then we would expect that a scientist must try to determine the causes for those things he observes. We would expect that a historian must try to determine what causes exist for various historical events, such as the American Revolution or the Civil War. Anytime we try to establish the cause for a particular event, we are engaged in *causal* thinking and may make *causal arguments*.

As you might guess, there are a number of ways in which we can fall into a fallacy when making causal arguments. We call a fallacy in a causal argument the **false cause fallacy**, or **causal fallacy**. The oldest and perhaps most widely recognized type of false cause fallacy is called the *post hoc ergo propter hoc* fallacy, which is Latin for "after this, therefore because of this." In brief, this simply means that people are prone to think that because one event follows another event, that the first event must have caused the one following it. However, just because one thing follows another thing in time doesn't mean that the first thing caused the second. In symbolic terms, if A is followed by B, that doesn't not mean that A caused B. In other words, **mere sequence or chronology does not equal causality**. For example, if you get a headache after drinking a soda, did the soda cause the headache? If you run your fastest time at a track meet right after dancing a little jig, is the jig the cause of your faster speed?

Consider the following examples.

**Example 1 (Fallacy)**
Right after the phone rang, Olivia started sneezing. She must be allergic to phone calls.

**Example 2 (Not a Fallacy)**
Almost immediately after receiving the injection of anesthesia, he fell asleep.

Example 1 should strike you as silly. We are not likely to think a phone ringing is the cause of a sneeze just because the ring came right before the sneeze. On the other hand, as example 2 shows, often one thing that follows another in time *does* involve a causal connection. If I pinch you and then you shout "Ouch!" I would be hard-pressed to argue that my pinch did not cause your shout. The point here, however, is that the mere fact that one event follows another does not *always* prove causation. Scientists are often trying to understand causal connections or relationships, and they have to work hard to avoid making mistakes when reasoning about what thing is causing another.

This is particularly true in a field in which certain laws or principles are not fully understood. Sometimes, sequence or chronology is the only tool at a scientist's disposal as she tries to determine what thing may be causing another. In such cases as this, the scientist will try to test her hypothesis about causation by creating controlled experiments that will allow her to isolate certain factors, which help her prove which thing is, in fact, causing another.

For the historian, however, carefully controlled and reproducible experiments aren't possible, because the historian studies specific events that have occurred in the past and therefore can't be reproduced again in exactly the same way in which they occurred. Even in the social sciences, such as sociology, that deal mainly in the present, it is still difficult to determine what thing is causing another. This is because the field of study is so large and complex (what motivates people in individual and group behaviors) that it usually prevents the sort of precise study that can be attained in the natural sciences. We must remember that establishing a causal connection is a tricky endeavor, since many factors can be present, making it hard to know just what is causing what.

The following are several different types of false cause fallacies, beginning with the partial cause.

### PARTIAL CAUSE

Whenever we assert that one factor is the complete cause for an event when there are other causes involved, we commit the "partial cause" fallacy. Consider the following examples.

#### Example 3 (History)

It was General Patton's stirring speech and leadership that led to the successful Allied invasion of France in June, 1944.

#### Example 4 (Sociology)

American students have been steadily watching more television over the last five years, and their math scores have steadily fallen during the same time period. Increased TV watching is resulting in poor math scores.

By most accounts, General Patton was a great speech giver and military leader. However, there were no doubt many other contributing factors that caused his army to be victorious in the Allied invasion—factors such as the army's previous training and experience; the leadership of his officers; and abundant food, supplies, and equipment.

While watching a lot of television may not be wise for numerous reasons, the argument in example 4 does not show a causal connection between increased TV watching and lower math scores. Again, there may be many other factors leading to falling math scores, such as the quality of schools, teachers, math textbooks, and materials, to name just a few.

#### Example 5 (Public Policy)

The availability of handguns is responsible for high rates of violent crime. If we significantly restrict access to handguns, the rates of violent crime will drop.

Let's consider this political and sociological example of false cause. Gun-control advocates (those people who want to restrict access to hand guns in particular) often make the argument that America's high crime rate could be reduced by limiting the availability of weapons, especially hand guns, since other countries (such as Japan) that have strict gun control also have low crime rates. Is there a causal connection between strict gun control and a low rate of crime?

There are many factors that cause violent crime, and one could argue that if weapons were not available to citizens, criminals would still find a way to get them and use them, or simply revert to using other weapons (such as knives) to commit violent crimes. While Japan has strict gun control and a low rate of violent crime, Switzerland has little gun control (citizens serving as reserve army soldiers often have army-issue automatic weapons in their homes) and also has a low rate of violent crime. In order to establish a causal link between the availability of firearms and violent crime, one would have to provide evidence that within the same country or region, violent crime either went down when strict gun control was implemented or up when it was ended. The different cultures of Japan and Switzerland may have a significant influence on crime rates and the way guns are used and misused. Large cultural or policy changes within the same country could also be the causes for increasing or decreasing crime, not just the availability, or lack thereof, of guns.

## False Cause

**Genus:** Fallacies relating to problems in inductive reasoning.
**Difference:** These arguments are based on insufficiently justified causal connections.

Now let's examine three other types of false cause fallacies and examples of each one.[1]

### CONFUSING A NECESSARY AND SUFFICIENT CONDITION

Sometimes an event won't occur without a certain factor or condition being present. This fallacy assumes that because something cannot occur without that certain factor or condition being present, it will necessarily occur if that factor is present. For example, it won't snow without the temperature being thirty-two degrees Fahrenheit (the temperature at which water freezes) or less. A freezing temperature may be necessary for it to snow, but is not sufficient to cause it to snow. Therefore, we would say that a freezing temperature is a necessary but not a sufficient condition for snow.

Consider this example of confusing a necessary and sufficient condition.

**Example 6**
> **Rachel:** The employer who interviewed me said that a college degree was required for the position. I have a college degree, so why didn't I get the job?

Rachel has learned that having a college degree is a necessary condition for getting the job, but not a sufficient condition to ensure that she will actually get it. After all, there were others who had college degrees that applied for the job, and the job could only be offered to one person.

### CONFUSING A CAUSE AND AN EFFECT

It is not always easy to see the difference between a cause and an effect. This is a fallacy in which a causal relationship exists between two elements, and an argument is based on the misunderstanding that the effect is the cause and the cause is the effect. Consider the following example.

**Example 7**
> **Jeff:** Mr. Clark, the company CEO, visits our office every year when we're serving the steak lunch. He obviously checks to see when we have the steak lunch every year, and then comes on that day!

---

1. One of the best sources for examples of causal fallacies is T. Edward Damer's *Attacking Faulty Reasoning*. See Damer's text for additional examples of causal fallacies.

Jeff is assuming that the cause of Mr. Clark's visit is the steak lunch. It is more likely that the cause of the steak lunch is Mr. Clark's visit! The office manager may plan a special steak lunch on the day that Mr. Clark visits.

### NEGLECT OF A COMMON CAUSE

We often think that one thing is causing another thing, when in fact a third factor is causing both. Put another way, we may think that A is causing B, when actually C is causing both A and B. Consider this example.

### Example 8

Lisa is depressed. It must because she is so obese.

Perhaps both Lisa's depression and her obesity are the result of a third factor, such as a troubled family life.

See if you can find examples of false cause from your study of history or current events.

Answers will vary.

_____

_____

_____

_____

_____

# False Cause

| | |
|---|---|
| FALLACIES OF PRESUMPTION | Arguments that make unwarranted assumptions about either the data or the nature of a reasonable argument. |
| Fallacies of Induction | Arguments that misuse empirical data or don't follow proper methods of inductive reasoning. |
| False Cause | An argument that uses any sort of weak causal connection as the basis of an argument. |

# Fallacy 25:
## Fake Precision

DEFINITION: Arguments that use numbers or statistics in a way that is too precise to be justified by the situation.

We live in a world that greatly values being scientific and demonstrating matters with mathematical precision. Unfortunately, many people are unaware of or ignore the limits of numbers and statistics. Statistics are very commonly used in ways that mislead and deceive us. One of the most common abuses of statistics is the fallacy of fake precision. Fake precision occurs when either questionable statistics are used or unjustified conclusions are drawn from them.

Consider the following examples of fake precision.

**Example 1**
"**Dear Friend:** In the past 5,000 years, men have fought 14,523 wars. One out of four persons living during this time have been war casualties. A nuclear war would add 1,245,000,000 men, women and children to this tragic list."[1]

**Example 2**
A total of 33.4 million Americans will die of heart disease in the next decade. Don't you think it is time to start caring for your heart?

**Example 3**
The SuperTec Z-1 tablet computer is preferred by three out of four college students seeking a new tablet computer.

In Example 1, it is clearly a case of fake precision to think that we can know exactly how many wars have been fought over the last 5,000 years and ridiculous to be so precise about how many people would be killed in a future event. Similarly, in example 2, it is dubious indeed to predict precisely how many people will die of heart disease in the next ten years. We should certainly doubt the truthfulness of the claim in example 3 that three out of four college students prefer the new SuperTec Z-1. How were these numbers determined? How many students were surveyed? What kinds of questions were on the survey?

Polls present us with another classic example of how statistics can be used in misleading ways. It is very difficult to put a number on public opinion, since people's opinions are complex and interwoven into a larger web of belief systems. When all the many details of an individual are taken into account, we find that his opinions are complex and often unique. This makes it difficult for those conducting polls. How do they measure the complex opinions of many individuals and reduce them to statistics? Those conducting

---

1. Howard Kahane. *Logic and Contemporary Rhetoric*, 6th ed. (Belmont, CA: Wadsworth Publishing Company, 1992), 100.

the polls often ask yes-or-no questions that distort the complexity of people's opinion simply by the way the questions are asked. As demonstrated below in Example 4, the way the questions in a poll are written can greatly affect its outcome.

**Example 4**

From the options below, please indicate whether you agree or disagree with the stated reasons for why people have an unfavorable opinion of President Brown.
1. He is not as patriotic as he should be.
2. He is an elitist who doesn't understand the needs of ordinary people.
3. He is not sufficiently concerned about helping American businesses prosper.
4. He lacks sufficient experience to be leading the United States.
5. He is pushing an agenda that is disapproved of by many Americans.

You can see from the way this question is posed that it suggests that President Brown is already deficient. The person being polled is forced to choose from five statements that are obviously critical of the president. Further, the fifth option could be true of any president, but is listed as if it were a fault of only President Brown. You can see how the results of this poll would be devastating to President Brown no matter who was polled. The results might be announced in this fashion: "Of those polled, 67 percent said that President Brown is pushing an agenda that is disapproved of by Americans, and 58 percent said that he was either unpatriotic, elitist, lacked sufficient experience to be president, or was not concerned with helping American businesses prosper."

In summary, remember that numbers or statistics have limitations. Be skeptical of those presenting comfortable, precise statistics, tempting you to think that the statistics speak for themselves. As with any other piece of evidence, statistics must be carefully interpreted.

## Fake Precision

**Genus:** Fallacies relating to problems in inductive reasoning.
**Difference:** These arguments misuse statistics in various ways.

Invent your own example of fake precision.

Answers will vary. Example: The average house contains 12,428 types of germs. Shouldn't you treat your house with Germ-Away spray today?

# Fake Precision

| FALLACIES OF PRESUMPTION | Arguments that make unwarranted assumptions about either the data or the nature of a reasonable argument. |
| --- | --- |
| Fallacies of Induction | Arguments that misuse empirical data or don't follow proper methods of inductive reasoning. |
| False Precision | An argument that uses numbers in a way that is too precise to be justified by the situation. |

6 out of 10 babies prefer our vegetables to those of the leading competition.

GREEN LEAF BABY FOOD

GARDEN VEGETABLES IN EVERY JAR!

# Fake Precision

125.2 million people suffer from bad breath.

Don't be a statistic!

# Chapter 5 Review

**A. DEFINE:**

1. Sweeping Generalization (Accident):

An argument that overextends a generalization to include facts or cases that are

exceptions to it.

2. Hasty Generalization (Converse Accident):

An argument that makes an unwarranted generalization on the basis of too few samples.

3. False Analogy:

An argument that fails because it creates an analogy between two things that are not

similar enough to warrant an analogy.

4. False Cause:

An argument that is based on a weak cause-and-effect connection.

5. Fake Precision:

An argument that uses numbers or statistics in a way that is too precise to be

justified by the situation.

**B. EXAMPLES:** Name the fallacy committed in the following examples. State reasons why you believe your answers to be correct.

1. I saw Bobby putting gum under the table. Jim is a young teenager, too, so I think that if I give him a piece of gum, he'll do the same thing.

false analogy (note that the reason is moving from one specific case to another specific case)

2. Since Jim and Bobby both stuck their gum under the table, we can be pretty sure that any teenager would do the same.

hasty generalization (note that the reasoning is moving from two examples toward a

generalization)

3. Studies show that 90 percent of teenagers stick their gum under the table when given the opportunity. Therefore, we can be pretty sure that Susie will do the same. (Hint: ignore the bogus statistic and focus on the fallacy being committed.)

sweeping generalization (note that the reasoning is moving from a generalization to one specific

case)

4. The average person tells a lie every twelve hours.

fake precision

5. Every time the copier breaks down, it seems to be right after you use it. You must be jinxing it.

false cause

**C. IN DEPTH:** Find three examples of fake precision. Use recent newspapers, magazines, or website articles. Be prepared to discuss how and why the examples use the fallacy of fake precision.

Answers will vary.

# Cumulative Fallacy Worksheet

**DIRECTIONS:** Identify each fallacy. (Hint: Some examples may commit more than one.)

1. Don't tell me your sob stories about terrorism. You Americans killed plenty of innocent civilians during the campaign in Afghanistan.

   Presumption, false analogy (as sad as accidental casualties are, they are a very different

   thing from the deliberate targeting of civilians)

2. I've always been favorably disposed toward people named Jonathan. That's the name of my wonderful brother, and I've never known someone named Jonathan that wasn't a pretty good guy.

   Presumption, hasty generalization (the sample size is likely too small)

3. You simply can't convict this man! Think of his wife, of his children, crying even now in this courtroom and pining at home without him if you choose to send him off to jail.

   Relevance, appeal to pity

4. Official sources indicate that an attack against Iraq is nearly certain before year's end.

   Relevance, appeal to illegitimate authority (since the sources are unknown it would be

   unwise to take their word for it)

5. You can't give Dr. Jones's theories any credence. He's not a real scholar! He's just a journalistic hack! Why, I wouldn't be surprised if he got his degree out of a Cracker Jack box.

   Relevance, *ad hominem* abusive

6. Lowenbrau beer: A German tradition!

_Relevance, chronological snobbery (appeal to tradition)_

7. I went to a chiropractor and he didn't help me. Those guys are just a bunch of quacks.

_Presumption, hasty generalization (not enough information)_

8. I don't care if that guy weighed 300 pounds! You're a Boy Scout, and Boy Scouts help those in need! You should have jumped right into that lake to try to save him!

_Presumption, sweeping generalization (it might be a good general rule to jump in and save a_

_drowning man, but there are exceptions when there is no chance that it could be done without_

_having him pull you under as well. A better tactic would be to look for a life preserver or get help.)_

9. Every time I let you borrow my car, it breaks down. I'm sorry, but I can't let you use it any more.

_Presumption, false cause_

10. I know that Mussolini's rise to power was a bit brutal, but hey, you can't make an omelet without breaking a few eggs.

_Presumption, false analogy (people aren't eggs)_

# Unit 3: Clarity

In unit 1, we studied the fallacies of relevance and learned that there are several ways in which we can avoid the subject of an argument. We can try to discredit the source of an argument (*ad fontem* arguments); we can appeal to an emotion that distracts from the issue at hand (appeals to emotion); or we can introduce other irrelevant issues that evade the issue at hand (red herrings). We have learned that it is always wise to ask of a given argument: "Is it relevant to the issue at hand?"

In unit 2, we studied the fallacies of presumption and learned several ways in which we may assume something faulty or illegitimate in an argument (fallacies of presupposition). We also learned several ways we can misuse facts and data or improperly reason from facts and data (fallacies of induction). We have learned that it is always wise to ask of a given argument: "Is it assuming something illegitimate?"

Now, in unit 3, we will study fallacies of clarity. In the midst of a spirited debate, we often speak unclearly. That is because the nature of spirited debate provokes our emotions and tempts us to speak quickly without adequate thought, resulting in verbal sloppiness, unfinished arguments, and ambiguity. As well, some debaters are downright tricky and skillfully use ambiguity to their own advantage. Arguments that are unclear because of confusing word-use fall into the group we call fallacies of clarity. You will learn that it is wise to ask of a given argument: "Is it clear?"

Remember that the first or leading question we should ask of any argument is "What is the issue at hand?" After that, we should ask three questions that correspond to the concepts of relevance, presumption, and clarity. Is the argument relevant to the issue at hand? Is the argument assuming something illegitimate? Is the argument clear? By asking these questions, we should be able to quickly detect which fallacies are being used in an argument.

---

**First Question: What is the issue at hand?**

**Next Questions:**

| | | |
|---|---|---|
| Relevance | $\longrightarrow$ | Is the argument relevant to the issue at hand? |
| Presumption | $\longrightarrow$ | Is the argument assuming something illegitimate? |
| Clarity | $\longrightarrow$ | Is the argument clear? |

---

# Chapter 6
## Fallacies of Clarity

DEFINITION: Arguments that fail because they contain words, phrases, or syntax that distort or cloud their meanings.

Few enemies of sound reasoning can damage the strength of an argument like distorted, clouded, and confusing terms. When words are unclear we can call them **ambiguous**. Ambiguous words can be open to two or more interpretations and therefore do not have a clear meaning readily understood by the listener. The root of the word ambiguous is the Latin word *ambigere* which means "to wander about." Ambiguous words, as it were, wander about unable to decide on their meaning.

Everyone occasionally uses ambiguous speech, sometimes creating humorous or even embarrassing situations. Once at a family gathering a student commanded his dog Daisy to leave the room. "Daisy, get out of here!" he shouted. Unfortunately for my friend, his aged aunt was also in the room and was also named Daisy. She slowly rose with her cane to leave the room. It took a little while for her to understand that my friend was shouting at the dog, not her. As it turns out, "Daisy" can refer to a flower, a dog, or someone's aunt.

It is understandable that we will speak ambiguously from time to time in our everyday conversations. When we are making an argument, however, we should take special care to avoid ambiguous words. When someone does use ambiguous speech while making an argument it is likely that either the speaker doesn't really understand the issue, is just being sloppy and careless in his choice of words, or is deliberately trying to cloud the issue in order to gain the upper hand in an argument.

You will study three fallacies of clarity: **equivocation**, **accent**, and **distinction without a difference.** Some form of ambiguity characterizes all three of these fallacies.

**1. Equivocation:** An argument that fails because a key term is ambiguous.

### Example 1
> All stars are in orbit in outer space. The actor Miley Cyrus is a star. Therefore, Miley Cyrus is in orbit in outer space.

### Example 2
> The more you study, the more you know. The more you know, the more you forget. The more you forget, the less you know. So why study?[1]

---

1. Douglas Walton, *Informal Logic: A Pragmatic Approach* (Cambridge: Cambridge University Press, 2008), 252.

**2. Accent:** An argument that rests on an improper emphasis placed on certain words or phrases.

**Example 1**

The ZX-4 sedan is a relatively safe car.

**Example 2**

**Son:** Dad, I would buy this computer—it's *really* fast, has *great* graphics, a *huge* monitor, and *a lot* of memory.

**Dad:** I would buy this computer, but because it has a *huge* price tag and costs *a lot* of money, buying it would be a *great* mistake.

**3. Distinction Without a Difference:** An argument that makes a distinction between two things that are actually not different from each other.

**Example 1**

You really should join the cross-country team despite what you have heard about coach Higgins. He is not really a tough coach, he just knows that if we don't collapse after a work-out, we are not preparing well.

**Example 2**

Professional athletes should not really be role models for students—they should just show students what it means to live with integrity and honesty.

Before we dive into our study of these three fallacies, let's follow Tiffany who is on her way to ask Socrates if he can help her with a challenging school assignment.

## DISH IT UP

*Chapter 6: Fallacies of Clarity*

# Dialogue on Fallacies of Clarity

*Tiffany comes running up to Socrates as he strolls through the quad.*

**Tiffany:** Socrates! I'm so happy to see you. I need your help.

**Socrates:** Oh, dear, I hope it doesn't involve anything unpleasant.

**Tiffany:** Now, why would you think that? Of course it doesn't. I just want some philosophical advice.

**Socrates:** Well, I find that, too often, helping out a damsel in distress seems to involve slaying a dragon, or seven years of hard labor, or some sort of Herculean task. But I'm relieved that you merely want philosophical advice, because advice is always free (though one should note that one usually gets what one pays for) and philosophy, as you know, is my passion. So you are struggling with some sort of conundrum, I take it. Is it of an epistemological, ontological, or ethical nature?

**Tiffany:** You're going to have to fill me in, here. What exactly is the difference between an ontological and an epistemological dilemma?

**Socrates:** An ontological dilemma is one that involves issues of being, existence, or the fundamental nature of reality. **Ontology** is the branch of philosophy that answers the question, "What is real?" An epistemological dilemma, on the other hand, is one that concerns the issues of truth or knowledge. Epistemology is the branch of philosophy that answers the question, "How can we know what we know?" You know what ethics is, don't you?

**Tiffany:** Of course. It's the branch of philosophy that answers the question of what is right versus what is wrong and deals with questions of morality.

**Socrates:** Very good. I couldn't have said it better myself! So, which sort of dilemma are you struggling with?

**Tiffany:** It's definitely an ethical one. In my world history class, we're studying Confucius, and my teacher, Dr. Larsen, assigned us to write a short paper explaining whether Jesus or Confucius is right on a point about which they conflict.

**Socrates:** I would think that would be an easy question for you.

**Tiffany:** Not really. Confucius's saying asserts the opposite of what Jesus taught, but it seems to make so much sense. Jesus taught that we should repay evil with kindness, but when someone asked Confucius if one should do this, he answered, "Then what do you repay kindness with? Repay kindness with kindness, and repay evil with justice." That just seems to make so much sense, since so often repaying evil with kindness only leads to more evil being done. What would have happened, for example, if we had repaid Hitler's evil with kindness?

**Socrates:** My dear Tiffany, I think your teacher is deliberately presenting you with a false dilemma!

**Tiffany:** Why would he do a thing like that? That's not very nice of him!

**Socrates:** Don't be too hard on the old guy. I find that making students ponder over a false dilemma from time to time can be a good teaching technique. It gets the thoughts flowing and sometimes the creative juices, too. Do it too often, though, and they start to see right through it. Anyway, I think this is a false dilemma because whether or not you should repay evil with kindness depends on the situation.

**Tiffany:** But I don't believe in situation ethics.

**Socrates:** Well, maybe I do, but that all depends on what you mean by situation ethics.

**Tiffany:** Situation ethics is when you don't have any fixed ethical principles but only decide what is right and wrong based on the situation.

**Socrates:** Well, if that's what it means, then I don't believe in situation ethics either. I fear, however, that you're oversimplifying the situation. You need to have fixed moral principles, but you also need to be careful in applying them.

**Tiffany:** What do you mean?

**Socrates:** OK, here's an example. You believe murder is wrong, right?

**Tiffany:** Of course. Everyone does.

**Socrates:** Well, what is the definition of "murder?"

**Tiffany:** It's killing someone, of course.

**Socrates:** Well, does that mean it is murder when a policeman shoots and kills an armed robber who's pointing a gun at him?

**Tiffany:** Well, no. So, I guess we have to change the definition to say that it's the killing of an innocent human being when it's not self-defense.

**Socrates:** I think that we're making progress here, but we still have to rule out the killing of someone in an accident.

**Tiffany:** OK, so it's the intentional killing of an innocent human being.

**Socrates:** That's getting better, but even then there's some interpretation and application involved. Your state's legal code, for instance, defines murder as the killing of a person with malicious aforethought. There ends up being many legal battles about such things as what "malice" means and how to determine if the killing was done in self-defense. In all of these sorts of situations, it is very important not to equivocate on any terms. In fact, getting back to your original dilemma, there is a term or two in Confucius's statement that can easily be equivocated.

**Tiffany:** Equivocated? What does that mean?

**Socrates:** It means to use a word in more than one sense. Are there any words in there that have multiple meanings and senses?

**Tiffany:** I don't see it. "Evil" is evil, "kindness" is kindness, and "justice" is justice.

**Socrates:** I think you need to look more closely at the different shadings of meaning that those words can have. Take the word "evil," for instance. Isn't it true that there can be many different kinds and levels of evil? So, maybe some forms of evil are best addressed with kindness and others are best addressed with justice. In fact, sometimes people need a little "tough love" to straighten them out and, therefore, sometimes justice is the highest form of love!

**Tiffany:** Wow, I never thought about it that way before! Now I need to do some serious thinking about what forms of evil are best addressed with kindness and what forms are best addressed with justice. In fact, I think I'll write my paper on exactly that subject. Thanks, Socrates. You have a way of making things make sense by making them more simple.

**Socrates:** Ah, Tiffany, the Gordian knot of many a dilemma is best severed by the sword stroke of a little terminological clarity!

**Tiffany:** Huh? OK, well, I'm off to start writing now. Would you like to read it when I'm done?

**Socrates:** Of course, my dear. I'll be waiting under that tree over yonder.

**Tiffany:** It might take me a couple of hours to put together a rough draft.

**Socrates:** Oh, don't worry. I have many Gordian knots to untie. I don't mind waiting.

**Chapter 6: Fallacies of Clarity**
Dialogue on Fallacies of Clarity

# Fallacy 26:
## Equivocation

**DEFINITION: Arguments that fail because a key term is ambiguous.**

The word "equivocation" comes from the Latin *aequus* (equal) and *vox* (voice). The goal of a logician is to use terms "univocally" (with "one voice"), meaning that terms should be used with only one **consistent** meaning throughout an argument. If a term is used equivocally, more than one meaning is equally possible. When someone commits the fallacy of equivocation, an equivocal term is a key component in his argument, which may make the argument sound persuasive, but actually renders it deceptive and worthless. An equivocal term can also be called ambiguous, because it becomes unclear just how the term should be defined or understood.

Consider the following examples of equivocation.

**Example 1**
"**TV Evangelist:** All of you can stop sinning and be like Jesus.
**Member of the Studio Audience:** But how can we be sinless like Jesus? Jesus is different than us—He is the Son of God.
**TV Evangelist:** You are the son of God, too."[1]

**Example 2**
"**School District Board Member:** I don't see any reason why we should listen to the superintendent of schools on the textbook issue. We need to hear from someone who has some authority in the field of education. Our superintendent doesn't even have the authority to keep the students in line. Nobody respects her orders."[2]

**Example 3**
"The more you study, the more you know. The more you know, the more you forget. The more you forget, the less you know. So why study?"[3]

The TV evangelist in example 1 is using the phrase "Son of God" in two different senses. The traditional Christian reference to Christ as the *Son of God* is a divine title,

### Equivocation
**Genus:** An argument that fails due to a lack of clarity.
**Difference:** These arguments have ambiguous meanings for a specific word or words.

---

1. Kahane, 62.

2. Damer, 21.

3. Walton, 252.

whereas an individual Christian as a *son of God* is something far from a claim to deity. The school board member in example 2 uses the word "authority" in two different senses. To have *authority* in the field of education refers to scholarly expertise. To have *authority* to keep students in line refers to the ability to direct and guide students and their behavior.

The third example takes the form of a riddle. Each of the three statements, or premises, is true. The third statement, however, does not follow from the second statement. If you learn more, and therefore forget more, it does not mean that you know less. What is ambiguous or unclear in this argument is the amount of knowledge you can have. The phrases "more you know" and "less you know" take on different meanings in each statement depending on what they are being compared to. Ultimately, this fallacy tries to argue that the more you study, the less you know, which is clearly wrong.

Often equivocation is used for humor. You may be familiar with the famous Abbot and Costello routine "Who's on First," in which a reporter interviews a coach about his first baseman who happens to be named "Who." Here is an excerpt:

**Costello:** Well, then, who is on first?

**Abbott:** Yes.

**Costello:** I mean the fellow's name.

**Abbott:** Who.

**Costello:** The guy on first.

**Abbott:** Who.

**Costello:** The first baseman.

**Abbott:** Who!

**Costello:** The guy playing first base.

**Abbott:** Who is on first.

**Costello:** I'm asking you who's on first!

**Abbott:** That's the man's name.

**Costello:** That's whose name?

**Abbott:** Yeah.

**Costello:** Well, go ahead and tell me.

**Abbott:** That's it.

**Costello:** That's who?

**Abbott:** Yeah.[4]

Equivocation can also be used in riddles: "I see, I see" said the blind man, as he picked up a hammer and saw.

Words often do have several meanings, so it is therefore very important to carefully assess the meaning of key terms being used in an argument. In fact, carefully defining the meaning of key terms is one of the most important parts of learning to reason logically, and not doing so is one common way arguments become confusing or fallacious. Be sure to check every argument you evaluate for confusing or equivocal terms.

---

4. Bud Abbott and Lou Costello, "Who's on First." Available at: <http://www.baseball-almanac.com/humor4.shtml>.

**Chapter 6: Fallacies of Clarity**
*Fallacy 26: Equivocation*

# Equivocation

FALLACIES OF CLARITY | Arguments that fail because they contain words, phrases, or syntax that distort or cloud their meanings.

Equivocation | An argument that fails because a key term is ambiguous.

Do you ever get the feeling that your fund manager doesn't care?

WHM Mutual Fund always offers higher interest.

WHM Mutual Fund

# Equivocation

Our leather belts are for the hip

across from The Audio Shack

Banshee Accessories™

# Fallacy Discussion on Equivocation

**Socrates:** Here's another example of equivocation, which should be near and dear to the heart of anyone who has had to defend the teaching of logic, as I have had to do. Tiffany went to talk with her college advisor the other day and arrived as one of her fellow students was making this remark:

"You suggested that I take logic because logic would teach me how to argue. But I think that people argue too much as it is. Therefore, I do not intend to take any course in logic, and I am of the opinion that perhaps logic shouldn't be taught at all. It will only contribute to the increasing tension that already exists in the world."

How was Tiffany's classmate using the fallacy of equivocation in her argument?

The student is committing the fallacy of equivocation by using the word "argue" to mean

two different things. Further discussion follows on the next page.

**Socrates:** In logic, the term "argue" is used to indicate the act of making a reasoned defense of a conclusion, not the act of bitterly quarrelling. If anything, a more widespread knowledge of logic will help to reduce tension somewhat, as it will teach people to avoid many of the ambiguities that lead to misunderstanding. It will also teach them to fight fair in the arena of ideas.

**Chapter 6: Fallacies of Clarity**
Fallacy Discussion on Equivocation

# Fallacy 27:
## Accent

DEFINITION: Arguments that rest on an improper emphasis placed on certain words or phrases.

We have seen that when words are used in more than one sense in an argument they become equivocal and ambiguous. There is yet another way in which words can be used ambiguously in an argument—when we give words an improper accent, or emphasis, in such a way as to change the meaning of an argument.

Consider the ways the following examples change the meaning of a statement.

**Example 1**
>    *I* won't go to the movie tonight.

This statement implies that most likely someone else is going to the movie tonight.

**Example 2**
>    I won't go to the *movie* tonight.

This statement implies that you might be going somewhere else tonight.

**Example 3**
>    I won't go to the movie *tonight*.

This statement implies that you might be going to the movie some other time.

Note that this kind of accenting or emphasis works commonly in spoken arguments, in which your voice is used to accent or emphasize certain words or phrases. We can, however, accent words in print, too. We can do this by taking quotations out of context so that the original meaning is obscured. We can also simply omit certain words and lift out the words we want in order to create a misleading argument, distorting the original meaning.

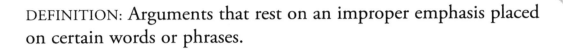

**Accent**
**Genus:** An argument that fails due to a lack of clarity.
**Difference:** These arguments rest on the foundation of an improper emphasis given to certain words or groups of words.

Consider the following examples.

**Example 4**
>    "**Newspaper Headline:** Teddy Confirms Rumor: Jackie Will Become a Kennedy Again"[1]

---

1. Damer, 27.

This newspaper headline made it appear as though Jackie Onassis (former wife of President John F. Kennedy) was going to marry back into the Kennedy family. To reinforce this false impression, the cover picture showed Jackie in a tender pose with Ted Kennedy (late US senator and brother of John F. Kennedy) and yet the article was merely about how the Kennedy family still considered her a member. The headline was obviously a ruse to get more people to purchase the paper. This kind of deliberate trickery is common among gossip magazines and tabloids.

**Example 5**

**Book Endorsement:** John Reynolds' new thriller is . . . filled with arctic adventure and surprising twists . . .

**Original Quotation:** John Reynolds' new thriller is a great disappointment, merely filled with arctic adventure and surprising twists that wreak havoc with what little plot exists.

When we compare the book endorsement with the original quotation, we see that the endorsement was taken out of context, distorting the original meaning from a negative review into a positive one. Note how taking a quotation out of context can also become a form of the straw man fallacy or an illegitimate appeal to authority, in addition to being a fallacy of accent.

**Chapter 6: Fallacies of Clarity**
Fallacy 27: Accent

# Accent

| FALLACIES OF CLARITY | Arguments that fail because they contain words, phrases, or syntax that distort or cloud their meanings. |
| --- | --- |
| Accent | An argument that rests on an improper emphasis placed on certain words or phrases. |

## Zutubyran™
### Breathe easy

Trouble with spring allergies?
With only a few side effects,* Zutubyran can help you breathe easy again.

Consult your doctor about taking Zutubyran.

*Side effects may include but are not limited to headache, abdominal pains, lower gestational discomfort, general aches and pains (elbow), amnesia, sore feet and trouble bending your third toe, trouble remembering your teacher's middle name, Latin vocabulary words may begin to drop from your memory, you'll start seeing red spots and occasionally plaid stripes, a heightened sense of smell especially toward steamed vegetables, bladder issues, nausea, hearing loss, fatigue, loss of sleep (drowsiness during class), desire to read more comic books, tendinitis, a general itchiness all over (especially a tendency to scratch scabs), intensified dizziness, a chronic need to stir your chocolate milk more than is necessary, soft stools, heightened irritability toward siblings, left eye twitching, a growing fascination with watching big honking chunks of steel roll down an airport runway and actually lift off the ground, wrist soreness, welts, scurvy, missing socks will begin to appear but when you reach out for them it will only be like going to one of those 3D IMAX theaters and you will grab for air, discomfort with aunts who like to hug and kiss a lot, bunions, arthritis but only when grabbing the last cookie that you know you should share with your younger sibling, and panic attacks.

# Fallacy 28:
## Distinction Without a Difference

DEFINITION: Arguments that make a linguistic distinction between two things that are actually not different from each other.

It is a vital part of logical argument to make distinctions between things that may seem alike but are actually different. We saw this when we studied the fallacy of false analogy because a false analogy involves the comparison of two things that are not similar enough for valid comparison.

If we can commit a fallacy by calling two things similar when they really are not (false analogy), we can also commit a fallacy by trying to insist that one thing is something else when it is not. In other words, a presenter may try to make a distinction by using different words to describe something, but in effect he ends up saying the same thing. We call this fallacy making a distinction without a difference.

Consider the following examples.

**Example 1**
It is not that I don't like her; I just think she is a miserable, hateful person.

**Example 2**
He's not really a bully. He just enjoys beating people up.

**Example 3**
**News Commentator:** Senator Johnson is not lying to the public, he is simply releasing information to the American people that they can handle.

**Example 4**
**Reggie:** I am not really a bad driver; I just don't pay much attention to the road.

The first two examples are so obvious as to be humorous, and indeed this kind of fallacy is often used to make jokes. However, the third example, featuring Senator Johnson, is not a joke. The commentator seems to be excusing misleading comments by Senator Johnson by qualifying those comments as "releasing information ... that they can handle." We may all like or "handle" a comfortable lie as opposed to a disturbing truth, but false information that we can handle is still a lie.

In the last example, Reggie is simply finding better-sounding words for describing his poor driving. One acceptable definition of a bad driver is someone who does not pay attention while driving. It may be that Reggie has ample ability and experience to actually drive with skill and caution, but if he habitually chooses not to concentrate and "pay attention to the road" his ability will not ensure that he is a good driver.

### Distinction Without a Difference
**Genus:** An argument that fails due to a lack of clarity.
**Difference:** These arguments rest on distinctions that don't represent real differences.

# Distinction Without a Difference

| FALLACIES OF CLARITY | Arguments that fail because they contain words, phrases, or syntax that distort or cloud their meanings. |
| --- | --- |
| Distinction Without a Difference | An argument that makes distinctions that are actually only linguistic distinctions and not real ones. |

## Kildorn Mufflers

Makes your **vroom, vroom** sound like **purr, purr**

Our mufflers aren't expensive, they just cost a little more.

# Distinction Without a Difference

# Fallacy Discussion on Distinction Without a Difference

Sir Robert Chiltern, a character in Oscar Wilde's play *An Ideal Husband*, is a distinguished member of England's House of Commons. He is known for living by impeccable principles, and he is wealthy, successful, and well respected. However, it is revealed that as a young man he sold a state secret to a stock market speculator. The money he made by selling that secret is the source of his wealth, and his wrong actions are about to be revealed to London society by blackmail. The following conversation takes place between him and his friend, Lord Goring, just before the scandal is about to break.

> **Sir Robert Chiltern:** Every man of ambition has to fight his century with its own weapons. What this century worships is wealth. The God of this century is wealth. To succeed one must have wealth. At all costs one must have wealth.
>
> **Lord Goring:** You underrate yourself, Robert. Believe me, without wealth you could have succeeded just as well.
>
> **Sir Robert Chiltern:** And if it is all taken away from me now? If I lose everything over a horrible scandal? If I am hounded from public life?
>
> **Lord Goring:** Robert, how could you have sold yourself for money?
>
> **Sir Robert Chiltern:** [Excitedly.] I did not sell myself for money. I bought success at a great price. That is all.[1]

Identify and give your thoughts on the fallacy of distinction without a difference that is committed in the dialogue.

Sir Robert Chiltern commits the fallacy of distinction without a difference in order to

defend his wrong actions. By "buying success at great price" he traded his integrity.

Further discussion follows on the next page.

1. Oscar Wilde, *The Importance of Being Earnest and Other Plays* (New York: Oxford University Press, 2008), 159–246.

**Socrates:** Sir Robert Chiltern made an unfortunate decision in his youth, and as he indicates in his first line, he considers life without wealth worthless. He was willing to trade his integrity, which is arguably the most valuable thing a human can possess, in order to gain wealth. As a weak defense, he insists that he did not sell his integrity for money, but rather "bought success at a great price." "Buying success" certainly sounds better that "selling one's integrity," but is there really any legitimate difference between the two? Not really, for he "bought success" by sacrificing his integrity, honesty, and now his reputation. He changes the language to describe his misdeed, but language only makes a distinction that amounts to no real difference.

**Chapter 6: Fallacies of Clarity**
Fallacy Discussion on Distinction Without a Difference

# Chapter 6 Review

**A. DEFINE:**

1. Fallacies of Clarity:

Arguments that fail because they contain words, phrases or, syntax that distort or cloud

their meanings.

2. Equivocation:

An argument that fails because a key term is ambiguous.

3. Accent:

An argument that rests on an improper emphasis placed on certain words or phrases.

4. Distinction Without a Difference:

An argument that makes a linguistic distinction between two things that are actually not

different from each other.

**B. IDENTIFY:** Name the fallacy that is being described by the following definitions.

1. Ambiguity that is created by the fact that a word has more than one meaning.

equivocation

2. Confusion that is created by placing emphasis on certain words or phrases.

fallacy of accent

3. Confusion caused by treating a purely semantic distinction as if it were a real distinction.

distinction without a difference

**C. EXAMPLES:** Name the fallacy that is being described by the following examples. State reasons why you believe your answer is correct.

1. But, Mom, you said that I shouldn't take any cookies. That's why I'm eating them right here by the cookie jar.

Equivocation (on "take"): Clearly the mother instructed her child not to take any cookies out of

the jar—and eat them. The child wants to equivocate the term "take" to mean taking the cookie

out of the room, therefore justifying the eating of the cookie.

2. Dagwood isn't really lazy. He just likes to sleep all the time.

Distinction Without a Difference: Sleeping all of the time certainly is a form of laziness. This

statement makes a verbal distinction that is not a real distinction.

3. The paparazzi always seem to get a bum rap. What they are doing is clearly in the public's interest. After all, if it wasn't pictures and information about celebrities, it wouldn't be such a profitable commodity.

Equivocation: This fallacy equivocates on the word "interest." While taking pictures of celebrities

might be "of interest" to much of the public, it may not be "in their best interest" to have these

photos. We are not sure just what the speaker is arguing for.

4. **Father to Son:** Why haven't you mowed the lawn yet today?
   **Son to Father:** Dad, you said that I should mow the lawn *before* my soccer game—and my soccer game has been rescheduled for tomorrow. So, I don't have to mow the lawn until tomorrow.

Accent: The son is arguing that he can delay mowing the lawn another day by purposely

accenting the word "before" used by his father. By emphasizing the word "before," he invests it

with meaning that his father did not intend.

# Cumulative Fallacy Worksheet

**DIRECTIONS:** For each example, write the name of the fallacy category (relevance, presumption, or clarity) and the name of the specific fallacy represented by the example. (Hint: Some examples may commit more than one fallacy.)

1. Take it easy, boss! It's not that I'm just standing around. I'm supervising!

 Clarity, distinction without a difference

2. The world couldn't have been created by God because matter has always existed; therefore, there is no need for a Creator-God.

 Presumption, begging the question (the question of whether matter has always existed is

 precisely what is at issue)

3. **James:** It is clear that man is descended from the apes.
 **Bryan:** So, on which side of the family are you descended from the apes, your mother's side or your father's side?

 Relevance, *ad hominem* abusive (Bryan deflects the issue by ridiculing his opponent)

4. Want war? If not, vote for Goldwater!

 Relevance, appeal to fear

5. The end of a thing is its perfection. Death is the end of life; therefore, it is life's perfection.

 Clarity, equivocation (on "end"; end can either mean simply chronological end or

 it can mean goal; when we say that death is the end of life, we generally mean the former,

 not the latter)

6. Socialism is clearly the only way to fully realize the principles of the Declaration of Independence, for does it not say that all men are created equal? Socialism is the only system that recognizes the natural human yearning for equality by mandating that "from each according to his ability, to each according to his need." Only socialism tries to make sure that equality extends to the realm of economics!

Clarity, equivocation (on "equality"; the Declaration didn't intend to mean that all men are

created equal in every material aspect, but rather in their political rights)

7. **Mom:** "Billy, you need to be polite to your uncle!"
   **Billy:** "But Mom, you told me to be courteous to strangers."

Clarity, accent (on "strangers")

8. He's not really a criminal. He just likes to "borrow" a few items now and then from the store.

Clarity, distinction without a difference

9. I don't believe you! You're just a meany head!

Relevance, *ad hominem* abusive

10. Why do you want to major in history? You already said that you don't want to be a teacher.

Relevance, irrelevant goals or functions

# APPENDIX A

# Bill and Ted's Excellent Election
## A Theatrical Play Demonstrating the Common Fallacies

*Bill and Ted are standing near three candidates for class president.*

*Bill:* Dude, I have no idea who to vote for.

*Ted:* I have an idea; let's go to our time machine and bring back Socrates.

*Bill:* Excellent!

*The boys get into the time machine. Soon they emerge from the time machine with Socrates.*

*Socrates:* Theodore, William, it's good to see you boys again.

*Ted:* Dude! It's Ted.

*Bill:* And call me Billiam . . . I mean Bill.

*Socrates:* So why did you bring me here?

*Bill:* It's like this: Our college is having this election for class president and we can't decide who to vote for.

*Socrates:* Well, I'm certainly happy to be of assistance. Let's go talk to the candidates.

*The three go up to Ben.*

*Bill:* Dude, so why should we vote for you?

*Ben:* Well, I've been class president for five years. I'm practically an NYUK tradition all by myself.

*Bill:* But dude, college is only four years.

*Ted:* Yeah, dude. Did you flunk or something?

*Ben:* No, man, I'm on the ten-year plan.

*Socrates:* Well, you seem to have some experience, anyway. Tell us about your policies.

*Ben:* Well, like, dude, every year I lobby to keep the grading scale really easy, so everyone can get an "A."

*Socrates:* So what does this "A" mean?

*Ben:* It represents excellent work.

*Socrates:* So does everyone at NYUK do excellent work?

*Ben:* No, look at me, man; I'm on the ten-year plan.

*Socrates:* So, if everyone getting A's doesn't represent reality, why is it a good thing?

*Ben:* Because it makes everyone happy.

*Socrates:* But, we mustn't forget that just because a thing is popular that doesn't make it a good thing. To think this way is to commit the *argumentum ad populum*, or mob appeal, fallacy. To hide reality under a popular illusion isn't often a good idea, in my judgement. Is there any other reason to do this other than its mere popularity?

*Ben:* Why, sure. It's an NYUK tradition. We've been doing it since the sixties, man.

*Socrates:* Well, just because it's been done for a long time, that doesn't mean that the practice should necessarily continue. To assume so is to commit the chronological snobbery fallacy. I recommend that we question one of the other candidates.

*The trio walk up to Zoe.*

*Ted:* So why should we vote for you?

*Zoe:* Because, like, I'm way popular, dudes!

*Bill:* Dude! She knows the lingo.

*Socrates:* Maybe so, but her reasoning is faulty. She is making another *ad populum* fallacy. Her popularity in and of itself doesn't make her the best candidate. Perhaps we should move on again.

*As they turn to go, Zoe accosts them and then begins to plead.*

*Zoe:* You just *have* to vote for me. If I don't win, I'll be sooo sad, I just might cry.

*Socrates:* Now she's making the *argumentum ad misericordiam*, or appeal to pity, fallacy.

*Zoe:* Please, you have to support me. You see, I'm a very emotional person.

*Ted:* Dude! That's enough for me.

*The trio walk up to Jen, who is holding a sign with a poster of Orlando Bloom, with a speech bubble that says: "Vote Jen."*

*Jen:* Vote for me. Orlando Bloom thinks I'd be a good candidate.

*Socrates:* Who's Orlando Bloom?

*Jen:* He's a *totally dreamy* movie star!

*Socrates:* What's a movie, and how can he be a star?

*Jen:* It's a thing Orlando Bloom stars in. He's sooo dreamy.

*Socrates:* We seem to be going in circles, young lady. Tell me more about this thing you call a "movie."

*Jen:* Well, it's sort of like a play.

*Socrates:* So this Bloom character is some sort of actor?

*Jen:* Yes, he's a totally *dreamy* actor.

*Socrates:* But what is it about him that makes him an expert?

*Jen:* Because he's totally dreamy!

*Socrates:* We seem to be bumping up against some question begging here. And yet I don't see anything about the job or experience of an actor that makes him an expert on being a class president. I suspect that we're also seeing an *argumentum ad verecundiam* fallacy, an appeal to illegitimate authority.

*Ted:* Like, dude, I don't know if I want to vote for any of these characters.

*Bill:* I know! Let's run for class president ourselves!

*Bill and Ted (together):* Excellent!

# APPENDIX B

## Love Is a Fallacy

from *The Many Loves of Dobie Gillis*
by Max Shulman

Cool was I and logical. Keen, calculating, perspicacious, acute and astute—I was all of these. My brain was as powerful as a dynamo, as precise as a chemist's scales, as penetrating as a scalpel. And—think of it!—I was only eighteen.

It is not often that one so young has such a giant intellect. Take, for example, Petey Bellows, my roommate at the university. Same age, same background, but dumb as an ox. A nice enough fellow, you understand, but nothing upstairs. Emotional type. Unstable. Impressionable. Worst of all, a faddist. Fads, I submit, are the very negation of reason. To be swept up in every new craze that comes along, to surrender yourself to idiocy just because everybody else is doing it—this, to me, is the acme of mindlessness. Not, however, to Petey.

One afternoon I found Petey lying on his bed with an expression of such distress on his face that I immediately diagnosed appendicitis. "Don't move," I said, "Don't take a laxative. I'll get a doctor."

"Raccoon," he mumbled thickly.

"Raccoon?" I said, pausing in my flight.

"I want a raccoon coat," he wailed.

I perceived that his trouble was not physical, but mental. "Why do you want a raccoon coat?"

"I should have known it," he cried, pounding his temples. "I should have known they'd come back when the Charleston came back. Like a fool I spent all my money for textbooks, and now I can't get a raccoon coat."

"Can you mean," I said incredulously, "that people are actually wearing raccoon coats again?"

"All the Big Men on Campus are wearing them. Where've you been?"

"In the library," I said, naming a place not frequented by Big Men on Campus.

He leaped from the bed and paced the room. "I've got to have a raccoon coat," he said passionately. "I've got to!"

"Petey, why? Look at it rationally. Raccoon coats are unsanitary. They shed. They smell bad. They weigh too much. They're unsightly. They—"

"You don't understand," he interrupted impatiently. "It's the thing to do. Don't you want to be in the swim?"

"No," I said truthfully.

"Well, I do," he declared. "I'd give anything for a raccoon coat. Anything!"

My brain, that precision instrument, slipped into high gear. "Anything?" I asked, looking at him narrowly.

"Anything," he affirmed in ringing tones.

I stroked my chin thoughtfully. It so happened that I knew where to get my hands on a raccoon coat. My father had had one in his undergraduate days; it lay now in a trunk in the attic back home. It also happened that Petey had something I wanted. He didn't have it exactly, but at least he had first rights on it. I refer to his girl, Polly Espy.

I had long coveted Polly Espy. Let me emphasize that my desire for this young woman was not emotional in nature. She was, to be sure, a girl who excited the emotions, but I was not one to let my heart rule my head. I wanted Polly for a shrewdly calculated, entirely cerebral reason.

I was a freshman in law school. In a few years I would be out in practice. I was well aware of the importance of the right kind of wife in furthering a lawyer's career. The successful lawyers I had observed were, almost without exception, married to beautiful, gracious, intelligent women. With one omission, Polly fitted these specifications perfectly.

Beautiful she was. She was not yet of pin-up proportions, but I felt sure that time would supply the lack. She already had the makings.

Gracious she was. By gracious I mean full of graces. She had an erectness of carriage, an ease of bearing, a poise that clearly indicated the best of breeding. At table her manners were exquisite. I had seen her at the Kozy Kampus Korner eating the specialty of the house—a sandwich that contained scraps of pot roast, gravy, chopped nuts, and a dipper of sauerkraut—without even getting her fingers moist.

Intelligent she was not. In fact, she veered in the opposite direction. But I believed that under my guidance she would smarten up. At any rate, it was worth a try. It is, after all, easier to make a beautiful dumb girl smart than to make an ugly smart girl beautiful.

"Petey," I said, "are you in love with Polly Espy?"

"I think she's a keen kid," he replied, "but I don't know if you'd call it love. Why?"

"Do you," I asked, "have any kind of formal arrangement with her? I mean, are you going steady or anything like that?"

"No. We see each other quite a bit, but we both have other dates. Why?"

"Is there," I asked, "any other man for whom she has a particular fondness?"

"Not that I know of. Why?"

I nodded with satisfaction. "In other words, if you were out of the picture, the field would be open. Is that right?"

"I guess so. What are you getting at?"

"Nothing, nothing," I said innocently, and took my suitcase out the closet.

"Where are you going?" asked Petey.

"Home for weekend." I threw a few things into the bag.

"Listen," he said, clutching my arm eagerly, "while you're home, you couldn't get some money from your old man, could you, and lend it to me so I can buy a raccoon coat?"

"I may do better than that," I said with a mysterious wink and closed my bag and left.

"Look," I said to Petey when I got back Monday morning. I threw open the suitcase and revealed the huge, hairy, gamy object that my father had worn in his Stutz Bearcat in 1925.

"Holy Toledo!" said Petey reverently. He plunged his hands into the raccoon coat and then his face. "Holy Toledo!" he repeated fifteen or twenty times.

"Would you like it?" I asked.

"Oh yes!" he cried, clutching the greasy pelt to him. Then a canny look came into his eyes. "What do you want for it?"

"Your girl," I said, mincing no words.

"Polly?" he said in a horrified whisper. "You want Polly?"

"That's right."

He flung the coat from him. "Never," he said stoutly.

I shrugged. "Okay. If you don't want to be in the swim, I guess it's your business."

I sat down in a chair and pretended to read a book, but out of the corner of my eye I kept watching Petey. He was a torn man. First he looked at the coat with the expression of a waif at a bakery window. Then he turned away and set his jaw resolutely. Then he looked back at the coat, with even more longing in his face. Then he turned away, but with not so much resolution this time. Back and forth his head swiveled, desire waxing, resolution waning. Finally he didn't turn away at all; he just stood and stared with mad lust at the coat.

"It isn't as though I was in love with Polly," he said thickly. "Or going steady or anything like that."

"That's right," I murmured.

"What's Polly to me, or me to Polly?"

"Not a thing," said I.

"It's just been a casual kick—just a few laughs, that's all."

"Try on the coat," said I.

He complied. The coat bunched high over his ears and dropped all the way down to his shoe tops. He looked like a mound of dead raccoons. "Fits fine," he said happily.

I rose from my chair. "Is it a deal?" I asked, extending my hand.

He swallowed. "It's a deal," he said and shook my hand.

I had my first date with Polly the following evening. This was in the nature of a survey; I wanted to find out just how much work I had to do to get her mind up to the standard I required. I took her first to dinner. "Gee, that was a delish dinner," she said as we left the restaurant. Then I took her to a movie. "Gee, that was a marvy movie," she said as we left the theatre. And then I took her home. "Gee, I had a sensaysh time," she said as she bade me good night.

I went back to my room with a heavy heart. I had gravely underestimated the size of my task. This girl's lack of information was terrifying. Nor would it be enough merely to supply her with information. First she had to be taught to think. This loomed as a project of no small dimensions, and at first I was tempted to give her back to Petey. But then I got to

**Appendix B**
Love Is a Fallacy

thinking about her abundant physical charms and about the way she entered a room and the way she handled a knife and fork, and I decided to make an effort.

I went about it, as in all things, systematically. I gave her a course in logic. It happened that I, as a law student, was taking a course in logic myself, so I had all the facts at my fingertips. "Polly," I said to her when I picked her up on our next date, "tonight we are going over to the Knoll and talk."

"Oo, terrif," she replied. One thing I will say for this girl: you would go far to find another so agreeable.

We went to the Knoll, the campus trysting place, and we sat down under an old oak, and she looked at me expectantly. "What are we going to talk about?" she asked.

"Logic."

She thought this over for a minute and decided she liked it. "Magnif," she said.

"Logic," I said, clearing my throat, "is the science of thinking. Before we can think correctly, we must first learn to recognize the common fallacies of logic. These we will take up tonight."

"Wow-dow!" she cried, clapping her hands delightedly.

I winced, but went bravely on. "First let us examine the fallacy called Dicto Simpliciter."

"By all means," she urged, batting her lashes eagerly.

"Dicto Simpliciter means an argument based on an unqualified generalization. For example: Exercise is good. Therefore everybody should exercise."

"I agree," said Polly earnestly. "I mean exercise is wonderful. I mean it builds the body and everything."

"Polly," I said gently, "the argument is a fallacy. Exercise is good is an unqualified generalization. For instance, if you have heart disease, exercise is bad, not good. Many people are ordered by their doctors not to exercise. You must qualify the generalization. You must say exercise is usually good, or exercise is good for most people. Otherwise you have committed a Dicto Simpliciter. Do you see?"

"No," she confessed. "But this is marvy. Do more! Do more!"

"It will be better if you stop tugging at my sleeve," I told her, and when she desisted, I continued. "Next we take up a fallacy called Hasty Generalization. Listen carefully: You can't speak French. Petey Bellows can't speak French. I must therefore conclude that nobody at the University of Minnesota can speak French."

"Really?" said Polly, amazed. "Nobody?"

I hid my exasperation. "Polly, it's a fallacy. The generalization is reached too hastily. There are too few instances to support such a conclusion."

"Know any more fallacies?" she asked breathlessly. "This is more fun than dancing even."

I fought off a wave of despair. I was getting nowhere with this girl, absolutely nowhere. Still, I am nothing if not persistent. I continued. "Next comes Post Hoc. Listen to this: Let's not take Bill on our picnic. Every time we take him out with us, it rains."

"I know somebody just like that," she exclaimed. "A girl back home—Eula Becker, her name is. It never fails. Every single time we take her on a picnic—"

"Polly," I said sharply, "it's a fallacy. Eula Becker doesn't cause the rain. She has no connection with the rain. You are guilty of Post Hoc if you blame Eula Becker."

"I'll never do it again," she promised contritely. "Are you mad at me?"

I sighed. "No, Polly, I'm not mad."

"Then tell me some more fallacies."

"All right. Let's try Contradictory Premises."

"Yes, let's," she chirped, blinking her eyes happily.

I frowned, but plunged ahead. "Here's an example of Contradictory Premises: If God can do anything, can He make a stone so heavy that He won't be able to lift it?"

"Of course," she replied promptly.

"But if He can do anything, He can lift the stone," I pointed out.

"Yeah," she said thoughtfully. "Well, then I guess He can't make the stone."

"But He can do anything," I reminded her.

She scratched her pretty, empty head. "I'm all confused," she admitted.

"Of course you are. Because when the premises of an argument contradict each other, there can be no argument. If there is an irresistible force, there can be no immovable object. If there is an immovable object, there can be no irresistible force. Get it?"

"Tell me more of this keen stuff," she said eagerly.

I consulted my watch. "I think we'd better call it a night. I'll take you home now, and you go over all the things you've learned. We'll have another session tomorrow night."

I deposited her at the girls' dormitory, where she assured me that she had had a perfectly terrif evening, and I went glumly home to my room. Petey lay snoring in his bed, the raccoon coat huddled like a great hairy beast at his feet. For a moment I considered waking him and telling him that he could have his girl back. It seemed clear that my project was doomed to failure. The girl simply had a logic-proof head.

But then I reconsidered. I had wasted one evening; I might as well waste another. Who knew? Maybe somewhere in the extinct crater of her mind a few embers still smoldered. Maybe somehow I could fan them into flame. Admittedly it was not a prospect fraught with hope, but I decided to give it one more try.

Seated under the oak the next evening I said, "Our first fallacy tonight is called Ad Misericordiam."

She quivered with delight.

"Listen closely," I said. "A man applies for a job. When the boss asks him what his qualifications are, he replies that he has a wife and six children at home, the wife is a helpless cripple, the children have nothing to eat, no clothes to wear, no shoes on their feet, there are no beds in the house, no coal in the cellar, and winter is coming."

A tear rolled down each of Polly's pink cheeks. "Oh, this is awful, awful," she sobbed.

"Yes, it's awful," I agreed, "but it's no argument. The man never answered the boss's question about his qualifications. Instead he appealed to the boss's sympathy. He committed the fallacy of Ad Misericordiam. Do you understand?"

"Have you got a handkerchief?" she blubbered.

I handed her a handkerchief and tried to keep from screaming while she wiped her eyes. "Next," I said in a carefully controlled tone, "we will discuss False Analogy. Here is an example: Students should be allowed to look at their textbooks during examinations. After all, surgeons have X rays to guide them during an operation, lawyers have briefs to guide them during a trial, carpenters have blueprints to guide them when they are building a house. Why, then, shouldn't students be allowed to look at their textbooks during an examination?"

"There now," she said enthusiastically, "is the most marvy idea I've heard in years."

"Polly," I said testily, "the argument is all wrong. Doctors, lawyers, and carpenters aren't taking a test to see how much they have learned, but students are. The situations are altogether different, and you can't make an analogy between them."

"I still think it's a good idea," said Polly.

"Nuts," I muttered. Doggedly I pressed on. "Next we'll try Hypothesis Contrary to Fact."

"Sounds yummy," was Polly's reaction.

"Listen: If Madame Curie had not happened to leave a photographic plate in a drawer with a chunk of pitchblende, the world today would not know about radium."

"True, true," said Polly, nodding her head "Did you see the movie? Oh, it just knocked me out. That Walter Pidgeon is so dreamy. I mean he fractures me."

"If you can forget Mr. Pidgeon for a moment," I said coldly, "I would like to point out that statement is a fallacy. Maybe Madame Curie would have discovered radium at some later date. Maybe somebody else would have discovered it. Maybe any number of things would have happened. You can't start with a hypothesis that is not true and then draw any supportable conclusions from it."

"They ought to put Walter Pidgeon in more pictures," said Polly, "I hardly ever see him any more."

One more chance, I decided. But just one more. There is a limit to what flesh and blood can bear. "The next fallacy is called Poisoning the Well."

"How cute!" she gurgled.

"Two men are having a debate. The first one gets up and says, 'My opponent is a notorious liar. You can't believe a word that he is going to say. Now, Polly, think. Think hard. What's wrong?"

I watched her closely as she knit her creamy brow in concentration. Suddenly a glimmer of intelligence—the first I had seen—came into her eyes. "It's not fair," she said with indignation. "It's not a bit fair. What chance has the second man got if the first man calls him a liar before he even begins talking?"

"Right!" I cried exultantly. "One hundred per cent right. It's not fair. The first man has poisoned the well before anybody could drink from it. He has hamstrung his opponent before he could even start . . . Polly, I'm proud of you."

"Pshaw," she murmured, blushing with pleasure.

"You see, my dear, these things aren't so hard. All you have to do is concentrate. Think—examine—evaluate. Come now, let's review everything we have learned."

"Fire away," she said with an airy wave of her hand.

Heartened by the knowledge that Polly was not altogether a cretin, I began a long, patient review of all I had told her. Over and over and over again I cited instances, pointed out flaws, kept hammering away without letup. It was like digging a tunnel. At first, everything was work, sweat, and darkness. I had no idea when I would reach the light, or even if I would. But I persisted. I pounded and clawed and scraped, and finally I was rewarded. I saw a chink of light. And then the chink got bigger and the sun came pouring in and all was bright.

Five grueling nights this took, but it was worth it. I had made a logician out of Polly; I had taught her to think. My job was done. She was worthy of me, at last. She was a fit wife for me, a proper hostess for my many mansions, a suitable mother for my well-heeled children.

It must not be thought that I was without love for this girl. Quite the contrary. Just as Pygmalion loved the perfect woman he had fashioned, so I loved mine. I decided to acquaint her with my feelings at our very next meeting. The time had come to change our relationship from academic to romantic.

"Polly," I said when next we sat beneath our oak, "tonight we will not discuss fallacies."

"Aw, gee," she said, disappointed.

"My dear," I said, favoring her with a smile, "we have now spent five evenings together. We have gotten along splendidly. It is clear that we are well matched."

"Hasty Generalization," said Polly brightly.

"I beg your pardon," said I.

"Hasty Generalization," she repeated. "How can you say that we are well matched on the basis of only five dates?"

I chuckled with amusement. The dear child had learned her lessons well. "My dear," I said, patting her hand in a tolerant manner, "five dates is plenty. After all, you don't have to eat a whole cake to know that it's good."

"False Analogy," said Polly promptly. "I'm not a cake. I'm a girl."

I chuckled with somewhat less amusement. The dear child had learned her lessons perhaps too well. I decided to change tactics. Obviously the best approach was a simple, strong, direct declaration of love. I paused for a moment while my massive brain chose the proper words. Then I began:

"Polly, I love you. You are the whole world to me, and the moon and the stars and the constellations of outer space. Please, my darling, say that you will go steady with me, for if you will not, life will be meaningless. I will languish. I will refuse my meals. I will wander the face of the earth, a shambling, hollow-eyed hulk."

There, I thought, folding my arms, that ought to do it.

"Ad Misericordiam," said Polly.

I ground my teeth. I was not Pygmalion; I was Frankenstein, and my monster had me by the throat. Frantically I fought back the tide of panic surging through me. At all costs I had to keep cool.

"Well, Polly," I said, forcing a smile, "you certainly have learned your fallacies."

"You're darn right," she said with a vigorous nod.

"And who taught them to you, Polly?"

"You did."

"That's right. So you do owe me something, don't you, my dear? If I hadn't come along you never would have learned about fallacies."

"Hypothesis Contrary to Fact," she said instantly.

I dashed perspiration from my brow. "Polly," I croaked, "you mustn't take all these things so literally. I mean this is just classroom stuff. You know that the things you learn in school don't have anything to do with life."

"Dicto Simpliciter," she said, wagging her finger at me playfully.

That did it. I leaped to my feet, bellowing like a bull. "Will you or will you not go steady with me?"

"I will not," she replied.

"Why not?" I demanded.

"Because this afternoon I promised Petey Bellows that I would go steady with him."

I reeled back, overcome with the infamy of it. After he promised, after he made a deal, after he shook my hand! "The rat!" I shrieked, kicking up great chunks of turf. "You can't go with him, Polly. He's a liar. He's a cheat. He's a rat."

"Poisoning the Well," said Polly, "and stop shouting. I think shouting must be a fallacy too."

With an immense effort of will, I modulated my voice. "All right," I said. "You're a logician. Let's look at this thing logically. How could you choose Petey Bellows over me? Look at me—a brilliant student, a tremendous intellectual, a man with an assured future. Look at Petey—a knothead, a jitterbug, a guy who'll never know where his next meal is coming from. Can you give me one logical reason why you should go steady with Petey Bellows?"

"I certainly can," declared Polly. "He's got a raccoon coat."

# GLOSSARY

## A

• **Accent:** an argument that rests on an improper emphasis placed on certain words or phrases.

• *Ad Baculum:* from the Latin, meaning "to the stick." See **Appeal to Fear**.

• *Ad Fontem:* from the Latin, meaning "against the source"; this subgroup of the fallacies of relevance consists of arguments that focus on the source of the argument, rather than on the issue itself.

• *Ad Hominem:* from the Latin, meaning "to the man." See *Ad Hominem* **Abusive** and *Ad Hominem* **Circumstantial**.

• *Ad Hominem* **Abusive:** an *ad fontem* argument that attempts to avoid the issue by insulting an opponent with abusive language. See *Ad Hominem*.

• *Ad Hominem* **Circumstantial:** an *ad fontem* argument that tries to discredit an opponent because of his background, affiliations, or self-interest in the matter at hand. See *Ad Hominem*.

• *Ad Misericordiam:* from the Latin, meaning "to pity." See **Appeal to Pity**.

• *Ad Populum:* from the Latin, meaning "to the people." See **Mob Appeal**.

• *Ad Verecundiam:* from the Latin, meaning "to shame." See **Appeal to Illegitimate Authority**.

• **Appeal to Fear:** an appeal to emotion argument that distracts by making the audience afraid of the consequences of disagreeing with the speaker. This fallacy seeks to arouse a fear of harm that is not realistic or related to the issue at hand. See *Ad Baculum*.

• **Appeal to Ignorance:** a red herring argument that claims that since a proposition cannot be disproven, it must therefore be true or likely.

• **Appeal to Illegitimate Authority:** an appeal to emotion fallacy that distracts by attempting to shame the listener into agreement by citing an illegitimate authority. See *Ad Verecundiam*.

• **Appeal to Pity:** an appeal to emotion argument that distracts by making the audience feel sorry for the speaker or someone on behalf of whom the speaker is arguing. This fallacy appeals to our sense of compassion. Like the other appeals to emotion, it tries to get us to accept certain views or courses of action by causing us to sympathize with the speaker rather than by providing good and careful reasoning. See *Ad Misericordiam*.

• **Appeals to Emotion:** a subgroup of the fallacies of relevance. These arguments attempt to sway the opinions of people by compelling them to feel emotions such as pity, anger, fear, joy, peer pressure, intimidation, etc.

• **Argue:** to provide rational reasons for or against an idea or action.

• **Argument:** providing examples or rational reasons for or against an idea or action with the intent to persuade.

• **Aristotle:** Greek philosopher and student of Plato who went on to found his own school, the Lyceum. His writings on logic are the earliest known attempt to explain logic in a systematic way.

• **Axiom:** a foundational principle upon which an argument rests.

## B

• **Begging the Question:** a fallacy of presupposition argument that assumes the very thing that one is trying to prove. See *Petitio Principii*.

• **Biased Expert:** an appeal to illegitimate authority that suggests we accept the opinions of one who has an unreasonable bias or prejudice.

• **Bifurcation (False Dilemma):** a fallacy of presupposition argument that frames the debate in such a way that only two options are possible, when other possibilities may exist. Also called a false dichotomy.

• **Burden of proof:** the obligation to present evidence to prove an argument is clearly stronger than the alternative.

**C**

• **Categorical Logic:** the branch of logic pioneered by Aristotle, which deals primarily with categories of things. In a categorical argument an argument can be represented with symbols, and each of these symbols represents a term, word, or phrase that describes a category of things. Categorical logic is always deductive logic, so only the structure or form of the argument is used to determine validity. Example: "All men are mortal" becomes "All S are P."

• **Celebrity Expert:** an appeal to illegitimate authority that suggests we accept the opinion of a celebrity who has no real expertise relating to the issue or product being promoted.

• **Chronological Snobbery:** an appeal to emotion argument that distracts by making the audience want to either be part of an old tradition or part of the latest cool, new thing. In other words, this fallacy distracts by rejecting or accepting something merely on the basis of its age, making an appeal to tradition or to novelty.

• **Circular Reasoning:** a category of begging the question. A circular argument may simply present a conclusion while trying to trick us into thinking that we are also being given a real premise that leads to this conclusion. What a circular argument actually does, however, is restate the conclusion in other words.

• **Clarity:** one of the three principles of critical thinking in which language used in an argument is clear and not open to multiple interpretations.

• **Conclusive:** having the property of certainty.

• **Confusing a Necessary and a Sufficient Condition:** a type of false cause fallacy (fallacy of induction) in which it is assumed that because something cannot occur without a certain factor being present, it will necessarily occur if that factor is present.

• **Confusing a Cause and an Effect:** a fallacy of induction in which a causal relationship exists between two elements, and an argument is based on the misunderstanding that the effect is the cause and the cause is the effect.

• **Consistent:** not in contradiction.

• **Credibility:** believability.

**D**

• **Debate:** a structured argument between two parties.

• **Deductive Reasoning:** a method of determining the validity of a formal argument (see **Formal Logic**) in which the conclusion must, necessarily, be true if the premises used to support it are true. It is whole-to-part reasoning. Deductive arguments are said to be black or white and cannot be gray.

• **Demagogue:** from the Greek *demagogos*; a person, especially an orator or political leader, who gains power and popularity by arousing the emotions, passions, and prejudices of the people.

• **Dialectic:** having to do with a back-and-forth interchange.

• **Dilemma:** a situation in which one must choose between two unpleasant alternatives.

• **Distinction Without a Difference:** an argument that makes a linguistic distinction between two things that are actually not different from each other.

• **Distributive:** characteristic of every individual member of a group.

**E**

• **Empirical Data:** data that comes to us by observation or experience.

• **Enthymeme (Hidden Assumption):** an argument in which at least one statement (either premise or conclusion) is assumed rather than explicitly stated.

• **Epistemology:** from the Greek, *episteme*, meaning "knowledge"; used in the modern sense to refer to the basis for knowledge, or how we know what we know. Also, the branch of academic philosophy that deals with the question, "How can we know what we know?"

• **Epithet:** a label (often a negative one).

• **Equivocation:** an argument that fails because a key term is ambiguous.

- **Euphemistic:** using "nicer" words to soft-pedal a statement that may seem negative.

- **Evidence:** a piece of data that supports a conclusion.

- **Explanation:** a series of statements in which a cause is given for an effect.

# F

- **Fake Precision:** a fallacy of induction argument that uses numbers or statistics in a way that is too precise to be justified by the situation.

- **Fallacies of Clarity:** arguments that fail because they contain words, phrases or, syntax that distort or cloud their meanings.

- **Fallacies of Induction:** arguments that misuse empirical data or don't follow proper methods of inductive reasoning.

- **Fallacies of Presumption:** arguments that make unwarranted assumptions about either the data or the nature of a reasonable argument.

- **Fallacies of Presupposition:** A subgroup of the fallacies of presumption. These arguments contain hidden assumptions that make them unreasonable.

- **Fallacies of Relevance:** arguments that have premises that do not "bear upon" the truth of the conclusions. In other words, they introduce an irrelevancy into the argument.

- **Fallacy:** The word "fallacy" comes from the Latin word *fallacia*, which means "deceit," "trick," or "fraud." The Latin verb *fallo, fallere, fefelli, falsum* means "to deceive." From *fallacia* and *fallo* we also get our English words "fallacious" and "false." The Latin roots of "fallacy" remind us that a fallacy can be both a deception and a trick. A commonly recognized bad argument failing to meet the requirements of relevance, clarity, or presumption.

- **Fallacy of Composition:** a fallacy of presupposition argument based on a hidden assumption that the properties of the whole will be the same as the properties of the parts.

- **Fallacy of Division:** a fallacy of presupposition argument that is based on the hidden assumption that a collective whole determines that all of its parts will be like the whole.

- **Fallacy of Moderation:** a fallacy of presupposition argument that assumes the correct answer is always the middle ground or a compromise between two extremes.

- **False Analogy:** a fallacy of induction argument that fails because it creates an analogy between two things that are not similar enough to warrant an analogy.

- **False Cause:** a fallacy of induction argument that is based on a weak cause-and-effect connection.

- **Formal Logic:** one of the two branches in the study of logic (see **Informal Logic**); it is reasoning in the abstract, focusing on deductive reasoning, in which the validity of an argument is based solely on the structure (form) of the argument and the premises imply a necessary conclusion.

# G

- **Genetic Fallacy:** an *ad fontem* argument that states that an idea should be discounted simply because of its source or origin.

# H

- **Hasty Generalization (Converse Accident):** a fallacy of induction argument that makes an unwarranted generalization on the basis of too few samples.

# I

- **Implication:** a relationship between statements in which the truth of one statement necessarily requires the truth of another.

- **Inconsistent:** a relationship between statements in which they cannot both be true.

- **Inductive Reasoning:** a method of determining the validity of an informal argument which tends to start with evidence that can be observed (with the senses) and compiled and works toward generalizations that are reasonably accurate with more or less probability (part-to-whole reasoning). Inductive arguments are said to be either strong or weak.

- **Informal Fallacies:** Informal fallacies are weak, poor, and fallacious arguments that occur in common language. These fallacies are not fallacious because of matters of form or structure, but because they violate principles such as relevance, presumption, and clarity.

- **Informal Logic:** one of the two branches in the study of logic (see **Formal Logic**). Informal logic deals with ordinary-language arguments that tend to emphasize inductive rather than deductive reasoning. The structure or form of an argument is less the issue than the weight of the evidence, and the arguments are generally determined to be reasonably accurate with more or less probability.

- **Irrelevant Goals or Functions:** a red herring argument that distracts by measuring a plan or policy according to goals it wasn't intended to achieve.

- **Irrelevant Thesis:** a red herring argument that distracts by making a case for the wrong point.

- **Is-Ought Fallacy:** a fallacy of presupposition argument that assumes that just because something *is* a certain way, it *ought* to be that way.

- **Issue:** the thing that the argument is really about; what is at stake in the argument.

# J

- **Justify, Justification:** to give a reason for; the reason for.

# L

- **Legitimate:** justified.

- **Loaded Question:** a category of begging the question in which a question is phrased in such a way as to limit the number of responses to the question and to cast a negative light on any answer that might be given (e.g., Have you stopped beating your wife yet?).

- **Locke, John:** an Enlightenment-era English philosopher known for his championing of empiricism, an epistemology based on inductive reasoning.

- **Logic:** from the Greek word *logos*, meaning "reason." The art and science of reason, usually divided into two subdivisions, or areas of study: "formal" and "informal."

- **Logical:** having the quality of being reasonable from the point of view of the discipline of logic.

# M

- **Majority:** representing the larger number of people within any particular group.

- **Metaphysics:** The branch of academic philosophy that deals with the question, "What is really real?"

- **Mob Appeal:** an appeal to emotion argument that distracts by making the audience want to be part of the crowd or one of the "common people." To make up for a lack of solid evidence and sound reason, this argument appeals to the emotions of a crowd, the desire to be part of the majority, or the interests of the "common man." See *Ad Populum*.

- **Motives:** the internal reasons behind a human action.

# N

- **Neglect of a Common Cause:** a fallacy of induction in which one thing is said to cause another, when actually a third thing caused both.

- **Non-Argumentative Persuasion:** an attempt to convince without making an open argument.

# O

- **Ontology:** the branch of philosophy that answers the question, "What is real?"

# P

- **Persuasion:** the art of convincing others.

- *Petitio Principii:* a Latin phrase literally meaning "petitioning" (asking, requesting, demanding) "the principle" (beginning, foundation). See **Begging the Question**.

- *Philos:* an ancient Greek word meaning "love." See **Philosopher**.

- **Philosopher:** originally a combination of two ancient Greek words—*philos* and *sophia*—meaning "lover of wisdom." In a more technical and contemporary sense it means "student of philosophy." See *Philos* and *Sophia*.

- **Poisoning the Well:** a fallacy in which the speaker not only attacks his rival but also tries to frame the very terms of the debate in a way that is unfavorable to one side.

- *Post Hoc Ergo Propter Hoc:* a Latin phrase meaning "after this, therefore because of this"; a form of the false cause fallacy in which a causal argument is based solely on chronology.

• **Premises:** reasons or propositions given in an argument that support or leads to a conclusion. Example: All men are mortal (premise). Socrates is a man (premise). Therefore, Socrates is mortal (conclusion).

• **Presumption:** one of the three principles of critical thinking in which language used in an argument presents data fairly and does not make unnecessary assumptions.

• **Propaganda:** techniques used to influence the opinions of others to do or believe something that they otherwise might not. Example: advertisements.

• **Propositional Logic:** similar in form to categorical logic; however, in this case, the symbols represent entire propositions, or statements, which are often connected by "logical operators," which substitute for words like "and," "or," "not," and "implies." Example: "Either John is a teacher or he is not a teacher," becomes "P v ~P."

# Q

• **Question-Begging Definition:** a category of the begging the question fallacy, this is sometimes called a loaded definition. It is a fallacy in which a presenter will try to define terms in his argument in a way that assumes a conclusion that he is obligated to prove. This fallacy is also often referred to as the "no true Scotsman" fallacy after the following example: Suppose someone said that no true Scotsman could support the British monarchy. The example has set up a non-negotiable "stipulative definition" with which we do not agree, and we are thus at an impasse.

• **Question-Begging Label:** also called a question-begging epithet, this is a category of the begging the question fallacy that occurs when someone labels another person or thing in a way that assumes a conclusion without offering any evidence for that conclusion. This frequently occurs when a label that assumes what is being argued is used.

# R

• **Reason:** (noun) a basis or cause for some belief, action, fact, or event; a statement presented to justify or explain a belief or action; (verb) to think or argue in a logical manner.

• **Red Herrings:** a subgroup of the fallacies of relevance. These arguments make a more subtle appeal to emotion, but include types of proofs that are irrelevant to the case at hand.

• **Relevance:** one of the three principles of critical thinking in which the premises of an argument provide some support for the conclusion.

# S

• **Slippery Slope:** a variation in the fallacy of false cause in which it is assumed that one step in a given direction will lead much further down that path, without an argument being given for why one thing will inevitably lead to another.

• **Snob Appeal:** an appeal to emotion argument that distracts by making a person want to feel "special." This is an emotional appeal to a sense of elitism or to those of "discriminating taste."

• **Socrates:** a Greek philosopher and the mentor of Plato, who wrote down much of what Socrates taught in the form of dialogues. Socrates is considered by many to be one of the chief founders of Western philosophy.

• *Sophia:* ancient Greek word meaning "wisdom." See **Philosopher**.

• **Sound:** logically valid and free from error or fallacy.

• **Special Pleading:** trying to plead for special logical privileges that would not be granted to all debate participants in a similar context.

• **Straw Man Fallacy:** a red herring argument that attempts to disprove an opponent's position by presenting it in an unfair, inaccurate light.

• **Sweeping Generalization (Accident):** a fallacy of induction argument that overextends a generalization to include facts or cases that are exceptions to it.

• **Syllogism:** a deductive, formal argument consisting of two premises followed by a conclusion.

# T

• **Taxonomy:** a systematic organization of things into categories.

• *Tu Quoque:* from Latin, meaning "you too," it is an *ad fontem* argument that assumes that a rival's recommendation should be discounted because the rival does not always follow it himself.

## U

• **Unnamed Expert:** an appeal to illegitimate authority that suggests we accept the opinions of an unnamed source, official, or spokesperson, therefore relying on secondhand information from unknown sources.

## V

• **Valid:** in logic, having the characteristics of being a properly structured deductive argument and thus being necessarily true if the premises are granted.

• **Validity:** in logic, the property of being a properly-structured deductive argument and thus being necessarily true if the premises are granted.

## W

• **Wrong or False Expert:** an appeal to illegitimate authority that suggests that we accept the opinions of one who has no expertise in the field about which he is speaking.

# BIBLIOGRAPHY

**Abbott, Bud and Lou Costello.** "Who's on First." Available at: <http://www.baseball-almanac.com/humor4.shtml>.

**Aldisert, Ruggero.** *Logic for Lawyers: A Guide to Clear Legal Thinking* (3rd Edition). South Bend, IN: National Institute for Trial Advocacy, 1988.

**Bennett, G.H.** *Roosevelt's Peacetime Administrations, 1933-1941: A Documentary History of the New Deal Years.* New York: Manchester University Press, 2004.

**Boller, Paul F.** *Presidential Campaigns: from George Washington to George W. Bush.* New York: Oxford University Press, 1984, 1985, 1996, 2004.

**Clark, Gordon.** *Logic.* Unicoi, TN: The Trinity Foundation, 1985.

**Copi, Irving M. and Carl Cohen.** *Introduction to Logic* (9th Edition). New York: Macmillan Publishing Company, 1994.

**Damer, T. Edward.** *Attacking Faulty Reasoning* (2nd Edition). Belmont, CA: Wadsworth Publishing Company, 1987.

**Engel, S. Morris.** *With Good Reason* (5th Edition). New York: St. Martin's Press, 1994.

**Hamblin, C.L.** *Fallacies.* London: Methuen, 1970.

**Hoover, A.J.** *Don't You Believe It! Poking Holes in Faulty Logic.* Chicago: Moody Press, 1982.

**Kahane, Howard.** *Logic and Contemporary Rhetoric* (6th Edition). Belmont, CA: Wadsworth Publishing Company, 1992.

**Kneale, Martha and Kneale, William.** *The Development of Logic.* Oxford: Clarendon Press, 1962.

**Malabre, Alfred L.** *Lost Prophets: An Insider's History of the Modern Economists.* Boston: Harvard Business Press, 1995.

**Moore, Brooke Noel and Parker, Richard.** *Critical Thinking* (3rd Edition). Mountain View, CA: Mayfield Publishing Company, 1992.

**Sloan, Irving J.** *American Landmark Legislation Labor Laws*, 2nd ser., vol. 4. New York: Oceana Publications, 1984.

**Smith, Gary Scott.** *Faith and the Presidency: from George Washington to George W. Bush.* New York: Oxford University Press, 2006.

**Walton, Douglas.** *Informal Logic: A Pragmatic Approach.* Cambridge: Cambridge University Press, 2008.

**Ward, Laura.** *Perfect Put-Downs: A Collection of Acid Wit.* New York: Sterling Publishing Company, 2009.

**Wilde, Oscar.** *The Importance of Being Earnest and Other Plays.* New York: Oxford University Press, 2008.

**Ziff, Larzer.** *Mark Twain.* New York: Oxford University Press, 2004.

# CHAPTER AND UNIT TESTS

Below is a table of contents for the chapter and unit tests that follow. Each reproducible student may be copied for classroom use. Please see the test answers table of contents on page 259 to locate the answers to each test.

# Chapter 1 Test: *Ad Fontem* Fallacies

Includes material from all of chapter 1

## A. FALLACIES

Provide the fallacy name for each of the fallacy definitions listed below.

1. The speaker asserts that because of the self-interest of or the circumstances surrounding his rival, his rival's arguments should be discounted.

2. The speaker asserts that we should discount his rival's argument because his rival has not been entirely consistent in either advocating or practicing his argument.

3. The speaker says all sorts of mean and nasty things about his rival as evidence that his rival's argument should be discounted.

4. An idea is discounted only because of its origin.

## B. DEFINE

Choose the best answer to define the terms or answer the question.

1. Logic
   a. the study of metaphysics
   b. the art and science of reasoning
   c. the debate and interchange of ideas

2. Fallacy
   a. a premise of an argument
   b. an occurrence of bad or incorrect reasoning
   c. a persuasive technique that targets large numbers of people

3. Relevance
   a. a commonly held idea
   b. a persuasive technique that targets a large number of people
   c. having to do with the main idea, rather than distracting with a side issue

4. *Ad Fontem* Argument
   a. arguments "to the source," also sometimes called "personal attacks"
   b. arguments having to do with a fountain
   c. arguments which are sound and logical

5. What is the first question you should ask yourself when you are presented with an argument?
   a. Does it hurt my feelings?
   b. What is the issue at hand?
   c. Is the person doing the arguing a logical, intelligent person?

# Chapter 1 Test: *Ad Fontem* Fallacies

(continued)

## C. EXAMPLES

Name the fallacy committed in the examples below.

1. Don't listen to him. He is a no-good, dirty, rotten scoundrel.

2. I don't believe you; you got that information from *The New York Times*, which is almost always liberal.

3. How can you tell me to "just say no" today, Dad, when you said "yes" in the sixties?

4. Why should I give any weight to your arguments for legal reform? You're a lawyer and probably stand to benefit from such reforms.

## D. CREATE

Create your own example of a *tu quoque* fallacy.

# CHAPTER 2 MID-CHAPTER QUIZ (OPTIONAL)

Includes material from chapter 2, fallacies 5–8

## A. FALLACIES
Name the fallacy that is described, providing the Latin name where appropriate.

1. A speaker tries to persuade by making us feel sorry for him or others.

2. An appeal to possible bad consequences that will follow if one doesn't accept the speaker's argument, without showing a clear causal link.

3. Appealing to the emotions of a crowd or to the common man to make up for a lack of solid evidence or sound reasoning.

## B. DEFINITIONS
Define the following fallacy.

1. Snob Appeal

## C. EXAMPLES
Name the fallacy committed in the example below, providing the Latin name where appropriate.

1. If you don't speak up for the oppressed minorities in this country by enacting legislation against hate crimes, then prejudice and violence will increase.

2. You really ought to take Jen to the prom, Jon. I know that you're not dating her anymore, but just think of how sad and lonely she'll be all alone at home on the night of her senior prom.

3. Most people I know are discontinuing their home phone plans and are just using cell phones. You should consider it!

# CHAPTER 2 TEST: APPEALS TO EMOTION

Includes material from all of chapter 2 and cumulative review of chapter 1

## A. FALLACIES
Name the fallacy that is described, providing the Latin name where appropriate.

1. The speaker appeals to the mere fact that a belief is widely held to prove its truth.

2. The speaker appeals to the mystique of the common man or working class.

3. The speaker appeals to the mystique of those with discriminating tastes.

4. This fallacy occurs when the speaker depends on emotional appeals to make his audience feel sorry for him or others rather than using sound evidence.

5. The speaker appeals to the opinion of an expert. The most common situations in which this occurs are when the expert is not named, is biased, or is not really an expert.

6. The speaker appeals to the mere age of a belief, practice, or thing as evidence that it is better.

## B. EXAMPLES
Name the fallacy committed in the example below, providing the Latin name where appropriate.

1. Check out the Ford F-150; it's the best-selling vehicle in America.

2. Yuengling Lager: made by the oldest brewery in America.

3. If we do not take immediate action to curb vehicle emissions which pollute the air we breathe, we are greatly compromising the health of our environment, our children, and their children.

4. Twin Brook Winery: No other Lancaster County winery has dedicated itself to producing the classic French wine with such single-minded devotion. Only the best grapes make it into our bottles.

5. Hi, I'm Tim Banks and I just won an Oscar for best supporting actor. I've got a great idea. Why don't we all just respect each other's differences? Wouldn't that be a great political platform?

6. People who really know tea buy it from a specialty store. They do not drink the cheap tea from the grocery store.

7. Our educational system is in crisis right now, and you suggest we engage in risky experiments with untried ideas, such as vouchers? Surely you don't want our educational system to collapse around our ears and leave us all without enough schools to educate our children!

# CHAPTER 2 TEST: APPEALS TO EMOTION

(continued)

## C. APPEALS TO AUTHORITY EXAMPLES:

Identify the type of appeal to illegitimate authority fallacy that is being committed in the examples below.

1. According to sources close to the president, he is prepared to resign if articles of impeachment are passed.

2. Hi, I'm football player Dan Donaldson. If you need a loan, let me tell you, you won't get a better deal than what you'll get from the folks at the Money Store.

3. Hi, I'm Dr. James Smith. Through my many years of cancer research, I have finally developed a new medication, Cancer-Ex, that is the most successful medication for preventing cancer that is currently available. Ask your local doctor what Cancer-Ex could do for you.

## D. CREATE

Create your own example of an appeal to illegitimate authority fallacy.

_____

_____

_____

_____

_____

_____

## E. CUMULATIVE EXAMPLES

Name each of the fallacies committed in the examples below.

1. How can the mayor have any credibility when speaking of the dangers of alcohol? He admits to having had a problem with alcohol himself.

2. Of course those legislators from Tennessee are against this tobacco tax. Tennessee produces more tobacco than any other state in the country! They are in the pockets of the industry, and you cannot take their arguments seriously.

3. Ladies and gentlemen, those who are opposed to health care reform are the lowest kind of base cowards that could possibly be imagined. Do not allow their silly, stubborn refusal to join the twenty-first century to be voted into the Senate again!

# CHAPTER 2 TEST: APPEALS TO EMOTION

(continued)

## F. DISCUSSION QUESTION

Appeals to emotion are very common in marketing and advertising. Do you think that it is effective? Can you think of a time in your own life that you might have been affected by an appeal to emotion?

_____

_____

_____

_____

_____

_____

_____

_____

_____

_____

_____

_____

_____

_____

_____

_____

# CHAPTER 3 TEST: RED HERRING FALLACIES

Includes material from all of chapter 3 and cumulative review of chapters 1 and 2

## A. DEFINITIONS
Give the definition or description for each of the fallacies below.

1. Irrelevant Thesis

2. Irrelevant Goals or Functions

3. Straw Man Fallacy

4. Appeal to Ignorance

## B. EXAMPLES
Name the fallacy committed in the examples below.

1. **Brother:** No one believes that there is really a ghost haunting the old Maloney mansion.
   **Sister:** But you have no proof! I think it is haunted!

2. I can't support bailing out the big banks that are going bankrupt. The bailout just rewards the bad decisions of greedy Wall Street bankers.

3. **Presidential Candidate:** Don't make age an issue in this campaign. After all, I've never raised the issue of my opponent's youth and inexperience.

4. Why would you major in history? You probably won't get a good-paying job with a history degree.

5. A puritan is someone who is terribly afraid that somewhere, somehow, someone might be having some fun.

6. Don't give me all those lines about being an environmentalist. You also support hunting, and that is clearly killing wildlife.

## C. CREATE

1. Create your own example of an irrelevant thesis fallacy.

_____

_____

_____

# CHAPTER 3 TEST: RED HERRING FALLACIES

(continued)

## D. CUMULATIVE FALLACIES

Provide the fallacy name for each of the fallacy definitions listed below. Remember, the fallacies may come from chapters 1–3.

1. The speaker argues against an exaggerated or inaccurate version of an opponent's position.

2. The speaker argues that because someone cannot disprove his position then it must be right.

3. The speaker calls her opponent all sorts of nasty names rather than challenging her opponent's argument.

4. The speaker proves a different point than the one that is relevant to the issue at hand.

5. The speaker persuades his audience by appealing to the authority of a questionable source or expert.

6. The speaker argues that a position or choice is not the right one because it doesn't fulfill a certain purpose, even though it was really never intended for such a purpose.

## E. CUMULATIVE EXAMPLES

Name the fallacy committed in each of the examples below. Remember, the fallacies may come from chapters 1–3.

1. How can the prosecution seriously suggest that my client committed this brutal crime? He's a fine, upstanding man with a loving family who will be devastated if he is convicted.

2. The only reason you oppose this new tax legislation is that you are an accountant and it will cause you a lot more work.

3. St. Patrick's Day is an Irish holiday. Americans shouldn't celebrate it.

4. Don't major in philosophy. What will all of your uncles who are businessmen think?

5. Don't tell me I can't prove that the president has been involved in numerous conspiracies. You can't prove that he has not been.

6. There's nothing wrong with polygamy. After all, it was practiced in even the oldest civilizations.

# UNIT 1 TEST: FALLACIES OF RELEVANCE

Includes material from all of unit 1 (chapters 1–3)

## A. FALLACIES
Provide the fallacy name for each of the fallacy descriptions listed below.

1. The speaker insists that her rival has no room to criticize something, because he has done it himself.

2. The defense attorney tries to convince the jury not to find the defendant guilty by trying to make the jury feel sad for the plight of the defendant's difficult life and circumstances.

3. The speaker tries to convince you by presenting you with the opinion of a well-known movie star with no expertise relating to the issue at hand.

4. The speaker appeals to the age of something to get others to accept or reject it.

5. The speaker argues that if something has not been disproven, it must be likely.

6. The speaker judges something according to goals that are irrelevant or unrealistic.

## B. DEFINITIONS
Give a definition or description for each of the fallacies below.

1. *Ad Hominem* Abusive

2. *Ad Hominem* Circumstantial

3. Genetic Fallacy

4. Appeal to Fear

5. Mob Appeal

6. Snob Appeal

7. Irrelevant Thesis

# UNIT 1 TEST: FALLACIES OF RELEVANCE

(continued)

8. Straw Man

## C. SHORT-ANSWER QUESTIONS

Answer the questions below.

1. What are the positive and negative senses of the word "argument"?

2. How do arguments sometimes violate the principle of relevance?

## D. EXAMPLES

Name the fallacy committed in each of the examples below.

### The *Ad Fontem* Fallacies

1. "Filthy Story-Teller, Despot, Liar, Thief, Braggart, Buffoon, Usurper, Monster, Ignoramus Abe, Old Scoundrel, Perjurer, Robber, Swindler, Tyrant, Fiend, Butcher."
   —*Harper's Weekly* on Abraham Lincoln[1]

2. "Reader, suppose you were an idiot; and suppose you were a member of Congress; but I repeat myself."
   —Mark Twain[2]

3. Officer, why did you pull me over for speeding? Policemen are always driving way over the speed limit themselves.

4. Yes, Jasmine thinks everyone should purchase a hybrid electric instead of a car that only uses gas. But she got those ideas from her roommate, who fanatically argues for alternative sources of energy. She is just a mouthpiece for her roommate!

---

1. Paul F. Boller, *Presidential Campaigns: from George Washington to George W. Bush* (New York: Oxford University Press, 1984, 1985, 1996, 2004), 117.
2. Larzer Ziff, *Mark Twain* (New York: Oxford University Press, 2004), 59.

(continued)

### Appeals to Emotion Fallacies

5. Don't vote for these country-club, blue-blooded Republicans. Vote for John Jackson, champion of the American working man and strong leader in recent polls!

6. No! No son of mine will be allowed to hike for two days up into those mountains. Do you know how cold it could get up there? And you could easily fall and get seriously injured. Would you rather live a long and happy life or risk it all just for a hike up a mountain?

7. This Christmas, leave behind the packed malls and the tinsel. There are families right in your hometown who are struggling to make ends meet. Please support them by donating to Salvation Army.

8. In 1974, football great Joe Namath was in a commercial for women's pantyhose and even wore them to show how great they could make your legs look! Clearly, that makes Beautymist pantyhose the best you can buy!

9. If you read *Moby Dick*, you will join the exclusive ranks of well-read Americans. It is an accomplishment of which few can boast.

10. Any art from before the twentieth century is better than the modernist and abstract styles that no one can even understand.

11. Hershey's chocolate is the best-selling in America! Everyone loves a Hershey's Kiss.

### Red Herrings

12. I don't see why we are spending so much on the so-called "war on drugs." Alcohol is far more frequently abused and it's still legal.

13. Our political opponents have challenged us to give them evidence that there really is a health-care crisis. Well, I ask them to give us evidence that there is not.

14. The television is a terrible invention. You spend half your time watching annoying commercials and getting headaches from the glowing screen.

15. Let's get serious here, gentlemen. Giving the American people a tax cut is not going to solve all of their financial problems.

# CHAPTER 4 TEST: FALLACIES OF PRESUPPOSITION

Includes material from all of chapter 4 and cumulative review of chapters 1–3

## A. FALLACIES
Provide the fallacy name for each of the fallacy descriptions listed below.

This fallacy is committed when . . .

1. . . . the speaker makes the assumption that the parts will have the same properties as a collective whole.

2. . . . the speaker assumes the very thing that she is trying to prove.

3. . . . the speaker assumes that a collective whole will have the properties of its parts.

4. . . . the speaker assumes that something is the right thing simply because it is the way that things happen to be.

5. . . . the speaker assumes that the best solution to a problem must be a compromise between extremes.

6. . . . the speaker assumes that only two possibilities exist, when in fact there may be others.

## B. DEFINE
Circle the answer that best defines the terms or answers the question.

1. Fallacies of Presupposition
   a. fallacies that play on the emotions of an audience
   b. fallacies that contain hidden assumptions
   c. fallacies that distract from the issue at hand

2. Axiom
   a. a foundational principle upon which an argument rests
   b. a well-reasoned argument
   c. an example of a false dilemma

3. Enthymeme
   a. a deductive argument with a hidden assumption
   b. a fallacy of induction
   c. a compromise between two extremes

4. *Petitio principii*
   a. circular explanation
   b. petitioning the principle
   c. the small prince

# CHAPTER 4 TEST: FALLACIES OF PRESUPPOSITION

## C. EXAMPLES

Name the fallacy committed in each of the examples below.

1. If those two tribes can't live together, why don't we just split the land in half and give half to each of them?

2. America: love it or leave it.

3. I have always grown corn in that field, and so did my father. Corn should always be planted there.

4. "These three musketeers are valiant men and consummate swordsmen. If I had an army of such men, we would be unstoppable!"

5. **Mr. Engleton:** Dickens's works are much better literature than those of Tolkien.
   **Johnny:** How does one know what writings are great literature?
   **Mr. Engleton:** They are the ones recommended by the well informed.
   **Johnny:** How does one get to be well informed?
   **Mr. Engleton:** Why, by reading great works of literature such as those of Dickens, of course.

6. The men who wrote this program had worked for Microsoft, the most powerful, successful, hard-driving company in the software industry. They must have been great programmers themselves.

## D. CREATE

Create your own example of a bifurcation (false dilemma) fallacy.

_____

_____

_____

_____

_____

_____

_____

_____

_____

_____

# CHAPTER 4 TEST: FALLACIES OF PRESUPPOSITION

(continued)

## E. CUMULATIVE EXAMPLES

Name the fallacy committed in each of the examples below.

1. Our plumber just recommended that we replace our old pipes. Of course he would recommend that, because we will be paying *him* to do it!

2. Dr. Robert Hernandez is the best surgeon in Chicago. In the paper last night, he was quoted as saying that the economy is recovering, and it is time to invest in the stock market again.

3. Yes, Sugar Bombs cereal may contain a great deal of sugar, but at least it does not contain high-fructose corn syrup as Syrupy Snaps does.

4. Time after time, Lansdowne Country Day School is selected by highly discriminating parents who want the very best education for their children. Your child could belong here, too.

5. Lansdowne Country Day School may have decent academics, but do you really want your daughter to be influenced by a bunch of spoiled rich kids? Plus, you will spend all of your spare time helping with fundraisers.

6. The new bridge over the Susquehanna River is so boring. It will not attract more tourists to the city.

7. Dad, can't we get a new set of silverware? These forks and knives used to belong to your parents!

# CHAPTER 5 TEST: FALLACIES OF INDUCTION

Includes material from all of chapter 5 and cumulative review of chapters 1–4

## A. FALLACIES
Provide the fallacy name for each of the fallacy descriptions listed below.

1. The speaker makes an argument by comparing two things that really are not very similar.

2. The speaker makes an argument on the basis of too few examples.

3. The speaker makes an argument using a weak causal connection.

4. The speaker extends a generalization to exceptional cases.

5. The speaker misuses statistics.

## B. DEFINITIONS
Circle the correct definition for both of the terms below.

1. Inductive Reasoning
   a. observing particular facts to prove a general conclusion
   b. using all of the evidence available to create an argument
   c. reasoning that starts with premises which lead to a necessary conclusion

2. Empirical Data
   a. data that is collected and accepted by relevant scholars
   b. data that can be observed or experienced
   c. data that is unreliable because it changes depending on the situation

## C. EXAMPLES
Name the fallacy committed in each of the examples below.

1. It's no wonder that violent crime has increased considering all the violence that has been in movies and video games lately.

2. People who eat dark chocolate are 52 percent less likely to struggle with depression.

3. Did you hear that Lisa found a dead grasshopper in a salad she got from MacDougal's? They should stop selling those salads immediately!

4. I need to buy a birthday present for my teenaged niece, Sarah. Teenagers all like rock music, right? I will get her a Rolling Stones CD. I'm sure she will like it.

# CHAPTER 5 TEST: FALLACIES OF INDUCTION

5. Mr. Yamamoto, our science teacher, told us about rare birds that come to his bird feeder. He said he feeds them sunflower seeds, so I am going to start putting sunflower seeds out, too. Mom, do we have a jar of sunflower seeds in the cupboard?

6. Mom, just as the air force needs new planes to fight effectively, so I need a new computer in my battle for better grades!

7. Every time we go on vacation it rains. We should go somewhere where there is a drought, since we are sure to cause rain!

## D. CREATE

Create your own example of a hasty generalization fallacy.

_____

_____

_____

_____

## E. CUMULATIVE EXAMPLES

Name the fallacy committed in each of the examples below. (Hint: Some examples may commit more than one.)

1. You can't take seriously Mark's argument that we should start a small farm. He has been reading Wendell Berry—a small farm advocate—for the last three years!

2. This sculpture is a great work of art, but you wouldn't understand since you are an ignorant American, and you were probably raised on John Wayne movies.

3. **TV commercial:**
   **Scene One:** Features a teenaged boy at the bus stop with bad acne on his face. Girls grouped together look at him and snicker. He looks away, ashamed.
   **Scene Two:** He is now at the bathroom sink and washes his face with Nuetranol Acne-Free Face Cleanser. Water and suds splash against his face in slow motion.
   **Scene Three:** Clear-faced, he is smiling, with his arm around a beautiful girl who looks at him adoringly.

4. Sarah, if you don't start taking those calcium vitamins today, you are going to get osteoporosis. You could be all hunched up and barely able to walk by the time you are sixty.

5. We shouldn't let kids watch those violent Hollywood movies because it just isn't right to let them be exposed to such images of brutality.

6. I am trying to read one book per month. My mom tells me I should read *The Hobbit*, and my teacher tells me that I should read *The Scarlet Letter*. I will just read half of each.

# UNIT 2 TEST: FALLACIES OF PRESUMPTION

Includes material from all of unit 2 (chapters 4–5) and cumulative review of chapters 1–4

## A. FALLACIES

Provide the fallacy name for each of the fallacy descriptions listed below.

1. An argument that contains an important, hidden assumption, central to what is being proved but not justified by the argument.

2. An argument that assumes only two alternatives are possible when there may be others.

3. Assuming that a compromise is always the correct conclusion.

4. Assuming that just because something is a certain way that it ought to be that way.

5. Extending a generalization to all cases without recognizing exceptions.

## B. DEFINITIONS

Give the definition or description for each of the fallacies below.

1. Fallacy of Composition

2. Fallacy of Division

3. Hasty Generalization

4. False Analogy

5. False Cause

6. Fake Precision

# UNIT 2 TEST: FALLACIES OF PRESUMPTION

(continued)

## C. SHORT-ANSWER QUESTION

What are fallacies of presumption?

_____

_____

_____

_____

_____

_____

_____

_____

_____

## D. EXAMPLES

Name the fallacy committed in each of the examples below.

**PART 1:** Select from the following three possibilities: false analogy, hasty generalization, sweeping generalization.

1. People who make bad grades usually do so because they do not study. Since Jack is making bad grades, it's obvious that he doesn't study.

2. If you put fewer people in a hot air balloon, it will rise higher and faster; if Jack will sleep for fewer hours each night, he will get higher grades and work at a faster pace. Jack should sleep a lot less in order to increase his academic performance.

3. John and Susie just don't try very hard at school. Kids these days are just so lazy.

**PART 2:** Select from the following possibilities: false cause, fake precision, fallacy of composition, fallacy of division.

1. Dennis Rodman is a great basketball player. When they add him to Shaquille O'Neal and Kobe Bryant, they are sure to have a great team.

2. Any law preserving the nation's farmland will be very popular. After all, a recent study by the US Department of Agriculture showed that 82 percent of Americans believe in supporting America's Farmers.

# UNIT 2 TEST: FALLACIES OF PRESUMPTION

(continued)

3. Studies show that most elementary school teachers are parents. It must be because working with children stimulates an interest in parenthood.

4. John Elway should be elected MVP of the NFL. After all, his team is the best team in the league right now.

5. "It is strangely absurd to suppose that a million human beings, collected together, are not under the same moral laws which bind each of them separately."

—Thomas Jefferson[1]

**PART 3:** Select from the following possibilities: begging the question, is-ought fallacy, bifurcation (false dilemma), fallacy of moderation.

1. Of course smoking cigarettes is OK. It's a legal activity, isn't it?

2. Jenny wants peach ice cream and Justin wants coffee ice cream. We will compromise by getting a bowl of peach and coffee ice cream mixed together!

3. Since you started eight months ago, you have consistently had the lowest sales in the department. Either you have not worked hard to improve sales or you simply lack the ability to do this job well. Either way, you are not performing sufficiently, and we may have to remove you from this job.

4. We need an Explorer's History month because we should set aside four weeks to recall the great achievements of America's great explorers.

**PART 4:** Select from the following possibilities: hasty generalization, sweeping generalization, fallacy of composition, fallacy of division.

1. That blimp is a lighter-than-air vehicle. That must mean that everything on it is lighter than air.

2. People who live on Hickory Mountain are almost all quite wealthy. Your friend Greg lives on Hickory Mountain, so he must be loaded.

3. Jon, Mike, and I are not as athletic as those guys. There's no way we could put together a team that could beat them.

4. My Uncle Harry is a crazy driver. It must be a quality common to all people from Queens.

---

1. Gary Scott Smith, *Faith and the Presidency: from George Washington to George W. Bush* (New York: Oxford University Press, 2006), 81.

# UNIT 2 TEST: FALLACIES OF PRESUMPTION

(continued)

## E. CREATE

1. Create your own example of an is-ought fallacy.

_____

_____

_____

2. Create your own example of a false cause fallacy.

_____

_____

_____

## F. CUMULATIVE EXAMPLES

Name the fallacy committed in each of the examples below.

1. Please remember that the defendant was raised in a home without a father and had to care for his younger siblings. He had to become a man while he was still a boy. It is not surprising that he would have many difficult problems to overcome. Please do not punish him for the rest of his life.

2. "Douglas can never be president, Sir. No, Sir; Douglas never can be president, Sir. His legs are too short, Sir. His coat, like a cow's tail, hangs too near the ground, Sir."
   —Thomas Hart Benton on Stephen A. Douglas, presidential candidate[2]

3. You have no proof that high fructose corn syrup is a cause of the increased obesity in America; therefore we will continue to use it as a primary ingredient in Granny's brand pancake syrup until proven otherwise.

4. Schools in America should consider switching to a year-round school schedule. It would be much better for the tourism industry because it would provide steadier, year-round revenue, since families would be able to take their vacations throughout the year.

5. Your objections to the building of the new superstore are clearly just tree-hugging, save-the-whales, environmentalist propaganda. You would probably try to stop an ambulance rushing on its way in order to keep it from running over a caterpillar.

---

2. Laura Ward, _Perfect Put-Downs: A Collection of Acid Wit_ (New York: Sterling Publishing Company, 2009), 120.

# CHAPTER 6 TEST (OR UNIT 3 TEST): FALLACIES OF CLARITY

**Includes material from all of unit 3 and cumulative review of units 1 and 2**

## A. FALLACIES
Provide the fallacy name for each of the fallacy descriptions listed below.

1. Ambiguity that is created by the fact that a word has more than one meaning.

2. Confusion that is created by placing emphasis on one particular word or phrase.

3. Confusion caused by treating a purely linguistic distinction as if it were a real distinction.

## B. EXAMPLES
Name the fallacy committed in each of the examples below.

1. He said that this dress looks good on me. I can't believe he thinks that my other dress doesn't look good on me!

2. Mr. Jones must be a very responsible person. If anything goes wrong at Lewis Academy, he is held responsible.

3. Jack doesn't really get angry. He just flies into a rage and punches people every once in a while.

4. The art of argument is a silly thing to study! Don't we have enough trouble with argumentative students already?

5. I wouldn't say that the movie was bad, but it was a complete waste of time and money.

## C. CREATE
Create your own example of a fallacy of accent.

_____

_____

_____

_____

_____

_____

(continued)

## D. DEFINE

1. What is a fallacy of clarity?

_____

_____

_____

_____

_____

## E. CUMULATIVE EXAMPLES

Name the fallacy committed in each of the examples below.

1. The average homeowner who is refinancing a house while the interest rates are low will save $67,030 on the interest payments during the course of the loan! Don't miss your chance to refinance today!

2. Senator Neilson, the entire nation is fed up with closed-door, private negotiations. The American people want honesty and transparency from their legislators.

3. Of course Melissa wants Mrs. Cruz to curve the grades. She failed the last exam and will argue for anything that will improve her grade.

4. Yes, our company's computer system is a bit old and inefficient, but it works. This company has always managed with old technology and that's the way it's got to be.

5. All of McDonald's food is delicious. I bet if I crack open a packet of ketchup and eat it plain it will be delicious!

6. I wouldn't suggest going to a big state university if you want to be a serious student—all the students at those universities party more than they study!

# FINAL EXAM

Assessment of the entire text and all twenty-eight fallacies

## A. FALLACIES

Provide the fallacy name for each of the fallacy descriptions listed below.

**Unit 1: Fallacies of Relevance**

1. An argument that discounts a rival's position because the rival has not always been consistent in advocating or practicing his current position.

2. The speaker says all sorts of mean and nasty things about his rival as evidence that his rival's argument should be discounted.

3. The thing or idea being argued is discounted solely because of its origin.

4. An argument that tries to discredit an opponent because of his circumstances or potential self-interest in the matter at hand.

5. An appeal to those of "discriminating tastes."

6. This fallacy occurs when the speaker depends on emotional appeals to make his audience feel sorry for him or others rather than providing sound evidence to support his argument.

7. An appeal to the opinion of an "expert," whether an unnamed source, a celebrity, a biased expert, or an expert on an unrelated issue.

8. An appeal to the mere fact that a belief is widely held to prove its truth, or an appeal to the mystique of the "common man" or "the people."

9. An appeal to the mere age of a belief, practice, or thing as evidence that it is correct or preferable.

10. An argument that presents a caricatured, inaccurate, or exaggerated version of an opponent's position.

11. An argument that proves a different point than the one that is relevant to the issue at hand.

12. An argument that insists that because a position cannot be proven, it must be false or, alternatively, if a position cannot be proven wrong, it must be true.

13. An argument that judges something on the basis of a goal that it was never intended to achieve.

### Unit 2: Fallacies of Presumption

1. An argument that makes the assumption that the parts of a collective whole will have the same properties as the collective whole.

2. An argument that is either just restating the conclusion in other words or uses a justification that is more controversial than the original conclusion.

3. An argument that assumes that something is right simply because it is the way things happen to be.

4. An argument that assumes that a collective whole will have the same properties as its parts.

5. An argument that assumes that only two possibilities exist, when in fact there may be others.

6. An argument that assumes that the best solution to a conflict is a compromise between the two extremes.

7. An argument that is based on a comparison of two things that are not very similar.

8. An argument that is based on a weak causal connection.

9. An argument that is based on a misuse of statistics.

10. An argument that extends a generalization to exceptional cases.

11. An argument that creates a generalization on the basis of too few examples.

## B. DEFINITIONS

Give the definition or description for each of the fallacies below.

### Unit 3: Fallacies of Clarity

1. Equivocation

2. Accent

# FINAL EXAM

(continued)

3. Distinction Without a Difference

## C. EXAMPLES

Match the fallacies with the examples below by writing the letters of the examples in the blank spaces provided.

**UNIT 1:**

1. *Ad Hominem* Abusive _____     8. Snob Appeal _____

2. *Ad Hominem* Circumstantial _____     9. Appeal to Illegitimate Authority _____

3. *Tu Quoque* _____     10. Chronological Snobbery _____

4. Genetic Fallacy _____     11. Appeal to Ignorance _____

5. Appeal to Fear _____     12. Irrelevant Goals or Functions _____

6. Appeal to Pity _____     13. Irrelevant Thesis _____

7. Mob Appeal _____     14. Straw Man Fallacy _____

A. Our school starts training students to speak French in the first grade, since speaking French distinguishes one as an exceptionally well-educated individual.

B. Please give this young man another chance to become a good and law-abiding citizen. He is too young to be locked away in prison and separated from his family.

C. Safe and warm housing is a necessity for human life. The City of Harrisburg should provide housing for any citizen in need.

D. Why would anyone vote for Johnson? He is about as inspiring as bowl of soggy cornflakes.

E. Of course leprechauns exist. Can you prove they don't exist? Since you can't prove they don't exist you should stop criticizing me for my conviction that they do!

F. The movie has been a box-office smash and everyone loves it! We should go see it tonight!

G. **Artist:** That painting is an important and influential piece of modern art.
   **Critic:** That painting is crayon scribbled on a white canvas. There is nothing significant about that.

H. You cannot tell me that I should not smoke. You smoke a pack of cigarettes a day!

I. You heard that argument for preventing illegal immigration on Fox News last night, didn't you? Why should we give your argument a hearing when it comes from that biased network?

J. We must provide funds to prop up the banks immediately. If we do not act quickly, they may fail and bring the rest of the economy down with them.

K. They just don't build them like they used to.

L. In an interview today, actress Julie Marshall stated that she believes that the national debt will be paid back over the next thirty years. Isn't that great news?

M. You can't boil water in the new army helmets! They really are poorly designed.

N. Of course James is in favor of hiring an assistant. It will sure make his job a lot easier.

# FINAL EXAM

(continued)

**UNITS 2 & 3:**

1. Begging the Question _____
2. Bifurcation (False Dilemma) _____
3. Fallacy of Moderation _____
4. Is-Ought Fallacy _____
5. Fallacy of Composition _____
6. Fallacy of Division _____
7. Sweeping Generalization _____

8. Hasty Generalization _____
9. False Analogy _____
10. False Cause _____
11. Fake Precision _____
12. Equivocation _____
13. Accent _____
14. Distinction Without a Difference _____

A. I'm not a poor student. I just don't study very hard, when I study at all.

B. Congress has not gotten anything done this year. Each one of those congressmen is lazy.

C. My neighbor has an Australian Shepherd that bit his son! Don't get one of those dogs—they are vicious.

D. **Athlete:** But coach, I took you seriously when you said I had to get back on track, and I just ran seven miles! You've got to let me play!

E. You *can* live without coffee. *You* can live without coffee.

F. You like chicken noodle soup, and I like tomato. I will look for a recipe for chicken-tomato-noodle soup! That will be perfect.

G. Sarah is thinking of going to a different school that offers a nursing program. I think she should stay where she is—things will be best for her just as they are.

H. A piece of paper is as light as a feather. I can carry a case of paper—no problem!

I. "There is no such thing as knowledge which cannot be put in to practice, for such knowledge is no knowledge at all." —Confucius

J. If you eat too much candy, your teeth will decay. If you love someone too much the relationship will deteriorate. It is best not to love someone a lot, but only a little bit.

K. English majors are legendary for being lousy at math. Gordon is an English major, so he is not likely to do well in his algebra class.

L. I got the flu right after I ate at Tony's Pizza Shop last winter. They must not keep their restaurant clean.

M. If you study for your SAT with the SAT Super Duper Prep Guide, your score could increase by 42.7 percent.

N. There are two types of people in the world: those who own a Mercedes-Benz and those who wish they did.

# TEST ANSWERS

Below is a table of contents for chapter and unit test answers. Please see the chapter and unit tests section beginning on page 231 for a reproducible copy of each student test.

# ANSWERS
# CHAPTER 1 TEST: *AD FONTEM* FALLACIES

## A. FALLACIES
Provide the fallacy name for each of the fallacy definitions listed below.

1. The speaker asserts that because of the self-interest of or the circumstances surrounding his rival, his rival's arguments should be discounted.
**ad hominem circumstantial**

2. The speaker asserts that we should discount his rival's argument because his rival has not been entirely consistent in either advocating or practicing his argument.
**tu quoque**

3. The speaker says all sorts of mean and nasty things about his rival as evidence that his rival's argument should be discounted.
**ad hominem abusive**

4. An idea is discounted only because of its origin.
**genetic fallacy**

## B. DEFINE
Choose the best answer to define the terms or answer the question.

1. Logic
   a. the study of metaphysics
   b. the art and science of reasoning
   c. the debate and interchange of ideas

2. Fallacy
   a. a premise of an argument
   b. an occurrence of bad or incorrect reasoning
   c. a persuasive technique that targets large numbers of people

3. Relevance
   a. a commonly held idea
   b. a persuasive technique that targets a large number of people
   c. having to do with the main idea, rather than distracting with a side issue

4. *Ad Fontem* Argument
   a. arguments "to the source," also sometimes called "personal attacks"
   b. arguments having to do with a fountain
   c. arguments which are sound and logical

5. What is the first question you should ask yourself when you are presented with an argument?
   a. Does it hurt my feelings?
   b. What is the issue at hand?
   c. Is the person doing the arguing a logical, intelligent person?

(continued)

## C. EXAMPLES

Name the fallacy committed in the examples below.

1. Don't listen to him. He is a no-good, dirty, rotten scoundrel.
   **ad hominem abusive**

2. I don't believe you; you got that information from *The New York Times*, which is almost always liberal.
   **genetic fallacy**

3. How can you tell me to "just say no" today, Dad, when you said "yes" in the sixties?
   **tu quoque**

4. Why should I give any weight to your arguments for legal reform? You're a lawyer and probably stand to benefit from such reforms.
   **ad hominem circumstantial**

## D. CREATE

Create your own example of a *tu quoque* fallacy.

**Answers will vary. Example: How can you tell me that I should get eight hours of sleep a night? You told me yourself that when you were in college you pulled all-nighters at least once a week!**

Includes material from chapter 2, fallacies 5–8

## A. FALLACIES

Name the fallacy that is described, providing the Latin name where appropriate.

1. A speaker tries to persuade by making us feel sorry for him or others.
   **appeal to pity (*argumentum ad misericordiam*)**

2. An appeal to possible bad consequences that will follow if one doesn't accept the speaker's argument, without showing a clear causal link.
   **appeal to fear (*argumentum ad baculum*)**

3. Appealing to the emotions of a crowd or to the common man to make up for a lack of solid evidence or sound reasoning.
   **mob appeal (*argumentum ad populum*)**

## B. DEFINITIONS

Define the following fallacy.

1. Snob Appeal
   **An argument that distracts by making a person want to feel "special." This is an emotional appeal to a sense of elitism or to those of "discriminating taste."**

## C. EXAMPLES

Name the fallacy committed in the example below, providing the Latin name where appropriate.

1. If you don't speak up for the oppressed minorities in this country by enacting legislation against hate crimes, then prejudice and violence will increase.
   **appeal to fear (*argumentum ad baculum*)**

2. You really ought to take Jen to the prom, Jon. I know that you're not dating her anymore, but just think of how sad and lonely she'll be all alone at home on the night of her senior prom.
   **appeal to pity (*argumentum ad misericordiam*)**

3. Most people I know are discontinuing their home phone plans and are just using cell phones. You should consider it!
   **mob appeal (*argumentum ad populum*)**

# Answers
# Chapter 2 Test: Appeals to Emotion

Includes material from all of chapter 2 and cumulative review of chapter 1

## A. FALLACIES

Name the fallacy that is described, providing the Latin name where appropriate.

1. The speaker appeals to the mere fact that a belief is widely held to prove its truth.
   **mob appeal (*argumentum ad populum*)**

2. The speaker appeals to the mystique of the common man or working class.
   **mob appeal (*argumentum ad populum*)**

3. The speaker appeals to the mystique of those with discriminating tastes.
   **snob appeal**

4. This fallacy occurs when the speaker depends on emotional appeals to make his audience feel sorry for him or others rather than using sound evidence.
   **appeal to pity (*argumentum ad misericordiam*)**

5. The speaker appeals to the opinion of an expert. The most common situations in which this occurs are when the expert is not named, is biased, or is not really an expert.
   **appeal to illegitimate authority (*argumentum ad verecundiam*)**

6. The speaker appeals to the mere age of a belief, practice, or thing as evidence that it is better.
   **chronological snobbery**

## B. EXAMPLES

Name the fallacy committed in the example below, providing the Latin name where appropriate.

1. Check out the Ford F-150; it's the best-selling vehicle in America.
   **mob appeal (*argumentum ad populum*)**

2. Yuengling Lager: made by the oldest brewery in America.
   **chronological snobbery**

3. If we do not take immediate action to curb vehicle emissions which pollute the air we breathe, we are greatly compromising the health of our environment, our children, and their children.
   **appeal to fear (*argumentum ad baculum*)**

4. Twin Brook Winery: No other Lancaster County winery has dedicated itself to producing the classic French wine with such single-minded devotion. Only the best grapes make it into our bottles.
   **snob appeal**

5. Hi, I'm Tim Banks and I just won an Oscar for best supporting actor. I've got a great idea. Why don't we all just respect each other's differences? Wouldn't that be a great political platform?
   **appeal to illegitimate authority (*argumentum ad verecundiam*)**

6. People who really know tea buy it from a specialty store. They do not drink the cheap tea from the grocery store.
   **snob appeal**

7. Our educational system is in crisis right now, and you suggest we engage in risky experiments with untried ideas, such as vouchers? Surely you don't want our educational system to collapse around our ears and leave us all without enough schools to educate our children!
   **appeal to fear (*argumentum ad baculum*)**

(continued)

## C. APPEALS TO AUTHORITY EXAMPLES:

Identify the type of appeal to illegitimate authority fallacy that is being committed in the examples below.

1. According to sources close to the president, he is prepared to resign if articles of impeachment are passed.
   **unnamed expert**

2. Hi, I'm football player Dan Donaldson. If you need a loan, let me tell you, you won't get a better deal than what you'll get from the folks at the Money Store.
   **celebrity expert**

3. Hi, I'm Dr. James Smith. Through my many years of cancer research, I have finally developed a new medication, Cancer-Ex, that is the most successful medication for preventing cancer that is currently available. Ask your local doctor what Cancer-Ex could do for you.
   **biased expert**

## D. CREATE

Create your own example of an appeal to illegitimate authority fallacy.

**Answers will vary. Example (celebrity expert): Race car champion Andy White**

**recommends Zorba Mutual Funds as the best way to win the investment race!**

## E. CUMULATIVE EXAMPLES

Name each of the fallacies committed in the examples below.

1. How can the mayor have any credibility when speaking of the dangers of alcohol? He admits to having had a problem with alcohol himself.
   ***tu quoque* fallacy**

2. Of course those legislators from Tennessee are against this tobacco tax. Tennessee produces more tobacco than any other state in the country! They are in the pockets of the industry, and you cannot take their arguments seriously.
   ***ad hominem* circumstantial**

3. Ladies and gentlemen, those who are opposed to health care reform are the lowest kind of base cowards that could possibly be imagined. Do not allow their silly, stubborn refusal to join the twenty-first century to be voted into the Senate again!
   ***ad hominem* abusive**

(continued)

## F. DISCUSSION QUESTION

Appeals to emotion are very common in marketing and advertising. Do you think that it is effective? Can you think of a time in your own life that you might have been affected by an appeal to emotion?

**Answers will vary. Ask students if there have been times in their lives when they were persuaded to do something to "be like everyone else" (mob appeal) or to be part of the "popular, in crowd" (snob appeal). Ask students if they have ever been persuaded to do something out of fear for some bad consequence (appeal to fear) or out of pity for someone or something (appeal to pity).**

Includes material from all of chapter 3 and cumulative review of chapters 1 and 2

## A. DEFINITIONS

Give the definition or description for each of the fallacies below.

1. Irrelevant Thesis

   **An argument that distracts by making a case for the wrong point.**

2. Irrelevant Goals or Functions

   **An argument that distracts by measuring a plan or policy according to goals it wasn't intended to achieve.**

3. Straw Man Fallacy

   **An argument that attempts to disprove an opponent's position by presenting it in an unfair, inaccurate light.**

4. Appeal to Ignorance

   **An argument that claims that since a proposition cannot be disproven, it must therefore be true or likely.**

## B. EXAMPLES

Name the fallacy committed in the examples below.

1. **Brother:** No one believes that there is really a ghost haunting the old Maloney mansion.
   **Sister:** But you have no proof! I think it is haunted!
   **appeal to ignorance**

2. I can't support bailing out the big banks that are going bankrupt. The bailout just rewards the bad decisions of greedy Wall Street bankers.
   **straw man fallacy**

3. **Presidential Candidate:** Don't make age an issue in this campaign. After all, I've never raised the issue of my opponent's youth and inexperience.
   **irrelevant thesis**

4. Why would you major in history? You probably won't get a good-paying job with a history degree.
   **irrelevant goals or functions**

5. A puritan is someone who is terribly afraid that somewhere, somehow, someone might be having some fun.
   **straw man fallacy**

6. Don't give me all those lines about being an environmentalist. You also support hunting, and that is clearly killing wildlife.
   **irrelevant thesis**

## C. CREATE

1. Create your own example of an irrelevant thesis fallacy.

   **Answers will vary. Example: You suggest that I should vote for the re-election of Senator Lockwood to the US Senate. Well, why should I do that when our local government can't even keep our sidewalks maintained?**

(continued)

## D. CUMULATIVE FALLACIES

Provide the fallacy name for each of the fallacy definitions listed below. Remember, the fallacies may come from chapters 1–3.

1. The speaker argues against an exaggerated or inaccurate version of an opponent's position.
   **straw man**

2. The speaker argues that because someone cannot disprove his position then it must be right.
   **appeal to ignorance**

3. The speaker calls her opponent all sorts of nasty names rather than challenging her opponent's argument.
   ***ad hominem* abusive**

4. The speaker proves a different point than the one that is relevant to the issue at hand.
   **irrelevant thesis**

5. The speaker persuades his audience by appealing to the authority of a questionable source or expert.
   **appeal to illegitimate authority**

6. The speaker argues that a position or choice is not the right one because it doesn't fulfill a certain purpose, even though it was really never intended for such a purpose.
   **irrelevant goals or functions**

## E. CUMULATIVE EXAMPLES

Name the fallacy committed in each of the examples below. Remember, the fallacies may come from chapters 1–3.

1. How can the prosecution seriously suggest that my client committed this brutal crime? He's a fine, upstanding man with a loving family who will be devastated if he is convicted.
   **appeal to pity**

2. The only reason you oppose this new tax legislation is that you are an accountant and it will cause you a lot more work.
   ***ad hominem* circumstantial**

3. St. Patrick's Day is an Irish holiday. Americans shouldn't celebrate it.
   **genetic fallacy**

4. Don't major in philosophy. What will all of your uncles who are businessmen think?
   **irrelevant goals or functions**

5. Don't tell me I can't prove that the president has been involved in numerous conspiracies. You can't prove that he has not been.
   **appeal to ignorance**

6. There's nothing wrong with polygamy. After all, it was practiced in even the oldest civilizations.
   **chronological snobbery**

Includes material from all of unit 1 (chapters 1–3)

## A. FALLACIES
Provide the fallacy name for each of the fallacy descriptions listed below.

1. The speaker insists that her rival has no room to criticize something, because he has done it himself.
   **tu quoque**

2. The defense attorney tries to convince the jury not to find the defendant guilty by trying to make the jury feel sad for the plight of the defendant's difficult life and circumstances.
   **appeal to pity**

3. The speaker tries to convince you by presenting you with the opinion of a well-known movie star with no expertise relating to the issue at hand.
   **appeal to illegitimate authority**

4. The speaker appeals to the age of something to get others to accept or reject it.
   **chronological snobbery**

5. The speaker argues that if something has not been disproven, it must be likely.
   **appeal to ignorance**

6. The speaker judges something according to goals that are irrelevant or unrealistic.
   **irrelevant goals or functions**

## B. DEFINITIONS
Give a definition or description for each of the fallacies below.

1. *Ad Hominem* Abusive
   **An argument that attempts to avoid the issue by insulting an opponent with abusive language.**

2. *Ad Hominem* Circumstantial
   **An argument that tries to discredit an opponent because of his background, affiliations, or self-interest in the matter at hand.**

3. Genetic Fallacy
   **An argument that states that an idea should be discounted simply because of its source or origin.**

4. Appeal to Fear
   **An argument that distracts by making the audience afraid of the consequences of disagreeing with the speaker.**

5. Mob Appeal
   **An argument that distracts by making the audience want to be part of the crowd or one of the "common people."**

6. Snob Appeal
   **An argument that distracts by making a person want to feel "special," preying on a desire for elitism or "discriminating taste."**

7. Irrelevant Thesis
   **An argument that distracts by making a case for the wrong point.**

(continued)

8. Straw Man
**An argument that attempts to disprove an opponent's position by presenting it in an unfair, inaccurate light.**

## C. SHORT-ANSWER QUESTIONS

Answer the questions below.

1. What are the positive and negative senses of the word "argument"?
   **Positive: When people engage in discussion and debate without personal attack, bickering, or quarreling in order to discover, clarify, and more fully understand what is true, correct, or wise.**
   **Negative: When people engage in discussion and debate while also bickering, quarreling, and personally attacking each other, with little regard to actually discover, clarify, and more fully understand what is true, correct, or wise.**

2. How do arguments sometimes violate the principle of relevance?
   **Oftentimes people make arguments that are simply not relevant to the issue at hand. Whenever someone argues for something, or introduces facts, issues, testimonies, and evidence that do not truly bear on the issue at hand, he or she is violating the principle of relevance. Answers will vary.**

## D. EXAMPLES

Name the fallacy committed in each of the examples below.

**The *Ad Fontem* Fallacies**

1. "Filthy Story-Teller, Despot, Liar, Thief, Braggart, Buffoon, Usurper, Monster, Ignoramus Abe, Old Scoundrel, Perjurer, Robber, Swindler, Tyrant, Fiend, Butcher."
   —*Harper's Weekly* on Abraham Lincoln[1]

   ***ad hominem* abusive**

2. "Reader, suppose you were an idiot; and suppose you were a member of Congress; but I repeat myself."
   —Mark Twain[2]

   ***ad hominem* circumstantial (the situation of being in Congress is the reason for being considered an idiot. Or it could also be an ad hominem abusive fallacy as it is attacking the character of a member of Congress.)**

3. Officer, why did you pull me over for speeding? Policemen are always driving way over the speed limit themselves.
   ***tu quoque***

4. Yes, Jasmine thinks everyone should purchase a hybrid electric instead of a car that only uses gas. But she got those ideas from her roommate, who fanatically argues for alternative sources of energy. She is just a mouthpiece for her roommate!
   **genetic fallacy**

1. Paul F. Boller, *Presidential Campaigns: from George Washington to George W. Bush* (New York: Oxford University Press, 1984, 1985, 1996, 2004), 117.
2. Larzer Ziff, *Mark Twain* (New York: Oxford University Press, 2004), 59.

# Answers
## Unit 1 Test: Fallacies of Relevance

(continued)

### Appeals to Emotion Fallacies

5. Don't vote for these country-club, blue-blooded Republicans. Vote for John Jackson, champion of the American working man and strong leader in recent polls!
**mob appeal**

6. No! No son of mine will be allowed to hike for two days up into those mountains. Do you know how cold it could get up there? And you could easily fall and get seriously injured. Would you rather live a long and happy life or risk it all just for a hike up a mountain?
**appeal to fear**

7. This Christmas, leave behind the packed malls and the tinsel. There are families right in your hometown who are struggling to make ends meet. Please support them by donating to Salvation Army.
**appeal to pity**

8. In 1974, football great Joe Namath was in a commercial for women's pantyhose and even wore them to show how great they could make your legs look! Clearly, that makes Beautymist pantyhose the best you can buy!
**appeal to illegitimate authority (celebrity)**

9. If you read *Moby Dick*, you will join the exclusive ranks of well-read Americans. It is an accomplishment of which few can boast.
**snob appeal**

10. Any art from before the twentieth century is better than the modernist and abstract styles that no one can even understand.
**chronological snobbery**

11. Hershey's chocolate is the best-selling in America! Everyone loves a Hershey's Kiss.
**mob appeal**

### Red Herrings

12. I don't see why we are spending so much on the so-called "war on drugs." Alcohol is far more frequently abused and it's still legal.
**irrelevant thesis**

13. Our political opponents have challenged us to give them evidence that there really is a health-care crisis. Well, I ask them to give us evidence that there is not.
**appeal to ignorance**

14. The television is a terrible invention. You spend half your time watching annoying commercials and getting headaches from the glowing screen.
**straw man fallacy**

15. Let's get serious here, gentlemen. Giving the American people a tax cut is not going to solve all of their financial problems.
**irrelevant goals or functions**

Includes material from all of chapter 4 and cumulative review of chapters 1–3

## A. FALLACIES
Provide the fallacy name for each of the fallacy descriptions listed below.

This fallacy is committed when . . .

1. . . . the speaker makes the assumption that the parts will have the same properties as a collective whole.
   **fallacy of division**

2. . . . the speaker assumes the very thing that she is trying to prove.
   **begging the question**

3. . . . the speaker assumes that a collective whole will have the properties of its parts.
   **fallacy of composition**

4. . . . the speaker assumes that something is the right thing simply because it is the way that things happen to be.
   **is-ought fallacy**

5. . . . the speaker assumes that the best solution to a problem must be a compromise between extremes.
   **moderation**

6. . . . the speaker assumes that only two possibilities exist, when in fact there may be others.
   **bifurcation (false dilemma)**

## B. DEFINE
Circle the answer that best defines the terms or answers the question.

1. Fallacies of Presupposition
   a. fallacies that play on the emotions of an audience
   b. fallacies that contain hidden assumptions
   c. fallacies that distract from the issue at hand

2. Axiom
   a. a foundational principle upon which an argument rests
   b. a well-reasoned argument
   c. an example of a false dilemma

3. Enthymeme
   a. a deductive argument with a hidden assumption
   b. a fallacy of induction
   c. a compromise between two extremes

4. *Petitio principii*
   a. circular explanation
   b. petitioning the principle
   c. the small prince

(continued)

## C. EXAMPLES

Name the fallacy committed in each of the examples below.

1. If those two tribes can't live together, why don't we just split the land in half and give half to each of them?
   **fallacy of moderation**

2. America: love it or leave it.
   **bifurcation (false dilemma)**

3. I have always grown corn in that field, and so did my father. Corn should always be planted there.
   **is-ought fallacy**

4. "These three musketeers are valiant men and consummate swordsmen. If I had an army of such men, we would be unstoppable!"
   **fallacy of composition**

5. **Mr. Engleton:** Dickens's works are much better literature than those of Tolkien.
   **Johnny:** How does one know what writings are great literature?
   **Mr. Engleton:** They are the ones recommended by the well informed.
   **Johnny:** How does one get to be well informed?
   **Mr. Engleton:** Why, by reading great works of literature such as those of Dickens, of course.
   **begging the question**

6. The men who wrote this program had worked for Microsoft, the most powerful, successful, hard-driving company in the software industry. They must have been great programmers themselves.
   **fallacy of division**

## D. CREATE

Create your own example of a bifurcation (false dilemma) fallacy.

   **Answers will vary. Example: Mr. Johnson just bought a new riding lawn mower. He must be getting lazy. Either that or he just got a big tax refund.**

## E. CUMULATIVE EXAMPLES

Name the fallacy committed in each of the examples below.

1. Our plumber just recommended that we replace our old pipes. Of course he would recommend that, because we will be paying *him* to do it!
   **ad hominem circumstantial**

2. Dr. Robert Hernandez is the best surgeon in Chicago. In the paper last night, he was quoted as saying that the economy is recovering, and it is time to invest in the stock market again.
   **appeal to illegitimate authority (wrong or false expert)**

3. Yes, Sugar Bombs cereal may contain a great deal of sugar, but at least it does not contain high-fructose corn syrup as Syrupy Snaps does.
   *tu quoque*

4. Time after time, Lansdowne Country Day School is selected by highly discriminating parents who want the very best education for their children. Your child could belong here, too.
   **snob appeal**

5. Lansdowne Country Day School may have decent academics, but do you really want your daughter to be influenced by a bunch of spoiled rich kids? Plus, you will spend all of your spare time helping with fundraisers.
   **straw man fallacy**

6. The new bridge over the Susquehanna River is so boring. It will not attract more tourists to the city.
   **irrelevant goals or functions**

7. Dad, can't we get a new set of silverware? These forks and knives used to belong to your parents!
   **chronological snobbery**

## A. FALLACIES

Provide the fallacy name for each of the fallacy descriptions listed below.

1. The speaker makes an argument by comparing two things that really are not very similar.
   **false analogy**

2. The speaker makes an argument on the basis of too few examples.
   **hasty generalization**

3. The speaker makes an argument using a weak causal connection.
   **false cause**

4. The speaker extends a generalization to exceptional cases.
   **sweeping generalization**

5. The speaker misuses statistics.
   **fake precision**

## B. DEFINITIONS

Circle the correct definition for both of the terms below.

1. Inductive Reasoning
   a. observing particular facts to prove a general conclusion
   b. using all of the evidence available to create an argument
   c. reasoning that starts with premises which lead to a necessary conclusion

2. Empirical Data
   a. data that is collected and accepted by relevant scholars
   b. data that can be observed or experienced
   c. data that is unreliable because it changes depending on the situation

## C. EXAMPLES

Name the fallacy committed in each of the examples below.

1. It's no wonder that violent crime has increased considering all the violence that has been in movies and video games lately.
   **false cause**

2. People who eat dark chocolate are 52 percent less likely to struggle with depression.
   **fake precision**

3. Did you hear that Lisa found a dead grasshopper in a salad she got from MacDougal's? They should stop selling those salads immediately!
   **hasty generalization**

4. I need to buy a birthday present for my teenaged niece, Sarah. Teenagers all like rock music, right? I will get her a Rolling Stones CD. I'm sure she will like it.
   **sweeping generalization**

(continued)

5. Mr. Yamamoto, our science teacher, told us about rare birds that come to his bird feeder. He said he feeds them sunflower seeds, so I am going to start putting sunflower seeds out, too. Mom, do we have a jar of sunflower seeds in the cupboard?
**false cause**

6. Mom, just as the air force needs new planes to fight effectively, so I need a new computer in my battle for better grades!
**false analogy**

7. Every time we go on vacation it rains. We should go somewhere where there is a drought, since we are sure to cause rain!
**false cause**

## D. CREATE

Create your own example of a hasty generalization fallacy.

**Answers will vary, but should feature a generalization made from too few examples or too little evidence. Example: Hi, I'm Fred Barnhart with Real Estate Road to Wealth. I am not ashamed to say that I made $100,000 my first year using this wealth-building program and I know that everyone of you listening can, too.**

## E. CUMULATIVE EXAMPLES

Name the fallacy committed in each of the examples below. (Hint: Some examples may commit more than one.)

1. You can't take seriously Mark's argument that we should start a small farm. He has been reading Wendell Berry—a small farm advocate—for the last three years!
**genetic fallacy**

2. This sculpture is a great work of art, but you wouldn't understand since you are an ignorant American, and you were probably raised on John Wayne movies.
***ad hominem* abusive or genetic fallacy**

3. **TV commercial:**
**Scene One:** Features a teenaged boy at the bus stop with bad acne on his face. Girls grouped together look at him and snicker. He looks away, ashamed.
**Scene Two:** He is now at the bathroom sink and washes his face with Nuetranol Acne-Free Face Cleanser. Water and suds splash against his face in slow motion.
**Scene Three:** Clear-faced, he is smiling, with his arm around a beautiful girl who looks at him adoringly.
**false cause and irrelevant goals or functions. Clear skin won't ensure a boy will gain a girlfriend; expecting to gain a girlfriend is an irrelevant goal of face cleanser.**

(continued)

4. Sarah, if you don't start taking those calcium vitamins today, you are going to get osteoporosis. You could be all hunched up and barely able to walk by the time you are sixty.
**appeal to fear**

5. We shouldn't let kids watch those violent Hollywood movies because it just isn't right to let them be exposed to such images of brutality.
**begging the question**

6. I am trying to read one book per month. My mom tells me I should read *The Hobbit*, and my teacher tells me that I should read *The Scarlet Letter*. I will just read half of each.
**fallacy of moderation**

Includes material from all of unit 2 (chapters 4–5) and cumulative review of chapters 1–4

## A. FALLACIES
Provide the fallacy name for each of the fallacy descriptions listed below.

1. An argument that contains an important, hidden assumption, central to what is being proved but not justified by the argument.
**begging the question**

2. An argument that assumes only two alternatives are possible when there may be others.
**bifurcation (false dilemma)**

3. Assuming that a compromise is always the correct conclusion.
**fallacy of moderation**

4. Assuming that just because something is a certain way that it ought to be that way.
**is-ought fallacy**

5. Extending a generalization to all cases without recognizing exceptions.
**sweeping generalization**

## B. DEFINITIONS
Give the definition or description for each of the fallacies below.

1. Fallacy of Composition
**An argument based on a hidden assumption that the properties of the whole will be the same as the properties of the parts.**

2. Fallacy of Division
**An argument that is based on the hidden assumption that a collective whole determines that all of its parts will be like the whole.**

3. Hasty Generalization
**An argument that makes an unwarranted generalization on the basis of too few samples.**

4. False Analogy
**An argument that fails because it creates an analogy between two things that are not similar enough to warrant an analogy.**

5. False Cause
**An argument that is based on a weak cause-and-effect connection.**

6. Fake Precision
**An argument that uses numbers or statistics in a way that is too precise to be justified by the situation.**

## C. SHORT-ANSWER QUESTION

What are fallacies of presumption?

**Arguments that make unwarranted assumptions about either the data or the nature of a reasonable argument.**

## D. EXAMPLES

Name the fallacy committed in each of the examples below.

**PART 1:** Select from the following three possibilities: false analogy, hasty generalization, sweeping generalization.

1. People who make bad grades usually do so because they do not study. Since Jack is making bad grades, it's obvious that he doesn't study.
   **sweeping generalization**

2. If you put fewer people in a hot air balloon, it will rise higher and faster; if Jack will sleep for fewer hours each night, he will get higher grades and work at a faster pace. Jack should sleep a lot less in order to increase his academic performance.
   **false analogy**

3. John and Susie just don't try very hard at school. Kids these days are just so lazy.
   **hasty generalization**

**PART 2:** Select from the following possibilities: false cause, fake precision, fallacy of composition, fallacy of division.

1. Dennis Rodman is a great basketball player. When they add him to Shaquille O'Neal and Kobe Bryant, they are sure to have a great team.
   **fallacy of composition**

2. Any law preserving the nation's farmland will be very popular. After all, a recent study by the US Department of Agriculture showed that 82 percent of Americans believe in supporting America's Farmers.
   **fake precision**

3. Studies show that most elementary school teachers are parents. It must be because working with children stimulates an interest in parenthood.
**false cause**

4. John Elway should be elected MVP of the NFL. After all, his team is the best team in the league right now.
**fallacy of division**

5. "It is strangely absurd to suppose that a million human beings, collected together, are not under the same moral laws which bind each of them separately."

—Thomas Jefferson[1]

**fallacy of composition, though this may be a good and well-reasoned assumption of composition**

**PART 3:** Select from the following possibilities: begging the question, is-ought fallacy, bifurcation (false dilemma), fallacy of moderation.

1. Of course smoking cigarettes is OK. It's a legal activity, isn't it?
**is-ought fallacy**

2. Jenny wants peach ice cream and Justin wants coffee ice cream. We will compromise by getting a bowl of peach and coffee ice cream mixed together!
**fallacy of moderation**

3. Since you started eight months ago, you have consistently had the lowest sales in the department. Either you have not worked hard to improve sales or you simply lack the ability to do this job well. Either way, you are not performing sufficiently, and we may have to remove you from this job.
**bifurcation (false dilemma) (surely there are other possibilities for poor sales in the department)**

4. We need an Explorer's History month because we should set aside four weeks to recall the great achievements of America's great explorers.
**begging the question**

**PART 4:** Select from the following possibilities: hasty generalization, sweeping generalization, fallacy of composition, fallacy of division.

1. That blimp is a lighter-than-air vehicle. That must mean that everything on it is lighter than air.
**fallacy of division**

2. People who live on Hickory Mountain are almost all quite wealthy. Your friend Greg lives on Hickory Mountain, so he must be loaded.
**sweeping generalization**

3. Jon, Mike, and I are not as athletic as those guys. There's no way we could put together a team that could beat them.
**fallacy of composition**

4. My Uncle Harry is a crazy driver. It must be a quality common to all people from Queens.
**hasty generalization**

---

1. Gary Scott Smith, *Faith and the Presidency: from George Washington to George W. Bush* (New York: Oxford University Press, 2006), 81.

## E. CREATE

1. Create your own example of an is-ought fallacy.

   **Answers will vary. Example: That's right! We have been making handmade ice cream at Lenny's Creamery for over fifty years—the way ice cream should be made.**

2. Create your own example of a false cause fallacy.

   **Answers will vary. Example: The mechanics at Town Center Auto Repair are corrupt. A day after I got my car inspected there, it overheated and I had to replace my radiator. Clearly they did something to my radiator so that I had bring it back to them for an expensive repair.**

## F. CUMULATIVE EXAMPLES

Name the fallacy committed in each of the examples below.

1. Please remember that the defendant was raised in a home without a father and had to care for his younger siblings. He had to become a man while he was still a boy. It is not surprising that he would have many difficult problems to overcome. Please do not punish him for the rest of his life.
   **appeal to pity**

2. "Douglas can never be president, Sir. No, Sir; Douglas never can be president, Sir. His legs are too short, Sir. His coat, like a cow's tail, hangs too near the ground, Sir."
   —Thomas Hart Benton on Stephen A. Douglas, presidential candidate[2]
   ***ad hominem* abusive**

3. You have no proof that high fructose corn syrup is a cause of the increased obesity in America; therefore we will continue to use it as a primary ingredient in Granny's brand pancake syrup until proven otherwise.
   **appeal to ignorance (note: this could look like a defense against a false cause fallacy, but the argument is resting on the need for "proof" and ignoring any evidence short of proof)**

4. Schools in America should consider switching to a year-round school schedule. It would be much better for the tourism industry because it would provide steadier, year-round revenue, since families would be able to take their vacations throughout the year.
   **irrelevant goals or functions**

5. Your objections to the building of the new superstore are clearly just tree-hugging, save-the-whales, environmentalist propaganda. You would probably try to stop an ambulance rushing on its way in order to keep it from running over a caterpillar.
   **straw man fallacy combined with an *ad hominem* abusive fallacy**

---

2. Laura Ward, *Perfect Put-Downs: A Collection of Acid Wit* (New York: Sterling Publishing Company, 2009), 120.

Includes material from all of unit 3 and cumulative review of units 1 and 2

## A. FALLACIES
Provide the fallacy name for each of the fallacy descriptions listed below.

1. Ambiguity that is created by the fact that a word has more than one meaning.
**equivocation**

2. Confusion that is created by placing emphasis on one particular word or phrase.
**accent**

3. Confusion caused by treating a purely linguistic distinction as if it were a real distinction.
**distinction without a difference**

## B. EXAMPLES
Name the fallacy committed in each of the examples below.

1. He said that this dress looks good on me. I can't believe he thinks that my other dress doesn't look good on me!
**accent**

2. Mr. Jones must be a very responsible person. If anything goes wrong at Lewis Academy, he is held responsible.
**equivocation**

3. Jack doesn't really get angry. He just flies into a rage and punches people every once in a while.
**distinction without a difference**

4. The art of argument is a silly thing to study! Don't we have enough trouble with argumentative students already?
**equivocation**

5. I wouldn't say that the movie was bad, but it was a complete waste of time and money.
**distinction without a difference**

## C. CREATE
Create your own example of a fallacy of accent.

**Answers will vary. Example:**

**Linda: What did you think of the school play last night?**

**Paul: Well, all of the cast members certainly *played* their parts well.**

(continued)

## D. DEFINE

1. What is a fallacy of clarity?

__An argument that fails because it contains words, phrases or, syntax that distort or__
__cloud their meanings. Answers will vary.__

## E. CUMULATIVE EXAMPLES

Name the fallacy committed in each of the examples below.

1. The average homeowner who is refinancing a house while the interest rates are low will save $67,030 on the interest payments during the course of the loan! Don't miss your chance to refinance today!
   **fake precision**

2. Senator Neilson, the entire nation is fed up with closed-door, private negotiations. The American people want honesty and transparency from their legislators.
   **mob appeal**

3. Of course Melissa wants Mrs. Cruz to curve the grades. She failed the last exam and will argue for anything that will improve her grade.
   ***ad hominem* circumstantial, possibly false cause**

4. Yes, our company's computer system is a bit old and inefficient, but it works. This company has always managed with old technology and that's the way it's got to be.
   **is-ought fallacy**

5. All of McDonald's food is delicious. I bet if I crack open a packet of ketchup and eat it plain it will be delicious!
   **fallacy of division**

6. I wouldn't suggest going to a big state university if you want to be a serious student—all the students at those universities party more than they study!
   **sweeping generalization**

Assessment of the entire text and all twenty-eight fallacies

## A. FALLACIES

Provide the fallacy name for each of the fallacy descriptions listed below.

### Unit 1: Fallacies of Relevance

1. An argument that discounts a rival's position because the rival has not always been consistent in advocating or practicing his current position.
   **tu quoque**

2. The speaker says all sorts of mean and nasty things about his rival as evidence that his rival's argument should be discounted.
   **ad hominem abusive**

3. The thing or idea being argued is discounted solely because of its origin.
   **genetic fallacy**

4. An argument that tries to discredit an opponent because of his circumstances or potential self-interest in the matter at hand.
   **ad hominem circumstantial**

5. An appeal to those of "discriminating tastes."
   **snob appeal**

6. This fallacy occurs when the speaker depends on emotional appeals to make his audience feel sorry for him or others rather than providing sound evidence to support his argument.
   **appeal to pity**

7. An appeal to the opinion of an "expert," whether an unnamed source, a celebrity, a biased expert, or an expert on an unrelated issue.
   **appeal to illegitimate authority**

8. An appeal to the mere fact that a belief is widely held to prove its truth, or an appeal to the mystique of the "common man" or "the people."
   **mob appeal**

9. An appeal to the mere age of a belief, practice, or thing as evidence that it is correct or preferable.
   **chronological snobbery**

10. An argument that presents a caricatured, inaccurate, or exaggerated version of an opponent's position.
    **straw man fallacy**

11. An argument that proves a different point than the one that is relevant to the issue at hand.
    **irrelevant thesis**

12. An argument that insists that because a position cannot be proven, it must be false or, alternatively, if a position cannot be proven wrong, it must be true.
    **appeal to ignorance**

13. An argument that judges something on the basis of a goal that it was never intended to achieve.
    **irrelevant goals or functions**

### Unit 2: Fallacies of Presumption

1. An argument that makes the assumption that the parts of a collective whole will have the same properties as the collective whole.
   **fallacy of division**

2. An argument that is either just restating the conclusion in other words or uses a justification that is more controversial than the original conclusion.
   **begging the question**

3. An argument that assumes that something is right simply because it is the way things happen to be.
   **is-ought fallacy**

4. An argument that assumes that a collective whole will have the same properties as its parts.
   **fallacy of composition**

5. An argument that assumes that only two possibilities exist, when in fact there may be others.
   **bifurcation (false dilemma)**

6. An argument that assumes that the best solution to a conflict is a compromise between the two extremes.
   **fallacy of moderation**

7. An argument that is based on a comparison of two things that are not very similar.
   **false analogy**

8. An argument that is based on a weak causal connection.
   **false cause**

9. An argument that is based on a misuse of statistics.
   **fake precision**

10. An argument that extends a generalization to exceptional cases.
    **sweeping generalization**

11. An argument that creates a generalization on the basis of too few examples.
    **hasty generalization**

## B. DEFINITIONS
Give the definition or description for each of the fallacies below.

### Unit 3: Fallacies of Clarity

1. Equivocation
   **An argument that fails because a key term is ambiguous. Answers will vary.**

2. Accent
   **An argument that rests on an improper emphasis placed on certain words or phrases. Answers will vary.**

# ANSWERS
# FINAL EXAM

(continued)

3. Distinction Without a Difference
   **An argument that makes a linguistic distinction between two things that are actually not different from each other. Answers will vary.**

## C. EXAMPLES

Match the fallacies with the examples below by writing the letters of the examples in the blank spaces provided.

**UNIT 1:**

| | | | |
|---|---|---|---|
| 1. *Ad Hominem* Abusive | **D** | 8. Snob Appeal | **A** |
| 2. *Ad Hominem* Circumstantial | **N** | 9. Appeal to Illegitimate Authority | **L** |
| 3. *Tu Quoque* | **H** | 10. Chronological Snobbery | **K** |
| 4. Genetic Fallacy | **I** | 11. Appeal to Ignorance | **E** |
| 5. Appeal to Fear | **J** | 12. Irrelevant Goals or Functions | **M** |
| 6. Appeal to Pity | **B** | 13. Irrelevant Thesis | **C** |
| 7. Mob Appeal | **F** | 14. Straw Man Fallacy | **G** |

A. Our school starts training students to speak French in the first grade, since speaking French distinguishes one as an exceptionally well-educated individual.

B. Please give this young man another chance to become a good and law-abiding citizen. He is too young to be locked away in prison and separated from his family.

C. Safe and warm housing is a necessity for human life. The City of Harrisburg should provide housing for any citizen in need.

D. Why would anyone vote for Johnson? He is about as inspiring as bowl of soggy cornflakes.

E. Of course leprechauns exist. Can you prove they don't exist? Since you can't prove they don't exist you should stop criticizing me for my conviction that they do!

F. The movie has been a box-office smash and everyone loves it! We should go see it tonight!

G. **Artist:** That painting is an important and influential piece of modern art.
   **Critic:** That painting is crayon scribbled on a white canvas. There is nothing significant about that.

H. You cannot tell me that I should not smoke. You smoke a pack of cigarettes a day!

I. You heard that argument for preventing illegal immigration on Fox News last night, didn't you? Why should we give your argument a hearing when it comes from that biased network?

J. We must provide funds to prop up the banks immediately. If we do not act quickly, they may fail and bring the rest of the economy down with them.

K. They just don't build them like they used to.

L. In an interview today, actress Julie Marshall stated that she believes that the national debt will be paid back over the next thirty years. Isn't that great news?

M. You can't boil water in the new army helmets! They really are poorly designed.

N. Of course James is in favor of hiring an assistant. It will sure make his job a lot easier.

## UNITS 2 & 3:

| | | | | | |
|---|---|---|---|---|---|
| 1. Begging the Question | **I** | | 8. Hasty Generalization | **C** |
| 2. Bifurcation (False Dilemma) | **N** | | 9. False Analogy | **J** |
| 3. Fallacy of Moderation | **F** | | 10. False Cause | **L** |
| 4. Is-Ought Fallacy | **G** | | 11. Fake Precision | **M** |
| 5. Fallacy of Composition | **H** | | 12. Equivocation | **D** |
| 6. Fallacy of Division | **B** | | 13. Accent | **E** |
| 7. Sweeping Generalization | **K** | | 14. Distinction Without a Difference | **A** |

A. I'm not a poor student. I just don't study very hard, when I study at all.

B. Congress has not gotten anything done this year. Each one of those congressmen is lazy.

C. My neighbor has an Australian Shepherd that bit his son! Don't get one of those dogs—they are vicious.

D. **Athlete:** But coach, I took you seriously when you said I had to get back on track, and I just ran seven miles! You've got to let me play!

E. You *can* live without coffee. *You* can live without coffee.

F. You like chicken noodle soup, and I like tomato. I will look for a recipe for chicken-tomato-noodle soup! That will be perfect.

G. Sarah is thinking of going to a different school that offers a nursing program. I think she should stay where she is—things will be best for her just as they are.

H. A piece of paper is as light as a feather. I can carry a case of paper—no problem!

I. "There is no such thing as knowledge which cannot be put in to practice, for such knowledge is no knowledge at all." —Confucius

J. If you eat too much candy, your teeth will decay. If you love someone too much the relationship will deteriorate. It is best not to love someone a lot, but only a little bit.

K. English majors are legendary for being lousy at math. Gordon is an English major, so he is not likely to do well in his algebra class.

L. I got the flu right after I ate at Tony's Pizza Shop last winter. They must not keep their restaurant clean.

M. If you study for your SAT with the SAT Super Duper Prep Guide, your score could increase by 42.7 percent.

N. There are two types of people in the world: those who own a Mercedes-Benz and those who wish they did.

# Logic

We use logic every day, especially to distinguish *logical* arguments from those that are unreasonable. As a fundamental part of the trivium, logic is a paradigm subject by which we evaluate, assess, and learn other subjects, growing ever closer to their mastery.

**Informal Logic**
(Grades 7–12)

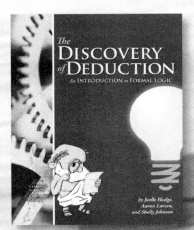

**Formal Logic**
(Grades 8–12)

**Logic/Pre-Rhetoric**
(Grades 8–12)

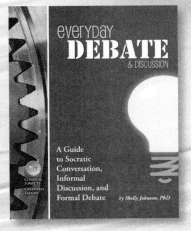

**Speech & Debate**
(Grades 8–12)

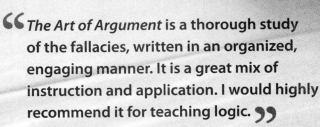

**❝** *The Art of Argument* **is a thorough study of the fallacies, written in an organized, engaging manner. It is a great mix of instruction and application. I would highly recommend it for teaching logic. ❞**
—Kathy Gelzer, *The Old Schoolhouse Magazine*